Lean & Green: Best Practice

Daniel Reichert

Lean & Green: Best Practice

How Companies Become More Efficient and Sustainable

Springer

Daniel Reichert
T&O Group
München, Germany

ISBN 978-3-658-49879-5 ISBN 978-3-658-49880-1 (eBook)
https://doi.org/10.1007/978-3-658-49880-1

Translation from the German language edition: "Lean & Green: Best Practice" by Daniel Reichert, © Springer Fachmedien Wiesbaden GmbH, ein Teil von Springer Nature 2025. Published by Springer Fachmedien Wiesbaden. All Rights Reserved.

This book is a translation of the original German edition "Lean & Green: Best Practice," 2nd edition, by Daniel Reichert, published by Springer Fachmedien Wiesbaden GmbH in 2025. The translation was done with the help of an artificial intelligence machine translation tool. A subsequent human revision was done primarily in terms of content, so that the book will read stylistically differently from a conventional translation. Springer Nature works continuously to further the development of tools for the production of books and on the related technologies to support the authors.

This Springer imprint is published by the registered company Springer Fachmedien Wiesbaden GmbH, part of Springer Nature.
The registered company address is: Abraham-Lincoln-Str. 46, 65189 Wiesbaden, Germany

Acknowledgments

Creating a book on success strategies and best practice approaches in industry is only possible with deep insights into companies and the ability to contextualize them. Therefore, our special thanks go to all the companies that contributed to this book or provided us with information. The willingness and excellent cooperation once again demonstrate that it is precisely the best companies that are characterized by their openness to exchange and their ability to benefit from mutual learning.

Thanks are also to the T&O Group and in particular to the Managing Director Marek Borgstedt. It was only through entrepreneurial foresight that it was possible to keep the award alive during challenging times such as the coronavirus pandemic and subsequently to strengthen it further.

Daniel Reichert
Head of Lean & Green
T&O Group, Munich

Contents

1 Introduction and Overview 1

2 Resource Efficiency and Sustainability 5
2.1 What Exactly is "Sustainability"? 7
2.2 What do Resources mean in the Context of Sustainability? 11
2.3 Sustainability at the Corporate Level 13
2.4 The Risks of Inaction 15
2.5 Transformation as Opportunity 19
2.6 The Current Challenges for Companies 22
References 27

3 The Underestimated Potential of Lean Management with regard to Sustainability 31
3.1 What is Lean Management, actually? 31
3.2 Anchoring Lean Management in Companies 35
3.3 Why Lean Management Systems Facilitate the Integration of "Green" 38
3.4 Lean = Green and vice versa? 46
References 47

4 Example methods for Industrial Companies 49
4.1 Approaches to Strategic Anchoring 49
4.2 Machine Effectiveness 51
4.3 Material Efficiency 57
4.4 Energy Management 62
References 69

5 Lean & Green Management Award 71
5.1 Award Process 72
5.2 Dynzamic Maturity Model and Benchmark 76

6 Best-practice examples from industry . . . 81
6.1 Fischer: Implementing Sustainability Management . . . 82
6.2 Südpack: Lean Management as a Fundamental Building Block for Sustainability . . . 89
6.3 DMG MORI: Sustainable Business = Successful Business . . . 93
6.4 BSH Slovenia: How a Culture of Continuous Improvement Enables Flexibility, Competitiveness, and Resilience . . . 98
6.5 ASMPT SMT Solutions: Value Stream-Oriented Lean Management—Achieving Economic and Environmental Excellence in Tandem . . . 102
6.6 Siemens: Synchronized Value Chain Design Lean vs. Agile Across the Entire Value Chain . . . 108
6.7 Festo Production EOOD: Operational Excellence through Digital Tools . . . 110
6.8 Hammerer Aluminium Industries: on the path to climate neutrality and circular economy . . . 119
6.9 Schaltbau: DC Factory NExT Factory Sets a New Standard for Green Production . . . 123
6.10 Festo: Resource Efficiency in the Construction of the Scharnhausen Technology Plant . . . 129
6.11 Siemens: Lean in the "Indirect" Area—Adapting Kata, Scrum, and Lean Methods . . . 133
6.12 TE Connectivity: How a Consistent Structure Can Make the Continuous Improvement Process Transparent and Measurable, Thus Securing the Achievement of Strategy andSustainability . . . 137
6.13 Welbilt Deutschland (Convotherm): Achieving "Green Production" Through Lean Management Projects . . . 138
6.14 Witte Automotive Bulgaria: Leading "Lean & Green" from the Bottom Up in a Fast-Growing Environment . . . 143
6.15 Volkswagen de México: How the Puebla plant is using "Lean & Green" best practices to improve resource efficiency in all areas . . . 150
References . . . 160

Conclusion . . . 161

Introduction and Overview 1

"Lean & Green" describes the intelligent integration of lean management approaches with environmental, energy, and sustainability aspects. The focus is on how a company's use of resources can be designed to support a Cooporate Sustainability.

"Lean & Green" approaches are therefore of central interest to companies across all sectors. Increasingly, in addition to economic figures, social and ecological factors are coming into focus for regulators, customers, the public and investors. Drivers of these developments include political frameworks and initiatives, increasingly conscious consumers, resource scarcity, and cost pressures. Moreover, in times of skilled labor shortages, it is becoming ever more important for many companies to have authentic answers regarding sustainability, thereby increasing their attractiveness as employers. The design of sustainable and resource-efficient business processes is thus becoming one of the critical success factors for companies.

Against this background, adjustments in business processes are crucial to finding answers to the increasingly urgent social and ecological challenges of our time. Companies are the main drivers of innovation, technology, and capital flow. Business processes determine how resources are used, products are manufactured, and services are delivered, thereby directly impacting the environment, society, and the economy. In addition, companies shape consumption patterns, working conditions, and global supply chains, giving them significant influence on sustainable development and the achievement of the so-called United Nations Sustainability Goals ("Sustainable Development Goals" [SDGs]). By adopting a more sustainable corporate orientation, for example, economic growth and decent working conditions are directly strengthened (SDG 8), industries and infrastructures are modernized (SDG 9), and production and consumption patterns are made more environmentally friendly (SDG 12). At the same time, reducing energy and material use supports climate protection measures (SDG 13). I am therefore very pleased that this book has been included in the second edition of the series *SDG – Research, Concepts, Solution Approaches for Sustainability*.

D. Reichert, *Lean & Green: Best Practice*, https://doi.org/10.1007/978-3-658-49880-1_1

To achieve a more sustainable corporate orientation, the core of the "Lean & Green" concept is to leverage synergies with the continuous improvement philosophy of lean management. The close connection between classic lean approaches and environmental and resource efficiency topics has long been recognized and is rooted in their shared focus on waste. One goal of lean management is to avoid or minimize waste (i.e., non-value-adding activities). This leads to more efficient processes and thus to lower resource consumption. "Lean & Green" thus highlights two sides of the same coin, which influence each other and have a direct impact on a company's resource efficiency. A particularly lean company is also more resource-efficient and thus "green."

However, the connection between "Lean" and "Green" gos far beyond this efficiency aspect. The core of lean management is to empower organizations across all levels for continuous improvement and change. Companies that have achieved a high level of maturity in lean management no longer limit themselves to the isolated application of individual methods from the lean toolbox, but instead pursue a systematic approach. In addition to internal solutions within departments, cross-functional improvements to overarching business processes also come into focus. Principles and practices are embedded in holistic management systems, and the philosophy of continuous improvement is deeply anchored in the organization and workforce. "Lean" thus becomes part of the corporate culture, strengthening participation and willingness to change. In addition, production and management systems provide guardrails that help support the company's long-term orientation and make strategic objectives operationally tangible.

Lean therefore helps companies adapt to market and sustainability challenges and build an organization that, with broad employee involvement, can effectively manage the necessary changes—qualities urgently needed by companies in the current and upcoming transformation toward a more sustainable economy.

Although this connection is fundamentally known, only a few companies have so far systematically applied it for mutual benefit. For example, lean management methods are rarely used to improve ecological or social performance. Conversely, it is also rarely demonstrated how process efficiency can be improved through more environmentally friendly or socially responsible practices. On the contrary, sustainability topics are usually seen as an additional investment that a company must make to manage market or compliance risks.

Organizationally, too, the overlaps between lean and green are minimal in many companies. While lean managers and continuous improvement coordinators (CIP = Continuous Improvement Process) do accompany and initiate process improvements, in many companies they have little contact with sustainability and environmental officers, energy managers, or facility managers, whose task it is to implement "green" improvements.

Yet the "Lean & Green" connection offers many points of contact to ensure that social and ecological aspects also become part of a company. In fact, it is especially the operational implementation of sustainability topics that many companies find challenging.

Much has changed since the first edition (2018), and especially in Europe, regulations introduced as part of the "European Green Deal" have led to sustainability now being structured more systematically and given greater priority and, in modern terms, "management attention" in many companies. Nevertheless, there is still much uncertainty about which specific methods can help achieve medium- and long-term sustainability goals.

As with the integration of lean management, the greatest effects are achieved when sustainability is seen as a mission for everyone, not just for support functions. The individual levers and opportunities for change necessary for a sustainable transformation are defined by the specific processes, supply chains, products, and services of the company, and thus also depend on the know-how of the employees and departments who manage these as part of their daily work.

Unfortunately, sustainability (and also lean management!) is still seen by many companies as an expert task, parked with individual people or staff units. In contrast, well-practiced lean philosophy has a very strong participative character. A core idea of lean management is that responsibility for one's own processes should be exercised as close as possible to the value creation itself. The task of support units and management functions should instead be to build systems and structures that enable and empower exactly this.

The path that companies take in successfully implementing lean management therefore offers many points of connection for advancing sustainability within their own organization and strengthening partnerships in the supply chain. If this succeeds, ecological and social topics can also be advanced as part of the continuous improvement process, and the operationalization of sustainability strategies can be described more concretely.

Since only a few companies have so far pursued such a close connection between "Lean" and "Green," cross-industry exchange and practical best-practice knowledge are of central interest to corporations as well as small and medium-sized enterprises. For the many companies from across Europe that have applied for the "Lean & Green Management Award" for years, this is a key motivation. Many of the participating top companies are pioneers in resource efficiency and pursue diverse and innovative "Lean & Green" approaches, which are shared as part of the best-practice exchange among participants.

To recognize these approaches and make best-practice knowledge accessible to a broader audience, this book aims to thematically address the connection between "Lean" and "Green" and present some success recipes from many years of corporate and consulting experience with "Lean & Green."

The introduction in Chap. 1 addresses the topic of sustainability and its implementation in the business environment. In addition to an explanation of the concept of sustainability, Chap. 2 examines the opportunities and risks this presents for companies and the specific challenges involved. Subsequently, Chap. 3 addresses the topic of lean management, explaining where synergies between lean and green can arise and how these can be developed for mutual benefit. Specifically, it is shown how lean management can help implement the sustainability transformation.

Based on four concrete topic examples, Chap. 4 illustrates how integrated "Lean & Green" approaches can be implemented within a company. The aim of this chapter is to demonstrate, using key levels of action, how to successfully implement "Lean & Green" step by step, anchor a sustainability strategy, improve machine effectiveness, increase material efficiency, and initiate the development of a holistic energy management system. Chap. 5 then presents the process and methodology of the "Lean & Green Management Award," explaining how companies can be compared across industries both in terms of Lean Management implementation and sustainability topics, and why this enables a practical transfer of knowledge between companies and industries.

In the final chapter, Chap. 6, approaches of individual companies are presented that rank among the top performers of the award, are distinguished by a high degree of "Lean Excellence," and succeed in deeply embedding sustainability aspects within the company. Specifically, the success stories and methods of the following companies are presented: fischer Group, SÜDPACK Group, DMG MORI, BSH Home Appliances (Slovenia), ASM Assembly Systems, Siemens Electronics, Festo Plant (Bulgaria), Hammerer Aluminium Industries, Schaltbau, Festo Technology n, TE Connectivity, Welbilt Germany (Convotherm), Witte Automotive (Bulgaria), Volkswagen de México (Mexico).

Resource Efficiency and Sustainability 2

Anyone who engages with the concept of sustainability quickly realizes that there is a multitude of concepts, discourses, and definitions, often with very different implications. The "elastic term" of sustainability is used in a wide variety of contexts. Depending on the context and intention, sustainability is invoked to indicate something lasting or enduring, usually with a positive connotation. For example, when a company speaks of sustainable growth, it usually means ongoing revenue increases rather than a reduction in the company's environmental impact. A sustainable management strategy tends to describe the effectiveness of defined measures rather than emphasizing efficient and resource-conserving decision-making. In the case of sustainable products, it is assumed that negative environmental impacts are reduced and that efficient use of resources is ensured or supported.

To assess the effectiveness of sustainability efforts or the "sustainability performance" of companies, sustainability reports, alongside traditional annual reports, are the central source of information provided by companies. Here, many companies publish data, statements, and definitions intended to demonstrate their own responsible—sustainable—actions. What was specifically understood by sustainability could, in the past, also be defined very differently here.

Against this Background, it is very welcome that in recent years, regulatory activities have increased to establish more universally valid sustainability standards. It is no coincidence that a large share of current sustainability regulation focuses on bringing more standardization and transparency to reporting. For example, the "Corporate Social Reporting Directive" (CSRD), which has been in effect since the beginning of 2023, is a key component of the European Union's (EU) Green Deal. Part of the directive is that, in the future, clear reporting standards—the so-called "European Sustainability Reporting

D. Reichert, *Lean & Green: Best Practice*, https://doi.org/10.1007/978-3-658-49880-1_2

Standards" (ESRS)—will apply to large European companies, which companies must comply with after staggered transition periods (European Union [EU], 2023).[1]

As a result, a comparable understanding of sustainability is increasingly emerging for the broad mass of companies—for example, the term "materiality analysis,"[2] at the time of the first edition of this book (2018), was more a topic for experts or those with a specific interest. Today, it is a term that most management teams are familiar with and have already encountered themselves. Furthermore, the harmonization of standards is leading to a fundamentally clearer understanding of what sustainability means in a corporate context and what measures and information are necessary to define authentic sustainability strategies. The previously more common "feel-good brochures," which often presented a collection of isolated individual measures for marketing purposes, will noticeably decrease as a result. It is clear that sustainability in the business environment has shifted from being a rather voluntary "nice-to-have" to a "must-have" perception.

The flip side for companies, however, is that this new regulation usually leads to increased effort, which is not directly value-adding in the traditional sense. Especially in Europe, we are currently in a transitional period that requires a major shift in thinking for many companies, auditors, consultants, and legislators, and is accompanied by a steep learning curve. This also means that the development and application of new standards require significant resources, which, in the first instance, do not directly lead to greater sustainability but initially only result in bureaucratic processes. In a time of multiple crises and considerable market uncertainties, this is a challenge for companies and for those who need to advocate for this internally. It is to be hoped that in the coming years, this will increasingly develop into effective and pragmatic processes and that the learning curves will ensure that sustainability becomes routine for the vast majority of companies, thereby initiating the necessary transformations. Because, just as with financial reporting (which is many times more resource-intensive), sustainability reporting is about creating transparency as to whether the company is using its limited resources sensibly. And this is not only in terms of "shareholder value," but in terms of an expanded "stakeholder value," that is, taking into account the interests of all relevant stakeholders such as employees, customers, suppliers, the environment, and society. This ensures that the company is not only financially successful but also acts sustainably and responsibly, which in the long term contributes to a more stable and resilient corporate structure and should be seen as an opportunity.

---

[1] Parallel to the finalization of this book, it is becoming apparent that some of the regulatory requirements are being adjusted, and the thresholds for when a company becomes subject to reporting obligations are being changed. It is expected that significantly fewer companies will be affected. Despite these developments, the author is convinced that sustainability reporting will gain importance worldwide.

[2] A crucial component of sustainability reporting, which determines which material topics a company reports on.

To contextualize the topic of Lean & Green and to describe the operational points of connection that exist in business, we will now turn to the concept of sustainability. "Even though, it seems, everything sensible and a good deal of the nonsensical has already been said about sustainability" (Uekötter, 2014), a classification is nevertheless necessary in order to identify the challenges and opportunities for companies that wish to engage with the topic of sustainability not only for direct compliance reasons, but have recognized it as a strategic long-term potential.

2.1 What Exactly is "Sustainability"?

The earliest origins of the term sustainability can be traced back to forestry. One of the founding fathers of the concept of sustainability was Hans Carl von Carlowitz, who, at the beginning of the 18th century, as "Oberberghauptmann of the Ore Mountains," was responsible for supplying wood to the mining and smelting industries of Saxony. In a time of energy crisis, when population growth and industrial demand increasingly threatened the availability of wood as a raw material, von Carlowitz recognized the need for action in 1713 (von Carlowitz, 1713).

For von Carlowitz, the focus was on the necessity of sustainable forestry, with the regenerative capacity of the existing system at its core. As von Carlowitz was responsible for the energy supply of the most important economic sector—metalworking—he had a direct economic interest and could estimate an immediate financial benefit. In this sense, sustainability was a resource-economic term describing the ongoing, long-term supply of necessary resources. This understanding of sustainability persisted into the 20th century and also found its way into everyday language in the sense of "durability."

From the second half of the 20th century onwards, the term sustainability was increasingly used in (economic) political contexts. It was significantly influenced by global environmental policy debates, such as those shaped by the work of the *Club of Rome*. In addition to the question of a lasting supply of resources, ethical questions increasingly came to the fore. No longer was only the resource-economic perspective considered; instead, holistic concepts were discussed that focused on the future viability of humanity. Through future scenarios and risk analyses, long-term, intergenerational challenges were to be highlighted and societal debates initiated to improve the future. Whereas for von Carlowitz the opposite of sustainability was "wood scarcity," from now on, sustainability could be contrasted with "total collapse" (Uekötter, 2014).

One of the most frequently cited definitions of sustainability was developed in this sense in 1987 by the so-called "Brundtland Commission." The Brundtland Commission (named after the chairwoman of the World Commission on Environment and Development) was commissioned by the UN to examine future development and environmental policy challenges and to identify innovative and realistic courses of action. In the final report—"Our Common Future"—sustainability or sustainable development was defined as a global, intergenerational responsibility:

> "Sustainable development is development that meets the needs of the present without compromising the ability of future generations to meet their own needs." (Brundtland Report, 1987a)

In addition to the permanent supply of required resources (the purely resource-economic component), the goal was formulated here to ensure the lasting satisfaction of *all* needs. This definition by the Brundtland Commission was subsequently cited or adopted in many international agreements. The report led to an ongoing discourse on sustainability. Among other things, following its publication, the "United Nations Conference on Environment and Development" (1992) was convened, which met in Rio de Janeiro (often simply called the Rio Conference). As a result of this conference, sustainability and sustainable development were now discussed internationally on a broad basis, and even a global right to sustainable development was mentioned in the final declaration.[3] Other outcomes of the Rio Conference included, among others, the Framework Convention on Climate Change, the Convention on Biological Diversity, and Agenda 21.

At the Rio Conference itself, as well as in the numerous subsequent discourses, the central question became that of "how" and, consequently, the question of political and economic imperatives for action. The Brundtland Commission's report had already suggested that sustainable development is not only an intergenerational challenge, but also a societal task that can only be realized through the cooperation of many actors at multiple levels (Brundtland Report, 1987a). However, in 1987, sustainability was primarily a green issue, with the focus on the management of natural resources. In business terms, it was the global commons where it was recognized that persistent market failure would occur. An example of such failure was quantified almost 20 years later by the British economist Nicholas Stern, who, on behalf of the British government, calculated that the economic consequences of global warming would rise to nearly EUR 5.5 trillion per year by 2100 (Stern & Richter, 2009). In his more recent analyses, Stern emphasizes that the economic costs of climate change are likely to be significantly higher than originally calculated, and that more comprehensive risks, particularly due to the presence of so-called tipping points, are still insufficiently incorporated into economic risk assessments (Stern, 2016). Such calculations vividly illustrate the implications that disregarding the ecological dimension can have for long-term economic conditions.

The realization that ecological challenges cannot be solved in isolation, but are interrelated with economic and social issues, was worked out in increasing detail over the course of the 1990s. It was quickly recognized that reducing the concept of sustainability to natural resources would lead to a narrow and misguided sustainability policy. For example, the Enquete Commission of the German Bundestag (1998) stated:

---

[3] The fact that discourses developed on a broad basis may be due, among other things, to the fact that at the conference, civil society groups and non-governmental organizations (NGOs) were involved in the negotiations to an extent previously unknown.

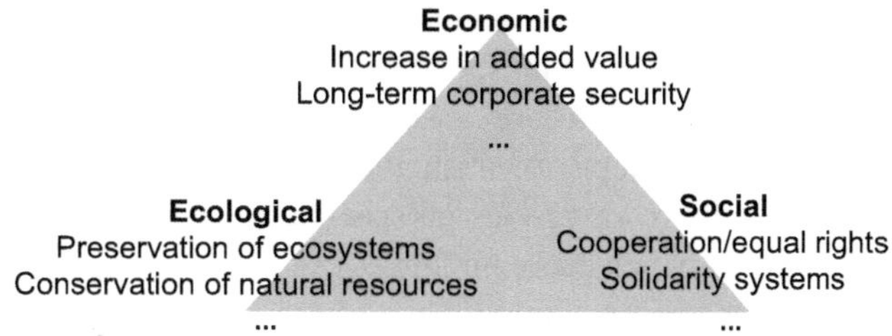

Fig. 2.1 Three-pillar model. (Own illustration)

> "A sustainability policy dominated by ecological concerns will always lose out in the societal process of weighing interests whenever other problems appear more immediate, tangible, and pressing, and thus are more urgent and attractive for political action." (German Bundestag, 1998, p. 18)

In order to nevertheless derive effective responses to long-term imperatives for action, the concept of sustainability is often described today using so-called three-pillar or three-level models (see Fig. 2.1). The understanding of sustainability is thus seen as a long-term harmony of ecological, economic, and social goals. Strategies, actions, and decisions that claim to be sustainable must not, in the long term, play these sometimes conflicting goals off against each other. Examples here would be the clearing of primeval forests for the cultivation of monocultures such as oil palms (ecological) or the use of child labor in Indonesia (social) due to monetary interests (economic). However, social and ecological projects must also not be in permanent contradiction to fundamental value and wealth creation, as the failure to meet basic needs would otherwise threaten the loss of support and necessary resources.

Some more recent definitions expand the three dimensions of sustainability to include additional levels of consideration. This allows the understanding of sustainability to be further differentiated, for example, distinguishing between ecological (e.g., renewable energies, environmental protection), socio-economic (e.g., working conditions), cultural-institutional (e.g., trust in institutions, corruption), socio-cultural (e.g., diversity, gender), and financial/economic (e.g., revenue, trade balances) sustainability (Moldaschl, 2007). Such extensions make it possible to more finely elaborate the interactions between the target dimensions and to make the concepts more operationalizable. However, the three-dimension model still forms the basis and today represents the foundation of almost all definitions of sustainability. Precisely because of its rather open interpretation, it is a widely accepted model in business and politics.

Closely linked to the three-dimension model is the concept of the "Triple Bottom Line" (TBL), often referred to as "People, Planet, Profit." This model was proposed by John Elkington in the 1990s and calls on companies to assess their performance not only by economic, but also by social and ecological criteria. The TBL expands the three-dimension model by emphasizing the responsibility of companies to pursue economic returns, ecological responsibility, and social justice simultaneously. The model, through its reference to the English "Bottom Line" (translatable in German as "Nettoergebnis"), already implies a more quantifiable reporting, in which financial assessments are placed on an equal footing with social and ecological criteria (Elkington, 2018).

In addition, there are a number of other models and approaches that define and expand the concept of sustainability. These models attempt to examine the concept of sustainability from various perspectives and to address specific challenges that may not be sufficiently considered in the classic three-dimension model.

One such approach to illustrate sustainability is the sustainability cross, also known as the concept of "Strong vs. Weak Sustainability." This model distinguishes between strong and weak sustainability. Strong sustainability assumes that natural capital (e.g., forests, biodiversity) cannot be replaced by other forms of capital (e.g., financial capital). Therefore, these natural resources must be preserved to secure the livelihoods of future generations. Weak sustainability, on the other hand, allows the substitution of natural capital with other capital, as long as the total capital stock does not decrease. One criticism is that the terms "strong" and "weak" sustainability are often interpreted differently, leading to confusion and inconsistent applications or even instrumentalization in politics and business. In particular, the concept of weak sustainability is heavily criticized, as many natural resources and ecosystem services are irreplaceable, and thus there are concerns that ecological limits will not be observed (Ott & Döring, 2008; Steurer, 2001).

Another model is the concept of "Planetary Boundaries," developed by a group of scientists led by Johan Rockström. This model identifies nine ecological boundaries within which humanity must operate to ensure a safe operating space for the planet. The idea is that crossing these boundaries can lead to irreversible environmental damage that destabilizes the balance of the Earth system. Compared to the three-dimensions model, the planetary boundaries concept places a stronger focus on ecological dimensions and emphasizes that maintaining these boundaries is the fundamental prerequisite for any form of sustainable development. While the three-dimensions model seeks a balance between ecological, economic, and social goals, the planetary boundaries model presents ecological limits as non-negotiable (Potsdam Institute for Climate Impact Research [PIK], 2023).

The "Donut Model," also known as "Doughnut Economics," was developed by the economist Kate Raworth and, in a sense, connects the three-dimensions model with the planetary boundaries (Raworth 2012). It represents sustainable development as a space enclosed by two boundaries: an ecological ceiling, defined by the planetary boundaries, and a social foundation, which describes the minimum requirements for a dignified human life. Between these two boundaries lies the "safe and just space for humanity" (Raworth 2012). The donut model expands the three-dimensions model by explicitly linking the social dimension to minimum requirements and placing these in an integrative context with ecological boundaries (Raworth, 2018).

Although these models differ in their approaches, they have overlaps and distinctions. Central to all concepts is the management of resources, although the term "resource" itself can be understood in very different ways. Therefore, the next chapter will address the topic of resources in the context of sustainability.

2.2 What do Resources mean in the Context of Sustainability?

Central to achieving sustainability goals in all concepts is the management of resources.[4] The key question is how best to use them to support sustainable development.

A closer look at resources across the different dimensions of sustainability quickly reveals that their nature can be very different. Natural raw materials, which we, for example, burn for energy production, are by nature finite/exhaustible. Here, a sustainability strategy must aim to enable resource-conserving use or to develop substitution options. However, there are also generative resources. Examples include human skills and competencies (human capital), intellectual property, or certain social relationships (such as trust). Strategies here should aim to enable an increase in these resources. Unlike in the classical economic sense, these resources have the property of being amplified/increased through their own use. This type of resource should therefore be used as extensively (liberally) as possible to best support prosperity and sustainable development. In addition to these two types, there are also renewable resources, which can be restored or reproduced through the use of energy and labor. These include manufactured goods, but also softer factors such as a company's reputation and brand value. Sustainable management of these resources should focus on efficiency, aiming to keep the use of energy and labor as low as possible.

It becomes clear that there is a particularly close relationship between finite and regenerative resources. By using finite raw materials, we are able to generate energy and provide raw materials for products. Goods can be reproduced through the use of finite resources, but are dependent on them as long as reuse and recycling or renewable energies are not employed.

To make these relationships tangible and to derive meaningful courses of action, sustainability debates also distinguish between the concepts of efficiency, consistency, and sufficiency. Efficiency describes the sensible or productive use of raw materials and energy. The decisive factor is the ratio between resources used (input) and resources or products produced (output). This ratio can be improved, for example, by changing processes through the use of technology and optimization measures. Consistency, on the other hand, describes the lasting impact of human material and energy flows on the environment and natural processes. From this perspective, resource use should be organized in such a way that it leaves no lasting, destructive impact on the environment (i.e., does not endanger the functioning of social and ecological systems). Ideally, sustainability strategies are designed so that only reusable and renewable resources are used. In this context, the term circular economy is often used, which, in contrast to the linear use of resources, enables the most closed possible flow of materials, substances, and energy (see Fig. 2.2).

[4] "Resources" and "capitals" are often used synonymously in this context.

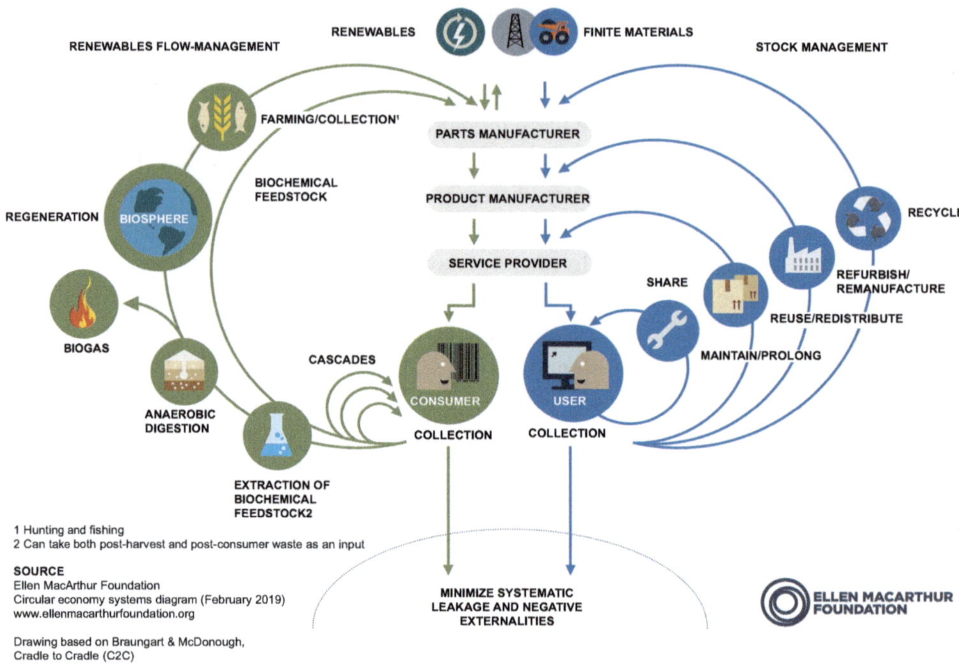

Fig. 2.2 Circular Economy Butterfly Diagram. (Ellen MacArthur Foundation 2019)

Arguably the most critically discussed concept regarding sustainable resource use is the concept of sufficiency. In sufficiency-oriented sustainability strategies, the central assumption is that reduced resource use can also enable a satisfactory (sufficient) life. Such approaches are fundamentally based on ecological limits, compliance with which can only be achieved through corresponding changes in awareness and consumption patterns (Fischer & Grießhammer, 2013). Unlike efficiency, sufficiency concepts are not about rationalizing resource use, but rather about rationing and avoiding overconsumption. Proponents of these approaches criticize efficiency-driven strategies by arguing that efficiency gains alone are not sufficient to achieve sustainable development. Reference is made, among other things, to rebound effects, which can offset or even overcompensate for efficiency gains (Göpel, 2020). An example here is air travel: thanks to numerous technical measures, airplanes today are much more efficient and consume significantly less fuel. Nevertheless, the absolute CO_2 emissions from air travel have increased disproportionately over the same period. The reason for this is the growing number of people taking flights. This, in turn, is partly due to the fact that airfares have become more affordable for a broader segment of the population, which is in part also due to the lower fuel costs for airlines. In this example, one would have to ask the difficult question of how many flights, for whom, and for what purpose could still be considered satisfactory (sufficient).

Sufficiency-based sustainability concepts therefore ask what "the truly needed amount of something" is in order to ensure sustainability with minimal loss of well-being. Since the definition of what constitutes a satisfactory life is highly normative, the question of sufficient resource use is hotly debated (Linz et al., 2002).[5]

Having examined the concepts of sustainability and resources, the next section will address how these are applied in the economic context and for individual companies.

2.3 Sustainability at the Corporate Level

Many companies have recognized that sustainability can be of strategic importance for several reasons. Departments that devote all their time to sustainability issues are no longer uncommon in large corporations. Over the years, this has led to the establishment of professional sustainability management. In parallel with the development of the concept of sustainability, terms such as "Corporate Citizenship," "Corporate Social Responsibility" (CSR), "Environmental, Social and Governance" (ESG), or "Corporate Sustainability" have increasingly emerged, aiming to transfer the concept of sustainability to the corporate context (see Fig. 2.3).

In particular, the term CSR has been a very popular buzzword in the business environment for many years. However, in the past, companies have interpreted it very differently and often used it to enhance their image depending on the situation. "Many companies include under this everything good they do: cultural and sports events or nature trails, donations, sponsorships, and the establishment of foundations" (Aachener Stiftung, 2017).

For a long time, there was no uniform definition of the term CSR, and in corporate practice it was often used synonymously with the term Corporate Citizenship (CC). However, CC and CSR differ in scope and focus. CC is understood as the social engagement of companies that goes beyond the actual business activities of the respective company. This includes the examples mentioned above, such as donations, sponsorships, or foundations (Loew et al., 2004).

In contrast, CSR can be defined not just as an additional activity, but as a holistic concept that encompasses all corporate activities and, in particular, the core business. What matters is not how profits are used, but that they are already generated in an environmentally and socially responsible manner (Pufé, 2014). The proximity to the concept of sustainability is evident here. The CSR concept is ultimately also about considering the three dimensions of economy, ecology, and social issues in an integrated way. The European Commission, for example, defined CSR

[5] See also concepts that distinguish between strong and weak sustainability (e.g., Ott & Döring, 2008; Steurer, 2001)—see Sect. 2.1.

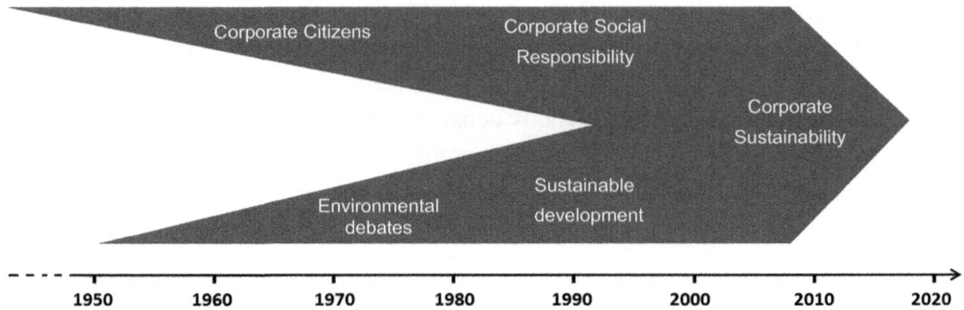

Fig. 2.3 Development towards Corporate Sustainability. (Own illustration)

> "as a concept whereby companies integrate social and environmental concerns in their business operations and in their interaction with their stakeholders on a voluntary basis." (EU Commission, 2011, p. 4)

CSR and sustainability in the business context are therefore closely related concepts. Both concepts consider the three dimensions, but CSR focuses only on the scope of action of the company and not the entire system in which it operates. This focus is intended to help concentrate on the truly company-specific requirements of sustainability.

In addition to CSR, the term ESG is also frequently encountered in companies and is closely linked to CSR. While in the past both terms were often seen as opposites—CSR as a voluntary framework and ESG as a set of quantifiable criteria—they are now increasingly being integrated together in everyday corporate practice (Tykkä, 2022). CSR provides the holistic framework in which a company defines its responsibility, while ESG delivers the structure of specific sustainability criteria.

> "While CSR aims to make a business accountable, ESG criteria make such business' efforts measurable." (Lexology, 2021, p. 1)

Thus, the topics that must be reported according to the European CSRD guidelines are structured according to the ESG distinction, that is, by environment, social, and governance (Kaźmierczak, 2022).

Occasionally, this is also referred to as "Corporate Sustainability," which particularly emphasizes the connection between societal and corporate challenges (see Fig. 2.4).

Against this background, the more recent term "purpose" should also be seen. In an increasingly competitive labor market, companies that can communicate a clear and authentic corporate purpose are better able to attract and retain talented professionals. In particular, younger generations are looking for employers who not only strive for economic success but also make a positive contribution to society. A strong purpose statement and its credible implementation strengthen the employer brand and make the company more attractive to qualified professionals. At the same time, this can increase

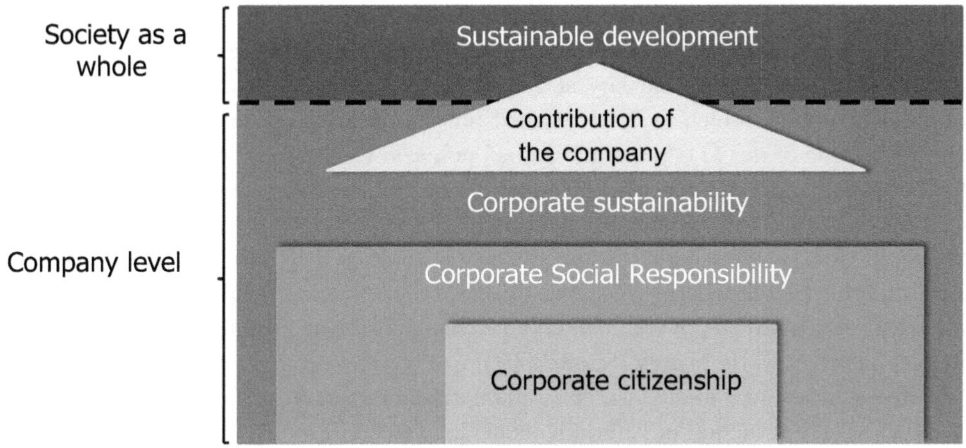

Fig. 2.4 Sustainability at the societal and corporate level. (Own illustration)

employee retention, as employees identify more strongly with the company's values and are more motivated to contribute to the company's long-term success.

A clearly defined corporate purpose also goes hand in hand with the sustainable use of resources. Even at the corporate level, the management of resources is crucial for the realization of sustainability strategies in the sense of CSR or corporate sustainability. In terms of sustainability, companies must ask themselves how they can use the resources available to them in such a way that they support efficiency, consistency, and sufficiency criteria in all three dimensions (economic, ecological, social) (see Sect. 2.2). The new reporting obligations in the EU are aimed precisely at this. They are intended to make transparent whether the company's resources are actually being used for the key issues in the three dimensions.

2.4 The Risks of Inaction

If you open the business section of a current daily newspaper, you will almost certainly find articles on topics such as environmental pollution, CO_2 emissions, fair trade, product life cycles, recycling, or similar. Sustainability is an omnipresent topic and its facets and challenges are widely discussed. The reason for this is that, on a global scale, numerous developments can be identified that will fundamentally change existing conditions and courses of action for most people and companies. These are so-called "megatrends" that make a shift in existing value creation processes toward more sustainable forms of business virtually imperative and put companies under pressure to act.

Arguably the most prominent and probably also the most urgent trend is climate change. Due to global warming, harvests are failing, floods are increasing, and hurricanes are causing ever more devastating damage. By now, it is not only the inhabitants of small island states who fear and experience the effects firsthand. The increasingly frequent heatwaves and heavy rainfall events are leading to extreme weather phenomena that are growing in both intensity and frequency. A shocking example is the flooding of the Ahr Valley, which in 2021 reached previously unimaginable proportions and is considered one of the worst natural disasters in recent German history. Such events illustrate how real and immediate the threats posed by climate change have become, even for countries like Germany. The consequences of climate change now affect a large part of the population, with the poorest segments in less developed countries suffering the most. According to Nicolas Stern, who investigated the economic impacts of climate change on behalf of the British government, climate change is the greatest and most far-reaching market failure in world history (Stern, 2007).

Closely linked to climate change is another major issue of our time: the loss of biodiversity. The destruction of natural habitats, the spread of monocultures, and the excessive use of pesticides are causing species to disappear at an alarming rate. Forests, coral reefs, and other sensitive ecosystems that serve as habitats for countless plant and animal species are shrinking or dying out, leading to an irretrievable loss of biological diversity. The decline of pollinators such as bees and butterflies threatens not only food production but also the stability of entire ecosystems. The loss of biodiversity does not only affect remote areas but also has direct impacts on human livelihoods and prosperity. Scientists warn that the disappearance of species and the resulting ecological imbalances will have profound consequences for the climate, food security, and human health (Intergovernmental Science-Policy Platform on Biodiversity and Ecosystem Services [IPBES], 2019).

At the international level, these problems have long been recognized, and numerous forums are seeking possible solutions. In terms of climate, the most important platform is the negotiations associated with the UN Framework Convention on Climate Change. Starting with its signing at the Rio Conference in 1992, the establishment of quantitative CO_2 targets in the Kyoto Protocol of 1997, and their development through subsequent climate conferences up to the Paris Agreement in 2015, the goals and commitments regarding global warming have been continuously tightened. The latest decision of the Paris Agreement limited global warming to well below 2 °C.[6]

Especially in the area of climate, the direct implications for companies can be clearly demonstrated. States are increasingly under pressure to intervene in specific economic sectors through regulation in order to achieve global climate targets. Under the Paris

[6] Initially, there was often talk of a 2-degree target—according to the agreement, however, it would be more accurate to speak of a 2-degree limit. The agreement defined 1.5 °C as the goal: "The universal agreement's main aim is to keep a global temperature rise this century well below 2 degrees Celsius and to drive efforts to limit the temperature increase even further to 1.5 degrees Celsius above pre-industrial levels." (United Nations Framework Convention on Climate Change [UNFCCC Newsroom]—(06.11.2017).

Agreement, the signatory states have committed to developing national action plans, known as "Nationally Determined Contributions" (NDCs), which set out their respective contributions to achieving the climate goal. These NDCs must be revised every five years according to the "progression principle," meaning that each subsequent contribution must be more ambitious than the previous one. The first global stocktaking process, known as the first "Global Stocktake," took place in 2023 to assess whether the cumulative greenhouse gas reductions are sufficient to achieve the goal of the Paris Agreement ("Übereinkommen von Paris") from 2015 (Federal Ministry for Economic Cooperation and Development [BMZ], 2025)—limiting global warming to well below 2 °C, ideally to 1.5 °C. The final report then made it clear that despite the increase in climate commitments, the world remains far from being on track to limit global warming to 1.5 °C.

In their action plans and climate strategies, states are therefore still required to set out how they intend to implement their own climate strategies and from which economic sectors the respective reductions are to be achieved. In the German government's Climate Action Programme 2030, which sets the path to greenhouse gas neutrality by 2045, it is precisely defined what contribution the energy, buildings, transport, industry, and agriculture sectors must make. In 2019, this was embedded in the national legal framework through the adoption of the Climate Protection Act (KSG) and was even tightened in terms of requirements and targets by a decision of the Federal Constitutional Court 2021.[7] However, the requirements for sectoral targets in Germany have recently been relaxed, meaning that individual sectors that fail to meet their targets now face less stringent sanctions. This has led to controversy, as particularly in the transport sector, which has made hardly any progress in reducing CO_2 emissions since 1990, significant improvements are still needed.

Nevertheless, the fact remains: companies that fail to anticipate these developments risk suffering direct economic competitive disadvantages. This may manifest itself through the loss of subsidies and tax relief or may even lead to direct penalties and compliance risks.

At the European level, the EU Commission made it clear early on that corporate sustainability in the sense of CSR is indeed the responsibility of companies, but can also be enforced by government regulation if necessary:

> "CSR should be company led. Public authorities can play a supporting role through a smart mix of voluntary policy measures and, where necessary, complementary regulation." (EU Commission, 2017)

[7] In 2021, the Federal Constitutional Court ruled that the original version of the Climate Protection Act was partially unconstitutional. The court found that the law could endanger the freedom rights of future generations by setting insufficient measures for the period after 2030. This decision is based on Article 20a of the Basic Law, which obliges the state to protect the natural foundations of life for future generations as well (Federal Constitutional Court, 2021).

While at the time of the last edition of this book (2018) it was still unclear how regulatory pressure would develop, the adoption of the EU Green Deal has now crystallized a whole set of requirements that are putting many companies under pressure to act. This regulation makes effective climate and sustainability management virtually indispensable for companies in the medium term.

But it is not only climate change that poses direct risks for businesses; other megatrends are also challenging industry to question existing practices and develop sustainability strategies. The increase in the world's population, for example, not only impacts climate change but also leads to further intensification of resource scarcity and other environmental burdens. It is not just the total number of people (according to UN estimates in 2017, about 9 billion people will inhabit this planet by 2050), but also the accompanying change in income distribution. Projections suggest that the number of people who can be classified as middle class will continue to grow in the coming years (Kharas, 2017). This is associated with enormous changes in the required material and energy flows. Increasing prosperity means that more and more people are demanding access to products and technological innovations, which will pose supply challenges for industry. If there are no economic policy adjustments, resource scarcity can lead to political and economic tensions, and additional consumption can threaten the integrity of the ecological system (see Sect. 2.2). This is especially true in urban areas, which are experiencing the highest growth rates and are already struggling with smog and waste problems.

In addition, the availability of certain finite resources, such as rare earths or raw materials, presents major challenges for companies, as availability and price volatility can jeopardize business models and pose financing risks. Against this background, it is not surprising that corporate environmental management is placing increased emphasis on recycling and re-use concepts. Converting finite resources into renewable resources (with the ideal of a circular economy) is a central task that will become more pressing with increasing consumption. In the long term, industries face the challenge of compensating for population and economic growth through altered value chains and improved energy and resource efficiency (see also the concept of sufficiency in Sect. 2.2).

In this context, it can be observed that the horizon of corporate responsibility seems to be continuously expanding. Whereas in the past the focus was primarily on companies' own manufacturing processes, companies, consumers, and regulators are increasingly considering entire value creation processes. As a result, the pressure on companies is rising to consider the impacts of their products along the entire life cycle, starting from the early design and development phases. Companies that are unable to present coherent sustainability concepts in this regard risk, in the long term, losing credibility and becoming the target of lawsuits or warranty claims.

These risks are further exacerbated by another megatrend. Digitalization and the information age have made global value flows more complex and information flows faster. This presents companies with the challenge of creating transparency in increasingly complex supply chains. If they fail to do so, it is now much easier and faster to lose credibility and market value. The networking of civil society movements, critical media, and concerned consumers can quickly lead to the consequences of irresponsible actions becoming directly accessible to a broad public (e.g., through protest actions or dissemination via social media). In addition to impacts on the capital market, there is a risk of permanently losing sustainability-conscious customers. Simply giving a company a green veneer is no longer enough to win the favor of the market. Today, informed customers know very well what it means to be sustainable and are increasingly sensitive in their purchasing decisions.

2.5 Transformation as Opportunity

Apart from the fact that sustainability strategies help reduce risks arising from global changes, a corporate strategy focused on sustainability also offers direct advantages for companies. Several studies have now shown that sustainability is also financially worthwhile for businesses (Ameer & Othmann, 2012; McKinsey & Company, 2019; Chen et al., 2023). Some studies even show that simultaneous engagement in all three dimensions of sustainability can yield a positive financial effect after two years (Wang & Sarkis, 2013). Even if the direct correlation between financial performance and sustainable business practices is not always easy to calculate, there are nevertheless causal relationships that open up a wide range of opportunities for companies.

A key advantage for companies in engaging with sustainability strategies lies in the opportunity to increase the company's brand value. A convincing presentation of a company's own sustainability can significantly enhance its reputation (Gidwani, 2013). Often, this is the decisive motivation for business leaders to address the issue (Accenture, 2013). As sustainability becomes more important to customers, it can also serve as a differentiating factor, helping to attract new customers and increase brand value. Ecological and socially responsible actions also promise stronger customer loyalty.

Sustainability in this sense is primarily an element that, as part of a marketing strategy, can bring a variety of benefits. However, this also entails the risk of "greenwashing." PR or marketing initiatives in which the appearance of sustainability does not match the substance can lead to far-reaching economic policy misjudgments or misguided consumer incentives. For consumers, it is usually not immediately apparent whether yogurt with a "natural" label or the donated square meter of rainforest for a crate of beer actually represents a more sustainable purchasing decision. Greenwashing can become even more critical for society and companies if the aim is to prevent or weaken government regulation. An extreme example, which ultimately also involved cases of fraud, is the discussion and impact of the so-called "Dieselgate scandal." Here it became clear that companies only appeared to have adapted to sustainability requirements, with far-reaching negative consequences for the environment, health, and ultimately the company itself.

Meanwhile, stricter regulations are also being implemented to prevent greenwashing. Particularly noteworthy is the so-called "Green Claims Directive" of the European Union. This directive aims to require companies to substantiate their sustainability claims with sound and verifiable evidence. False or misleading statements can not only damage consumer trust but are increasingly leading to legal consequences for companies. As a result, greenwashing is not only an ethical issue but also a significant legal risk.

Nevertheless, companies that do not use sustainability merely as misguided marketing, but have their sustainability verified through recognized standards and networks, can increase their reputation and brand value in the long term. Once this is achieved, not only do market shares usually rise, but profits as well, since higher prices can be charged for these products.

The reputation gained in this way affects not only customers and consumers. Increasingly, it is a critical success factor in attracting the right talent to a company or retaining good employees ("war on talents"). For more and more people, sustainability is an additional criterion in deciding for or against a company. A company that can convincingly demonstrate that it is more ecological and socially responsible than its competitors has a clear market advantage here (Walsh & Sulkowski, 2009).

Investors are also becoming increasingly sensitive to the issue of sustainability. Companies with lower ecological or social risks have better chances of obtaining loans. The demand for socially and ecologically sustainable investment opportunities ("Socially Responsible Investments" [SRIs]) is constantly increasing, as is the interest of investors in obtaining transparency about responsible capital deployment. This trend has been further intensified by the increasing regulation of the financial market as part of the Green Deal—especially the "Sustainable Finance Disclosure Regulation" (SFDR). This regulation requires financial market participants, such as fund managers and insurers, to provide detailed information on how they take sustainability risks into account in their investment decisions and what impact their investments have on the environment and society.

It is therefore not surprising that the market for sustainability ratings is booming. Worldwide, there are over 70 agencies comparing corporate ethics, and there is a confusing number of platforms offering ESG ratings for companies and supply chains. In addition, almost all major banks now offer consulting services through various sustainability departments. A sustainability strategy that also makes a company's ecological and social risks transparent and authentically demonstrates future opportunities can thus help reduce capital costs, generate investment funds, and improve shareholder relations.

Aligning a company with sustainability is usually also accompanied by direct competitive advantages in the traditional sense. Companies that focus on resource efficiency as part of their sustainability initiatives often achieve significant cost savings. Firms that participated in the evaluation of the Lean & Green Management Awards between 2013 and 2024 were able to reduce their energy costs by an average of 3% per year through resource efficiency projects. The best companies even achieved double-digit percentages, which they were able to maintain over several years. Companies that fail to keep pace with such developments will very soon feel the cost disadvantages (see also Chap. 4).

The topic of material efficiency is already a decisive success factor. The share of raw materials and operating supplies in manufacturing companies averages between 30% and 45% of total production costs (Sievers et al., 2013). According to data from the Federal Statistical Office (2016), the share of material costs in the gross production value of small and medium-sized enterprises has continuously increased over the past 30 years—from 36% in 1993 to around 41.5% in 2019. Interestingly, while material expenditures have risen, personnel costs have decreased over the same period from 27% to 19.5%. Energy costs, on the other hand, have remained almost unchanged at about 2% (VDI Center for Resource Efficiency [VDI ZRE], 2024). In addition to the supply risks already mentioned, which are emerging for some materials, efficient use of materials is thus one of the key levers for increasing company profitability. Sustainability concepts that improve the management of finite and renewable resources can provide crucial impetus here (see Sect. 2.2).

The efficiency advantages of sustainability initiatives are not limited to the company itself; sustainable supply chain management also offers significant economic and strategic benefits. Ecological and social standards and their enforcement can make a significant contribution to improving business relationships with suppliers and strengthening their employee motivation. This, in turn, leads to higher process and product quality, which directly benefits customers and can improve the performance of entire value chains.

Another connection that holds enormous potential for companies is the positive interplay between sustainability strategies, innovation potential, and new business models. Companies may decide to abandon previous practices and operate more sustainably for a variety of reasons. The most common reason is likely the tactical necessity for change—or that it opportunistically contributes to improving company performance. Assuming that social and ecological challenges will make sustainable business practices imperative in the long term, thereby increasing pressure on companies, those that respond early will have an innovation advantage ("first mover advantage"). Companies that cling to outdated business models for as long as possible risk being unable to respond to necessary changes in time. Early anticipation of future challenges and standards gives companies more time to experiment with materials, technologies, and processes.

This is especially true when entirely new industries emerge as a result of social and ecological challenges. The long-term perspective underlying sustainability concepts pushes companies to examine alternatives to existing business models and to understand how customer needs can be met in other ways. This drives innovation and can thus open up new markets. Renewable energies, smart grids, car-sharing concepts, organic products, or environmental technologies are examples where new business models have developed in direct response to social and ecological challenges.

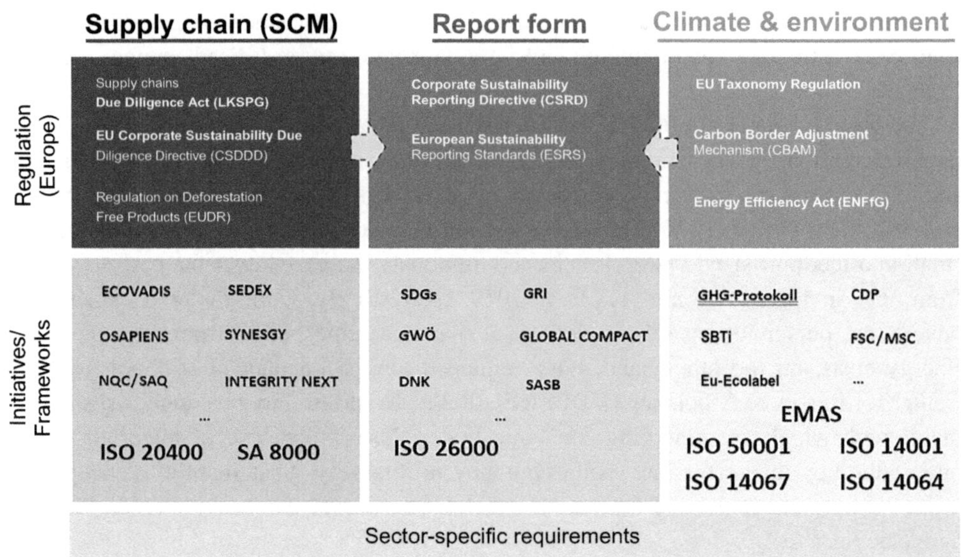

Fig. 2.5 Structure of current sustainability topics for industrial companies—selection. (Own illustration)

2.6 The Current Challenges for Companies

Companies across all industries are under pressure to act. The opportunities and risks outlined above imply that inaction can have serious consequences for companies. Yet many companies struggle to take the first step toward sustainability or become entangled in efforts to integrate sustainability substantively into existing corporate structures and strategies.

Broadly simplified, three main areas can currently be defined in which companies are required to orient themselves and manage sustainability issues. These three areas cannot be sharply separated and are mutually dependent (see Fig. 2.5). First, it is important to clarify what the future reporting format will be, in which the topics converge and which also allows for an assessment of one's own progress and sustainability performance. This is the pivotal point, as for many companies it means gaining a realistic picture of their current situation and, based on this, defining sustainability goals and strategies. Second, it is necessary to make transparent which risks and impacts exist in the company's supply chains and how these can be addressed. Especially due to the crises of recent years (corona crisis, chip crisis, supply chain crisis, energy crisis, war on Ukraine, etc.), it has become clear how interconnected and vulnerable global supply chains are. In addition, many social and ecological problems are cross-border and can only be solved through cooperation along the supply chains—explicitly including, for example, the preservation of biodiversity and the observance of human rights and social standards. Closely related is the third area, which can be described as environmental and climate management. In particular, there have long been numerous rules and standards in this area that a company must be aware of and must also provide very concrete targets and key figures.

1. Sustainability Reports

The starting point of any sustainability report should be an analysis of which individual sustainability topics are most significant or "material" for the company itself and the specific context in which it operates. The method of choice here is the so-called "materiality analysis." A materiality analysis is also a component of most international sustainability reporting standards and, with the adoption of the CSRD and the associated "European Sustainability Reporting Standards" (ESRS) in the EU, has taken on a new dimension. It is now not only a term familiar to a broader audience, but for the first time, it also defines the concept of double materiality as a mandatory requirement.

"Double materiality" means that two perspectives must be considered in the materiality analysis: on the one hand, the company's impacts on the environment and society (inside-out perspective), and on the other hand, the impacts of environmental and social issues on the company itself (outside-in perspective). This means that topics are not only assessed based on their financial relevance to the company, but also on whether the company's actions have significant effects on the environment and society.

Conducting a materiality analysis begins with a comprehensive review of the company context—including a stakeholder analysis. It is crucial to identify the relevant internal and external stakeholders and to understand their expectations and requirements of the company. These stakeholders may include employees, customers, suppliers, investors, non-governmental organizations (NGOs), governments, and society at large.

The next step is to create a "long list" of potential sustainability topics. This list includes all topics that could be relevant in the context of the company. To analyze these topics in more detail, they are specified by providing a detailed description of the so-called "Impacts, Risks and Opportunities" (IROs). IROs help to assess the specific risks, opportunities, and impacts of each topic, thereby enabling a better evaluation of their relevance for the company.

The final assessment and prioritization of the topics is then carried out using a scoring system. Positive or negative impacts are evaluated based on magnitude, scope, likelihood of occurrence, and irreversibility. Financial opportunities and risks are assessed based on likelihood of occurrence and magnitude. The result of this process is a list of material topics that are particularly important for the company and must therefore be addressed in the reporting.

Engaging with IROs and the associated identification of strategic topics helps the company to position itself more securely for the future. Through the systematic analysis of risks and opportunities arising from sustainability topics, the company can respond early to potential changes and proactively take measures to ensure its long-term resilience and success. This not only contributes to fulfilling reporting obligations, but also strengthens the company's sustainable orientation and competitiveness in the market.

However, the CSRD-ESRS standard is not the only sustainability reporting standard, although it is now the decisive one within the European legal framework. Globally, there are still a variety of other standards. For example, if companies want to take a broader approach, they can report in line with the "United Nations Global Compact." Here, they commit to regularly reporting on activities that support the UN Sustainable Development Goals (SDGs). However, the specific content of Global Compact reports is largely left to the companies themselves. The criteria of the "Global Reporting Initiative" (GRI), which for a long time were considered the gold standard for sustainability reports, are more specific. To mention another example: there is also the criteria catalog of the "German Sustainability Code" (DNK), which is primarily used in German-speaking countries. However, it does not see itself as an additional requirement, but rather seeks to make the criteria of the relevant standards simple and practical for medium-sized companies.

This brief overview of reporting standards, which is by no means exhaustive, illustrates how complicated orientation has been or still is for companies in this area. Against this background, it is very welcome that there is now a mandatory harmonization at the European level with the ESRS standard, although the ongoing negotiations on reducing bureaucracy will determine in the future the extent to which the European ESG regulation will gain real traction.

2. Sustainability in Supply Chains

Comprehensive CSR approaches require transparency across the entire supply chain and a sound risk management system, which is increasingly becoming mandatory due to regulatory requirements. German legislation, particularly the Supply Chain Due Diligence Act (LkSG), and the more recent EU Directive on "Corporate Sustainability Due Diligence" (CSDDD), are putting pressure on companies to systematically identify, assess, and minimize human rights and environmental risks in their supply chains. These regulations force companies to establish robust risk management systems, which has led to the emergence of numerous assessment platforms that confront companies with different questionnaires. Completing these questionnaires is often very time-consuming, and unfortunately, their terminology and focus are not standardized, which in the worst case can lead to duplication of work for companies. This approach also carries the risk of embellishment, as companies may try to present their sustainability performance as better than it actually is. It is not sufficient to focus solely on optimizing questionnaire responses.[8] Rather, companies should aim to derive concrete measures for the individually material topics. This also includes working closely with their own suppliers to improve sustainability standards along the value chain.

[8] Many consulting services currently focus precisely on such optimization, which carries the risk that while ratings may improve, more effort is invested in questionnaires than in actual transformation.

Another important aspect that is coming into focus in this context is the protection of biodiversity. The regulation on deforestation-free supply chains ("EU Deforestation Regulation" [EUDR]) plays a central role here, as it obliges companies importing certain products into the EU to ensure that their products do not contribute to deforestation.[9] This requires a deeper analysis and control of supply chains to ensure that no raw materials are sourced from ecologically sensitive areas.

Overall, companies are expected not only to make their supply chains more transparent, but also to establish systems that promote long-term improvements and sustainable partnerships with suppliers. Actively involving and developing suppliers with regard to sustainability (in addition to the classic aspects such as cost, quality, technological competence, or innovative strength) is therefore one of the central challenges currently facing many companies.

3. Environmental and Climate Management

Environmental and climate management are closely linked to the first two subject areas and must increasingly be brought into focus by companies. This is not only due to growing regulatory requirements, but also to the increasing societal and economic necessity. Various standards provide guidance here: the "EU Eco-Management and Audit Scheme" (EMAS) as well as the internationally recognized standards ISO 14001 for environmental management systems and ISO 50001 for energy management systems are well-established frameworks that help companies systematically record and improve their environmental and climate performance.

Another important method is the "Life Cycle Assessment" (LCA), which evaluates the environmental impacts of a product throughout its entire life cycle. The "little brother" of the LCA, the "Product Carbon Footprint" (PCF), focuses specifically on the greenhouse gas emissions of a product. Professionally conducted LCAs and PCFs make it possible to accurately determine environmental impacts along the entire value chain. Accordingly, approaches for sustainability strategies can also be derived from these findings. A challenge for companies in this context is finding the right level of transparency. LCAs can become extremely extensive and complex at a high level of detail, which does not always make operationalization easy and is usually associated with significant effort (especially in data preparation). This is particularly true for complex value chains, where it is also important to define the appropriate level of detail for the company.

Due to recent regulations under the EU Green Deal, it is becoming increasingly mandatory for companies to calculate their own "Corporate Carbon Footprint" (CCF), including "Scope 3" emissions. This comprehensive recording of all direct and indirect emissions of a company is intended to ensure that climate management is not only superficial, but is deeply integrated into the value chain. The main standards here are primarily

[9] These products mainly include raw materials and goods that can be linked to deforestation, such as soy, palm oil, timber, cocoa, coffee, beef, and certain products made from these.

the requirements of the "Greenhouse Gas Protocol" (GHG) and the ISO 14064 standard. In terms of environment and climate, the so-called "EU Taxonomy Regulation" also brings a new perspective into play. This very comprehensive classification system defines which economic activities are considered environmentally sustainable and compels companies to structure their environmental and climate measures in order to be "taxonomy-compliant." The advantage of taxonomy compliance is that companies able to demonstrate their activities as sustainable in the sense of the EU taxonomy gain access to a growing number of investors and financial resources that specifically want or are required to invest in sustainable projects. This can not only reduce financing costs but also strengthen the company's reputation in the market. Furthermore, the taxonomy enables companies to communicate transparently and credibly to stakeholders that they are actively contributing to achieving the EU's climate goals.[10]

Another element of current regulation is the "Carbon Border Adjustment Mechanism" Regulation (CBAM Regulation), which already applies to certain companies. This regulation aims to regulate the CO_2 emissions of imported goods into the EU by requiring importers to purchase certificates for the emissions of these goods. CBAM complements the "EU Emissions Trading System" (EU ETS) and ensures that companies within the EU are not disadvantaged by cheaper but more environmentally harmful imports. For companies, this means that in the future they will need to closely monitor their emission sources and, if necessary, make adjustments to remain competitive and minimize regulatory risks. Still under discussion

In addition to these regulatory requirements, there are also a number of private reporting frameworks. Central examples here include the "Carbon Disclosure Project" (CDP) and the "Science Based Targets Initiative" (SBTi). The CDP calls on companies to disclose their environmental impacts, such as greenhouse gas emissions and water consumption. The SBTi helps companies set scientifically based climate targets that are aligned with the goals of the Paris Agreement. The assessments of these two initiatives are becoming increasingly important for investors and customers and are being incorporated into ratings and supplier evaluations.

The complexity not only in the area of climate and environment, but across all three subject areas, makes it clear that companies face a whole range of challenges and that it is often not easy to keep track. This is especially true as developments in the field of sustainability are currently very dynamic and a rapid learning process is taking place on all sides.

The current focus of developments is primarily on creating transparency and implementing and aligning the many new regulations in such a way that substantial change and

[10] The main goal of the EU taxonomy is to direct capital flows towards sustainable investments and thus make a significant contribution to achieving climate neutrality in the EU by 2050. By establishing clear criteria for sustainable economic activities, the regulation creates a foundation for transforming the European economy towards ecological sustainability and resilience.

a sustainable transformation of the economy can occur in the future. For the majority of companies, the next step will be to translate the identified areas for action, guidelines, and goals into more operationalizable corporate strategies. If there are regular, standardized, and measurable reports on the successes and failures of sustainability activities in the future, the focus will increasingly shift to operational implementation. Almost all companies face the challenge of integrating sustainability strategies into existing business strategies at as many levels as possible. A target set at the corporate level should ultimately be broken down to the plant and department levels. In addition to operational business areas, the strategy must also be anchored in research and development departments as well as in procurement and sales. Once a strategy has been formulated, the question also arises as to how employees can be engaged with the new topic, since many sustainability concepts would fail without their involvement.

These requirements mean that companies are increasingly dependent on looking beyond their own horizons, even in the area of sustainability. This is not only about searching for the best available techniques (which are usually referred to as "Best Available Techniques" [BAT] in international negotiations), but especially about obtaining cross-industry suggestions and insights on how ecological and social strategies can be sensibly operationalized in a company and which methods help to achieve an optimum in all three dimensions of sustainability. A comparison of numerous leading companies in Europe shows that those with extensive experience in holistic management systems and a high level of implementation of lean management principles find it particularly easy to integrate the topic of sustainability into their own business processes.

References

Aachener Stiftung Kathy Beys. (2017). *Lexikon der Nachhaltigkeit.* https://www.nachhaltigkeit.info. Accessed 6. Nov 2017.

Abschlussbericht der Enquete-Kommission. (1998). *Schutz des Menschen und der Umwelt—Ziele und Rahmenbedingungen einer nachhaltig zukunftsverträglichen Entwicklung* (S. 18). Deutscher Bundestag: Drucksache 13/11200 vom 26. Juni 1998.

Accenture. (2013). *The UN Global Compact- CEO Study on Sustainability 2013.*

Ameer, R., & Othman, R. (2012). Sustainability practices and corporate financial performance: A study based on the top global corporations. *Journal of Business Ethics, 108*, 61–79.

Brundtland-Bericht. (1987a). S. 51, Absatz 49 und S. 54, Absatz 1.

Bundesverfassungsgericht. (2021). *Pressemitteilung Nr. 31/2021 vom 29. April 2021.* https://www.bundesverfassungsgericht.de/SharedDocs/Pressemitteilungen/DE/2021/bvg21-031.html. Accessed 17. May 2025.

Carlowitz, V. (1713). *Sylvicultura oeconomica. Leipzig, Braun 1713 mit dem Zitat „nachhaltende Nutzung" auf Seite 105.*

Chen S., Song Y., & Gao P. (2023). *Environmental, social, and governance (ESG) performance and financial outcomes: Analyzing the impact of ESG on financial performance. Journal of Environmental Management 345*(4):118829.

Deutscher Bundestag. (1998). *Abschlußbericht der Enquete-Kommission „Schutz des Menschen und der Umwelt—Ziele und Rahmenbedingungen einer nachhaltig zukunftsverträglichen Entwicklung“* (S. 18). Deutscher Bundestag: Drucksache 13/11200 vom 26. Juni 1998.

Elkington, J. (2018). 25 years ago I coined the phrase “Triple Bottom Line.” Here’s why it’s time to rethink it. Harvard Business Review. https://hbr.org/2018/06/25-years-ago-i-coined-the-phrase-triple-bottom-line-heres-why-im-giving-up-on-it. Accessed 10. Sept 2024.

Ellen MacArthur Foundation/Circular economy systems diagram. (2019, February). www.ellen-macarthurfoundation.org Zeichung basiert auf Braungart & McDonough, Cradle to Cradle (C2C).

EU Kommission. (2011). Eine neue EU-Strategie (2011–14) für die soziale Verantwortung der Unternehmen (CSR). https://eur-lex.europa.eu/LexUriServ/LexUriServ.do?uri=COM:2011:0681:FIN:DE:PDF. Accessed 7. Nov 2017.

EU Kommission. (2017). *Definition von CSR*. http://ec.europa.eu/growth/industry/corporate-social-responsibility_de. Accessed 7. Nov 2017.

EU Kommission. (2023). *Corporate sustainability reporting*. https://finance.ec.europa.eu/capital-markets-union-and-financial-markets/company-reporting-and-auditing/company-reporting/corporate-sustainability-reporting_en. Accessed 10. Sept 2024.

Fischer, C., & Grießhammer, R. (2013). *Working Paper. Mehr als nur weniger Suffizienz: Begriff, Begründung und Potenziale* (S. 7 ff). Öko-Institut e. V.

Gidwani, B. (2013). *The link between brand value and sustainability*. The Conference Board, Director Note October 2013.

Göpel, M. (2020). *„Unsere Welt neu denken“. Eine Einladung*. Ullstein Verlag.

IPBES. (2019). *Summary for policymakers of the global assessment report on biodiversity and ecosystem services of the Intergovernmental Science-Policy Platform on Biodiversity and Ecosystem Services*. IPBES secretariat. https://doi.org/10.5281/zenodo.3553579

Kaźmierczak, K. (2022). *A literature review on the difference between CSR and ESG*. https://managementpapers.polsl.pl/wp-content/uploads/2022/12/162-Ka%C5%BAmierczak.pdf. Accessed 10. Sept 2024.

Kharas, H. (2017). *The unprecedented expansion of the global middle class—An update*. Global Economy and Development program at the Brookings Institution.

Konferenz der Vereinten Nationen über Umwelt und Entwicklung. (1992). https://www.un.org/depts/german/conf/agenda21/rio.pdf.

Lexology. (2021). *p. 1/RHTLaw Asia LLP*. https://www.lexology.com/library/detail.aspx?g=80bbe258-a1df-4d4c-88f0-6b7a2d2cbd6a. Accessed 10. Sept 2024.

Linz, M., Bartelmus, P., Hennicke, P., Jungkeit, R., Sachs, W., Scherhorn, G., Wilke, G., & von Winterfeld, U. (2002). *Von nichts zu viel. Suffizienz gehört zur Zukunftsfähigkeit* (S. 7 ff). Wuppertal Institut.

Loew, T., Ankele, K., & Braun, S. (2004). *Bedeutung der internationalen CSR-Diskussion für Nachhaltigkeit und die sich daraus ergebenden Anforderungen an Unternehmen mit Fokus Berichterstattung* (S. 54 f).

McKinsey & Company. (2019). *Five ways that ESG creates value*. https://www.mckinsey.com/~/media/McKinsey/Business%20Functions/Strategy%20and%20Corporate%20Finance/Our%20Insights/Five%20ways%20that%20ESG%20creates%20value/Five-ways-that-ESG-creates-value.ashx. Accessed 10. Sept 2024.

Moldaschl, M. (2007). Polychrome Nachhaltigkeit. *Ökologisches Wirtschaften, 1*, 30–34.

Ott, K., & Döring, R. (2008). *Theorie und Praxis starker Nachhaltigkeit* (2. Aufl.). Metropolis.

PIK—Potsdam-Institut für Klimafolgenforschung. (2023). *Schwindende Widerstandskraft unseres Planeten: Planetare Belastungsgrenzen erstmals vollständig beschrieben, sechs von neun bereits überschritten.* https://www.pik-potsdam.de/de/aktuelles/nachrichten/schwindende-widerstandskraft-unseres-planeten-planetare-belastungsgrenzen-erstmals-vollstaendig-beschrieben-sechs-von-neun-bereits-ueberschritten-1. Accessed 10. Sept 2024.

Pufé, I. (2014). Was ist Nachhaltigkeit? Dimensionen und Chancen. In Bundeszentrale für politische Bildung (Hrsg.), *Aus Politik und Zeitung—Nachhaltigkeit (APuZ)* (Bd. 64, S. 16).

Raworth, K. (2012). *A Safe and Just Space for Humanity: Can We Live within the Doughnut?* Oxfam Discussion Papers.

Raworth, K. (2018). *Die Donut-Ökonomie: Endlich ein Wirtschaftsmodell, das den Planeten nicht zerstört.* Hanser.

Sievers, U., et al. (2013). Ressourceneffiziente Fertigung. Erfahrungen und Handlungsempfehlungen zur Verbesserung von Rohstoff- und Energie-Effizienz in der verarbeitenden Industrie. *WoMag, 3*(2), 4–6.

Statistisches Bundesamt. (2016). *Kostenstrukturerhebung, Kostenstruktur der Unternehmen des Verarbeitenden Gewerbes sowie des Bergbaus und der Gewinnung von Steinen und Erden* (Anmerkung: neben den Kosten für Roh-, Hilfs- und Betriebsstoffe sind auch Aufwendungen für fremdbezogene Vorprodukte in den Materialkosten enthalten).

Stern, N. (2007). *The economics of climate change. The Stern review.* Cambridge University Press.

Stern, N. (2016). Economics: Current climate models are grossly misleading. *Nature, 530*(7591), 407–409.

Stern, N., & Richter, M. (2009). *Der Global Deal. Wie wir dem Klimawandel begegnen und ein neues Zeitalter von Wachstum und Wohlstand schaffen.* C.H. Beck.

Steurer, R. (2001). Paradigmen der Nachhaltigkeit. *Zeitschrift für Umweltpolitik und Umweltrecht, 24.2001/4*, 537–566.

Tykkä, E. (2022). *CSR or ESG as a management tool for a company?* https://www.theseus.fi/bitstream/handle/10024/743999/Thesis_Final_ET_2.pdf?sequence=2&isAllowed=y. Accessed 10. Sept 2024.

Uekötter, F. (2014). Ein Haus auf schwankendem Boden: Überlegungen zur Begriffsgeschichte der Nachhaltigkeit. In Bundeszentrale für politische Bildung (Hrsg.), *Aus Politik und Zeitung—Nachhaltigkeit (APuZ)* (Bd. 64, S. 14, 16).

United Nations Framework Convention on Climate Change [UNFCCC Newsroom]. (2017, June 11). https://unfccc.int/most-requested/key-aspects-of-the-paris-agreement.

VDI-Zentrum für Ressourceneffizienz. (2024). *Einführung in die Ressourceneffizienz.* https://www.ressource-deutschland.de/themen/ressourceneffizienz/. Accessed 10. Sept 2024.

Walsh, C., & Sulkowski, A. J. (2009). *A Greener Company makes for happier employees more so than does a more valuable one: A regression analysis of employee satisfaction, perceived environmental performance and firm financial value* (December 10, 2009).

Wang, Z., & Sarkis, J. (2013). Investigating the relationship of sustainable supply chain management with corporate financial performance. *International Journal of Productivity and Performance Management, 62*(8), 871–888.

3 The Underestimated Potential of Lean Management with regard to Sustainability

Lean management is a holistic management philosophy aimed at optimizing costs, quality, and delivery capability. The term "Lean" is often used as a catch-all for optimization methods, continuous improvement processes, order and cleanliness, or excellence systems. If one wishes to formulate a fundamental definition of "Lean," the common basis of most approaches may be the creation of value without waste. Waste, in this context, refers to all non-value-adding activities. Value-adding, in turn, is everything for which the customer is willing to pay.

So why does lean management hold such great potential for sustainability? Since lean management is described as a corporate philosophy and not merely a toolbox of optimization tools, it provides a broad foundation for making processes leaner and more sustainable. The focus on waste, the idea of continuous and targeted improvement, the empowerment of employees, and the integration of suppliers and customers along the value chain are key elements that decisively support the implementation of sustainability strategies.

3.1 What is Lean Management, actually?

An important root of lean management lies in the "Training Within Industry" (TWI) program, which was developed in the USA during World War II. The goal of the TWI program was to increase efficiency in industrial production to meet the demand for war materials. To this end, a systematic training program for workers was introduced, focusing primarily on improving work methods, training supervisors, and promoting teamwork. The program consisted of three main modules: "Job Instruction" (JI), "Job Methods" (JM), and "Job Relations" (JR), each aimed at teaching employees to perform their work more efficiently and safely, develop better work methods, and foster positive working relationships (Müller, 2018).

D. Reichert, *Lean & Green: Best Practice*, https://doi.org/10.1007/978-3-658-49880-1_3

The principles of the TWI program had a significant impact on economic development after the war. Especially in Japan, where the TWI program became widespread after the war, the methods were very well received. The emphasis on continuous improvement, standardization of work processes, and efficient employee training were central elements and influenced the economic upswing after World War II. Competition was fierce, and many companies tried to assert themselves in international markets. Western companies focused primarily on mass production with large facilities and high volumes (Womack & Jones, 2003). Japanese companies, including Toyota, faced major challenges in competing internationally, as they simply lacked the funds to accumulate material inventories and produce in large quantities. The high volumes produced by Western companies reduced their unit costs ("economies of scale"). As a result, Toyota, for example, had a massive cost disadvantage compared to Western competitors. To keep up with the international automotive industry, Toyota developed the now world-famous "Toyota Production System" (TPS). The main goal of the production system is to produce the best quality in the shortest possible time at the best possible cost (Liker, 2004). To achieve this, Toyota sought to harmonize processes and eliminate all unnecessary activities and functions from its factories. Toyota chose an approach that optimally balanced "Muda" (waste), "Mura" (unevenness), and "Muri" (overburden) (Liker, 2004). "Muda" is probably the best-known element, which can be divided into seven types of waste (see Sect. 3.2). "Mura" refers to types of loss that arise, among other things, from production control, for example, when processes are not coordinated or when there are excessive fluctuations. "Muri" refers to both overburdening of employees, such as stress, fatigue, etc., and overburdening of machines. Simply eliminating waste is of little help if it introduces too much fluctuation (Mura) into the process and/or overburdens employees (Muri). In particular, the fear of overburdening employees was and still is a widespread argument, mistakenly used by critics against the introduction of "Lean." However, the concept of waste can only be reconciled with Muri and Mura, the fundamental philosophy of lean management, to improve processes.

The TPS is usually depicted in the form of a house (see Fig. 3.1). The foundation is "Kaizen" with its philosophy of continuous improvement. At Toyota, "Heijunka" and standardization build upon this as the basis of lean management. Heijunka is the Japanese term for leveling/smoothing and addresses Mura (unevenness). Standardization, in turn, helps prevent Muri (overburden) and ensures that achieved optimizations are sustained. The production house has two essential pillars: "Just-in-Time" and "Jidoka." While Just-in-Time aims to harmonize processes and avoid inventories and overproduction, Jidoka focuses on consistently preventing errors and deviations as soon as they occur in the process.

The success of the TPS attracted interest from academia, the public, and other international automobile manufacturers, especially in the USA. Central to translating the TPS into the more modern term "lean production" was a study commissioned by the Massachusetts Institute of Technology (MIT) in the late 1980s. For this study, the two

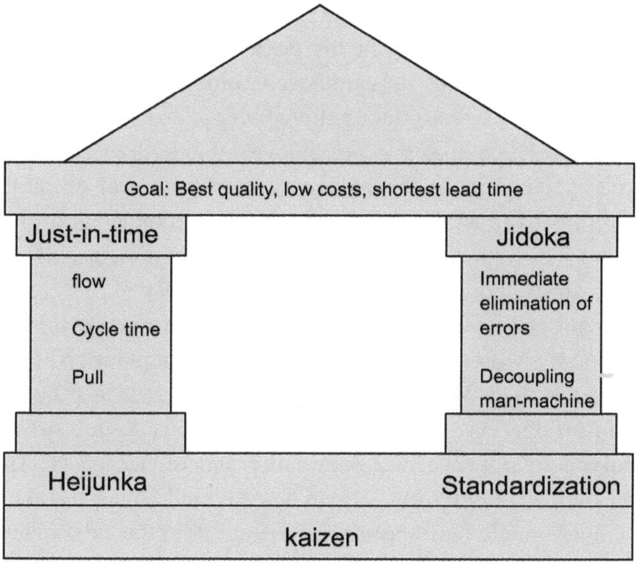

Fig. 3.1 Example of a production house based on Toyota. (Source: own illustration)

economists Womack and Jones collected information on various production approaches in North America, Japan, and South Korea. They quickly discovered that alternatives to the rigid system of mass and assembly line production offered clear advantages, and summarized their findings in the book *The Machine that Changed the World* (Womack, 1990). The book quickly spread internationally and, from the mid-1990s, became the foundation for the reorientation and development of holistic production systems in numerous companies. The focus on avoiding waste ultimately gave rise to the name "lean production."

Since 1990, lean management has continuously evolved and has been deepened and disseminated by various authors and practitioners. One of the most significant contributions came from Jeffrey Liker, who comprehensively described and analyzed the TPS in his book *The Toyota Way* (2004). Liker identified 14 management principles that made Toyota the leading automotive brand and form the foundation of modern lean management. A central element of Liker's work is the strong focus on processes and long-term systems thinking. Liker emphasized that sustainable success is not achieved through short-term gains or isolated improvements, but through the consistent optimization and harmonization of processes throughout the company. Decisions should always be made with long-term goals in mind, even if this means short-term losses. This underscores the importance of a stable, sustainable system built on long-term success and customer trust. Liker's emphasis on these aspects has strongly shaped modern lean management and contributed to the understanding of lean not just as a production method, but as a comprehensive management philosophy (Liker, 2004).

Another influential author in the further development of lean management is Mike Rother, who coined the term "Kata" in his book *Toyota Kata* (2009). Rother demonstrated how Toyota systematically integrated continuous improvement processes (Kaizen) into its daily routine. He introduced the concepts of the "Improvement Kata" and the "Coaching Kata," which make it possible to standardize improvement processes while simultaneously developing the ability of managers and employees to independently devise solutions to problems. Rother's work also contributed to the development of lean management into a more broadly applicable management philosophy that can be used in various industries and business areas (Rother, 2009).

Another significant concept that can be linked to lean management is "Six Sigma." Originally developed by Motorola in the 1980s and later popularized by General Electric under the leadership of Jack Welch, Six Sigma aims to reduce process variability and minimize errors in production and business processes. Six Sigma uses statistical methods and data analysis to improve process quality and reduce costs. The integration of lean management and Six Sigma into "Lean Six Sigma" began to take hold in the late 1990s. Michael George made an important contribution to the establishment of Lean Six Sigma with his book *Lean Six Sigma: Combining Six Sigma with Lean Speed* (2002), in which he described in detail the synergies between the two methods. Lean Six Sigma became especially popular in the early 2000s, as many companies worldwide adopted this approach to simultaneously reduce costs, accelerate processes, and improve quality (George, 2002; George et al., 2007).

"Agile methods," which originated in software development and are now used in many other fields, also aim to optimize business processes and have many overlaps with lean management. Ken Schwaber and Jeff Sutherland, the inventors of "Scrum," one of the best-known agile frameworks, emphasize—much like lean—the importance of flexibility, continuous improvement, and adaptability to change. Both approaches place great value on employee involvement and empowerment, as well as on continuous feedback loops to optimize processes (Scrum Guides, 2020).

"Business Process Management" (BPM), as described by authors such as Michael Hammer and James Champy, also has many overlaps with lean management. If one looks for distinguishing features between the approaches, BPM may take a more analytical and technology-driven approach to optimization, while lean focuses more on cultural change and the involvement of all employees. In addition, both approaches can also be understood as complementary: for example, lean management can identify the processes that should be automated and monitored through BPM (Hammer & Champy, 2003).

The intersection between lean management, agile methods, BPM, and Six Sigma lies in their shared goal of making business processes more efficient and customer-oriented. All four approaches strive to eliminate waste, improve quality, and increase flexibility. Moreover, all approaches now have a broad focus and apply to all business processes.

Thus, today the term "lean production" is rarely used; instead, "lean management" is more common. Lean management refers to a holistic approach that considers the entire value streams of a company. All business units are designed to ensure overall optimization along value streams. Lean approaches have also established themselves in "administrative" areas such as sales, procurement, research, or accounting, helping to optimize processes. In some companies, a distinction is still explicitly made here between "Operational Excellence" (OpEx) and "Administrative Excellence" (AdEx).

While lean production focuses on the physical manufacturing of products, reducing inventories, shortening production times, minimizing production errors, etc., "Lean Admin" focuses on improving information flows and reducing unnecessary administrative tasks to shorten processing times and minimize errors in office work. Even though the methods and the type of collaboration in optimization and control differ, both worlds pursue the fundamental lean principles (Brenner & Matyas, 2018). The increasing expansion to administrative processes has also led to lean being applied today in non-manufacturing companies. "Lean Banking" (Nestor D'Alessio & Oberbeck, 1994) or "Lean Hospital Management" (Angerer, 2015) are just two of many examples.

3.2 Anchoring Lean Management in Companies

The extent to which Lean Management is integrated into a company's processes can vary greatly between organizations. Unfortunately, Lean Management is still often viewed as a toolbox of methods that can be used to optimize processes in isolated instances. In most cases, these are isolated initiatives that address specific problems within defined areas and have a project-based character. Lean Management is more deeply embedded in daily processes in companies that, in addition to using methods and tools, also derive Lean principles (e.g., "Just-in-Time," "Zero Defects," etc.) and define guardrails for continuous development. In this way, Lean Management becomes not just a collection of individual initiatives, but the foundation for a holistic management system that can guide all activities.

A central component of such a system is effective policy deployment, which can be achieved through methods such as "Hoshin Kanri" or "Objectives and Key Results" (OKR). Both approaches aim to systematically and transparently translate a company's strategic objectives into operational measures and ensure that all levels of the organization are working toward the same overarching goals. The central question is then no longer what can be improved through isolated optimization activities, but rather what must be specifically optimized to achieve the desired (strategic) target states (see Fig. 3.2).

The specific individual target states can be concretized using a described excellence system (see TPS, Sect. 3.1). Lean principles help define how ideal processes and organizational structures should be designed to best support an individual market strategy. If, for example, the market environment requires high flexibility and fast response times, "Just-in-Time" could be a central principle to which all functional areas must align. Methods and improvement measures that follow this ideal then directly contribute to improving the company's strategic market position (see Fig. 3.3).

Fig. 3.2. Improvement with goal orientation. (Own illustration based on Aulinger)

Fig. 3.3 The path to capability in Lean Management. (Own illustration)

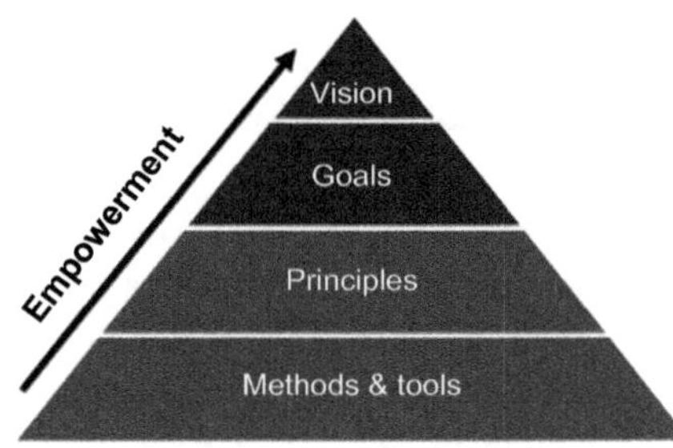

In this sense, Lean Management systems function as a kind of "transmission belt" through which strategic objectives can be translated into operational actions. It is therefore no longer just about the isolated application of Lean methods, but about the targeted application of Lean Management, which can only be achieved by harmonizing all functional areas. Starting from the "nucleus of production," other areas can also be developed in accordance with Lean principles. Harmonizing the various business processes with the goal of fulfilling customer requirements as waste-free as possible increases interface performance and also helps to operate more efficiently across departments. The unified language of a holistic management system makes it possible to interlink the different processes and align them toward an overall optimum.

Another crucial aspect of anchoring Lean Management is that Lean places a strong emphasis on employee participation and empowerment. Employees are encouraged to contribute their own ideas and take responsibility in their area. Therefore, team-based organizational forms are also closely linked to Lean Management. In order to realize lean processes and fast response times, operational problems should be decided and solved as independently and locally as possible. This enables management to gain time to focus on strategic matters and optimize the system as a whole. The more strategic a management position is, the greater the proportion of working time that should be

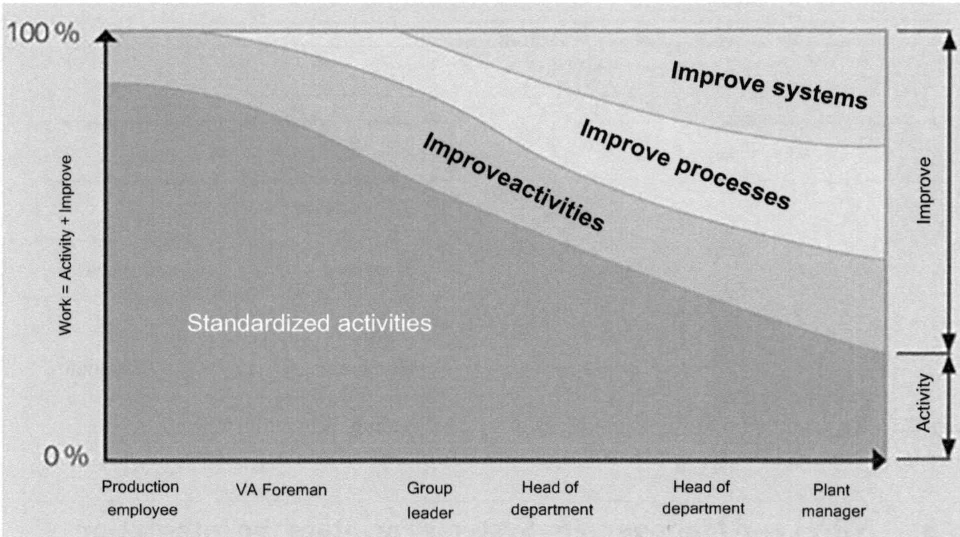

Fig. 3.4 Time allocation and tasks. (Winner of the Lean & Green Management Award)

devoted to system improvement. The systematic improvement of systems and processes corresponds to the fundamental Lean philosophy of continuous improvement and, in functioning Lean Management systems, is understood as a top management priority (see Fig. 3.4).

This requires, on the one hand, a team culture and, on the other, a certain level of problem-solving competence among all employees—both topics that are centrally influenced by the style of leadership. Empowering employees to solve problems independently is thus a key leadership element that should be continuously promoted in order to realize Lean as a corporate philosophy. It is not surprising that leadership culture and Lean leadership approaches are decisive building blocks in the implementation of Lean in companies. Other effective examples from this area, which also originated in Japan and were brought to the West, are discussed and implemented under the terms "Kata" or "Kata Coaching" (Rother, 2009).

It is clear that empowering employees will become even more important in the near future due to digitalization, automation, and "artificial intelligence" (AI). Increasingly, the "simple" processes are being automated and taken over by AI solutions. As a result, the requiered profiles and competences for employees is changing and becoming more demanding. Tasks that were previously easy to perform will have to be replaced by creative activities, which brings challenges in the selection and qualification of employees. If, as mentioned in the introduction to the book, one also considers that a sustainable orientation of the company requires competencies in all business areas, it becomes clear that Lean Management can make a decisive contribution to the future viability of companies.

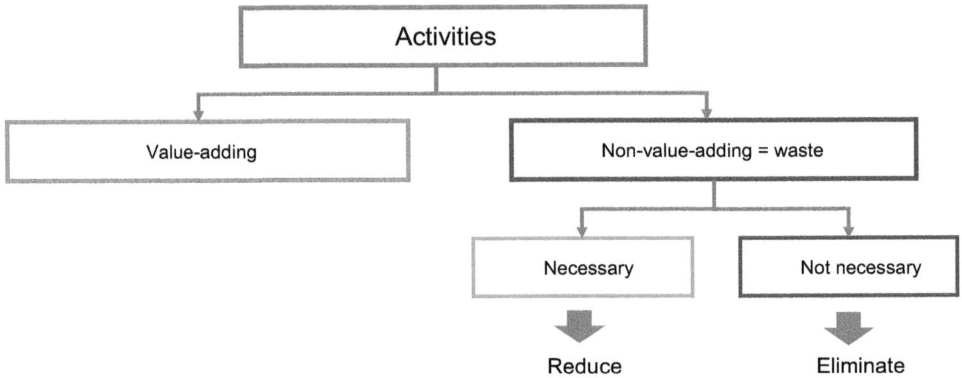

Fig. 3.5 Representation of value-adding vs. non-value-adding. (Own illustration)

3.3 Why Lean Management Systems Facilitate the Integration of "Green"

Various studies and the results of the Lean & Green Management Award show that companies with an integrated Lean Management system are, on average, "greener" than companies that have not implemented Lean Production (see Melnyk et al., 2003; Kovilage, 2021). Among others, one of the originators of the term "Lean," Jim Womack, already wrote in 2003:

> "This means that lean's role is to be green's critical enabler as the massive waste in our current industrial practices is reduced to free up resources for improving product technologies and production locations for free." (Womack, 2003)

The most well-known and also cited connection here is rooted in the concept of efficiency. A central goal of lean management is to categorize activities into value-adding and non-value-adding tasks in order to eliminate unnecessary activities from a process as much as possible and to use resources as efficiently as possible. This close link to the idea of resource efficiency explains why, for many, the connection between lean and green is established precisely here.

However, when distinguishing between value-adding and non-value-adding activities, it is important to note that there are activities which, although non-value-adding, are nevertheless necessary and therefore cannot be avoided given the current state of technology or production capabilities (see Fig. 3.5). An example of this are the change over times at a machine for a different products (e.g. changings tools). Change over as such is necessary in order to produce the products required by the customer. However, the setup process does not actively contribute to value creation, i.e., to customer benefit. In this case, it would make sense to reduce setup time to a minimum. Accordingly, the goal is to reduce this type of waste, not to eliminate it.

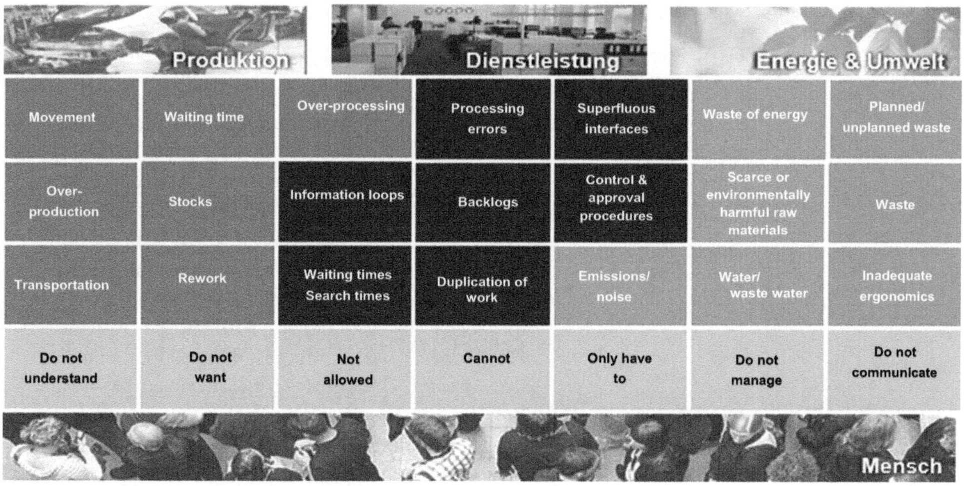

Fig. 3.6 Types of waste. (Own illustration)

There is a widespread understanding of the different types of waste in production, which is mostly based on the original approaches from Toyota and is structured in a very similar way. In order to make waste more tangible in administrative areas as well, in addition to the classic lean types of waste, specific wastes for the administrative sector are often defined. Since tasks and activities in this area are less physically observable and are mostly related to communication, the challenge here is to make process-relevant wastes visible. In the environmental field, there are also some approaches to defining specific types of waste, but so far these have only been implemented in practice by a few companies or consultancies (see Fig. 3.6). However, the successes show that there is great potential here, which will certainly help to continuously improve the resource efficiency of companies in the future.

However, the greatest effect on resource efficiency is achieved by approaches that link various types of waste. All classic Lean types of waste have an impact on the use of resources and can therefore be specifically applied methodically to optimize processes with regard to green applications (see Table 3.1).

The fact that the principle of waste thinking can be very well transferred to resource consumption is one reason why the topic of Lean & Green has become increasingly popular recently. However, this is only part of the picture. A holistic understanding of the Lean system offers a multitude of additional points of connection that help to advance sustainability topics and implement corresponding strategies.

The Strategic Component

A crucial building block for a functioning lean system is the ability to focus and prioritize—not just optimizing where we can, but above all where we must in order to achieve

Tab. 3.1 Lean types of waste and resource efficiency

Waste	(Classical meaning)	Impact on resource efficiency
Overproduction	Unnecessary investment of time, material, personnel, and financial resources	This involves the use of many unnecessary resources such as raw materials, energy, water, etc., to produce products that ultimately are not needed. Strict avoidance of overproduction therefore has a direct impact on resource efficiency. In addition, the unwanted products will eventually have to be disposed of, which, depending on the product, can also require significant resources
Waiting	Waiting times for tools, materials, output from upstream processes, etc.	During waiting, products may change their properties and thus become unusable. A generally greater effect, however, occurs with machines, which are often not switched off during waiting times. The resulting heat, cooling, and energy consumption are forms of waste. Waiting for upstream processes also means that capacities are not fully utilized. Better utilization of capacities directly increases resource efficiency
Transport	The materials required for a process are widely scattered or generally much too far from the actual place of value creation	It is obvious that reducing transport distances can save fuel, energy, and emissions. In particular, more efficient transport management from the supplier or to the customer has a major impact on a company's ecological footprint
Inventory	Similar to overproduction + additionally concealing problems such as poor planning and control, quality issues, etc.	More packaging material is needed to store the products. In addition, there may be consumption for, e.g., cooling or heating. There is also the risk that products may be damaged during handling in the warehouse or lose their properties over time
Motion	The employee is constantly on the move or making unnecessary movements during work	Similar to inventory, a large, distributed, and confusing workspace requires higher energy expenditure. Carrying parts or tools can also lead to damage

(continued)

Tab. 3.1 (continued)

Waste	(Classical meaning)	Impact on resource efficiency
Rework	Nonconforming parts/products that do not meet quality requirements. Waste similar to overproduction and potential additional investments (more work = higher costs) to replace defective parts	Rework requires more resources than originally planned. The contribution margin decreases, and material and energy consumption as well as emissions increase
Overprocessing	The product is overcomplicated or overengineered	Unnecessary features on the product usually mean more complexity and a higher demand for resources such as materials and energy. Increased complexity can also lead to quality problems, making rework necessary

our goals. This is fundamentally true for companies, but increasingly also applies to the topic of sustainability. In the future, this topic will receive more attention and thus bind more resources. All the more important, then, is to have a robust prioritization and goal-setting process.

Examples of effective tools for anchoring goals throughout the organization are the "Hoshin Kanri" and "OKR" approaches already mentioned in Sect. 3.2. These help ensure that strategic goals, including sustainability, are cascaded from top management down to all levels of the organization. An appealing aspect is that interdependencies between activities and projects are made transparent, and the impact of measures on all key objectives is considered. For example, a strategic project might focus on increasing the company's quality rates, but this could potentially conflict with another strategic goal, such as reducing lead times. Highlighting such interdependencies can be essential in ensuring that projects and activities not primarily aimed at sustainability still make their impact on strategic sustainability goals transparent. This prevents sustainability topics from being perceived as an isolated "add-on." Instead, such methods integrate sustainability into existing strategy processes, so that it is naturally considered in every project, investment decision, and target agreement. The overarching goal is to ensure that, through unified prioritization and focus, limited resources are not scattered across various parallel systems, but are instead purposefully deployed for projects and improvement activities that contribute to achieving strategic goals—including sustainability.

The topic of "policy deployment " also includes the so-called "goal transformation." The idea here is that strategic goals and key figures are not simply imposed on an organization as a whole, but that a process exists which precisely defines which specific influencing and control variables make sense at which level. For example, it makes little sense in a manufacturing company to post the monthly earnings figures (*"Earnings Before Interest and Taxes" [EBIT]*), even though this is a crucial strategic metric for the company. Far more suitable would be, for instance, the daily output rates, which do have a direct impact on profit, but not exclusively. Output rates, however, are generally directly influenceable by the manufacturing areas and are thus a better-suited target and control metric .

The process of determining which control metrics and KPIs are appropriate at which level is also highly relevant for sustainability topics. The process helps to make specific levers in different areas transparent and to clarify their contribution to overarching sustainability goals. Here, too, it makes little sense to apply overarching goals, such as climate neutrality, equally to everyone. Rather, the aim is to find target and control variables that can be influenced specifically by each area. For example, in procurement, the lever could be used to achieve a more sustainable supply chain or supplier base. Requirements for development could include leveraging design opportunities to make new products more sustainable according to defined criteria. Production targets would usually focus on material and energy efficiency. Even support areas such as Human Resources (HR) could be given goals, such as building sustainability competencies within the organization.

Fundamentally, it is about ensuring that all departments and teams align their goals with the overarching sustainability strategies, even if the levers may be very different. This is a key factor in ensuring that sustainability does not remain an "add-on," but is seen as an integral part of organizational priorities.

Process-Oriented Thinking

A challenge for such strategic anchoring of sustainability in the organization is, of course, knowing the relevant levers in the respective processes. This is where another dimension of a holistic lean system comes into play—namely, thinking in terms of horizontal processes. This includes understanding which levers exist within processes and what cross-functional impacts they have. Central methods in lean management are therefore process analyses, which examine how a process should be structured across interfaces to achieve the greatest possible customer value. This can be very effectively applied to sustainability topics as well, when processes are analyzed not only in terms of cost, quality, and delivery times, but also with regard to levers for sustainability. The range of process analyses is very broad. The analysis can focus on a manufacturing process, but just as well on administrative processes, such as the procurement process or, more broadly, the entire order fulfillment process. The product development process can also be analyzed for sustainability aspects using process analysis methods.

Lean methods in this sense, often referred to as "value stream analysis," can thus help to gain greater understanding of the individual levers for increased sustainability. The application of these tools is particularly attractive when classic process optimization is directly combined with improving sustainability performance. When it comes to redesigning a process or when improvements are needed, the resources of process participants usually have to be planned, the process is recorded with more or less structure, and improvements are derived—meaning time and effort are invested. In such cases, it is usually possible, with little additional effort, to integrate the sustainability perspective into these projects. This can be done by adding project objectives or by involving sustainability and environmental experts in the project team. The result can be a better process that both reduces costs and advances sustainability.

Process analysis can also be particularly relevant with regard to supply chains. In lean management, the integration and development of suppliers and partners play a major role. Successful companies do not limit the implementation of lean management to their own factories, but extend the focus to the processes of the entire supply chain. Active supplier development and collaborative exchange help to harmonize processes and implement continuous and mutual improvements. This, in turn, makes it possible to optimize quality, cost, or delivery time and generate additional customer value.

Companies that already have advanced supplier management and drive their production system beyond the boundaries of their own plants have a good starting point for integrating new "green" aspects into the value chain. Many companies are currently facing this challenge with regard to sustainability—not least because there are crucial levers in this area for improving the ecological and social performance of their own company. Experience with supplier development methods and tools can be effectively expanded to achieve a company's own sustainability strategy. Jointly defined targets can be set, and direct support can be provided through methods and expertise. This creates transparency about the environmental or social performance of the entire supply chain and enables targeted management through mutual exchange.

Performance Management

In addition to defining goals and identifying key levers for improvement, many companies currently face the challenge of being able to manage sustainability—that is, to ensure target achievement through target-actual comparisons. Here too, holistic lean systems offer many points of connection. For example, companies with extensive experience in implementing shopfloor or performance management systems have a solid foundation for moving toward a more short-cycle management approach in the area of sustainability as well.

Shopfloor and performance management systems help companies better manage the achievement of their goals by providing regular review and escalation cycles. These cycles make it possible to collect performance data at short intervals, identify deviations from targets, and initiate immediate corrective actions. The aim is to create interdisciplinary transparency about the current status, clearly assign responsibilities, and ensure proactive communication. This enables companies to respond more quickly to problems or negative developments and to take timely countermeasures.

"Shopfloor management" (or "officefloor management" in administrative areas) can help to more strongly integrate sustainability goals into day-to-day operations. This, in turn, leads to sustainability becoming a cross-functional topic rather than the responsibility of just a few.

The central challenge at present is the ability to define and make available relevant, actionable sustainability metrics. There is a significant overlap here with a key aspect of the current sustainability challenge for companies—the availability of data. It is not always necessary to collect or measure entirely new data. Often, the task is to combine existing data in a meaningful way and generate performance indicators from it. Until now, metrics such as CO_2 emissions, energy consumption, or environmental risks in the supply chain have mostly been "reporting metrics" that appear in annual reports, but have not served as management metrics like traditional performance indicators. There is certainly much potential in the coming years for companies to make better use of both existing and newly generated data. Ultimately, this leads to a more agile and continuous improvement process with regard to sustainability.

The Toolbox of Methods

If sustainability can be established as a target and management variable for more departments and functions within the company, the question also arises as to how to counteract deviations. Here too, a wide range of tools and methods from the lean management environment can help. Many approaches pursue the overarching goal of identifying and eliminating problems and root causes in processes. These tools and methods can often be applied in isolation and promise quick (cost) effects. Such methods and tools are suitable for specifically improving the efficiency of a process or business area. Based on green types of waste, these can also be analyzed in terms of sustainability to identify unnecessary resource consumption and then avoid or reduce it. Companies with many years of experience in the application and implementation of lean tools, and who have built up the corresponding methodological expertise, benefit from this. However, the prerequisite is that existing methodological expertise is not limited to individual areas or experts, but is broadly anchored within the company. On the one hand, it is advisable to sensitize lean method experts, if available in the company, to sustainability topics as well. On the other hand, technical departments (e.g., environmental or energy teams) should be qualified in lean methods. This leads to a shared understanding, and different competencies can complement each other very well. As with many approaches, it becomes clear that the greatest effects can be achieved in interdisciplinary workshops, and the mutual exchange of experience contributes to the qualification of all participants.

Examples of such adaptation of lean methods to sustainability topics include integrated "5S"[1] methods or the full range of problem-solving methods (the "5S" approach is a method for workplace organization aimed at creating efficient, safe, and sustainable work environments). In an integrated "5S" workshop, work areas can also be assessed and optimized with regard to environmental aspects. In addition to classic "5S" topics such as order and cleanliness, safety, and ergonomics, environmentally relevant points are also defined. Improvements that could be evaluated here include, for example, compressed air leaks, waste separation, break behavior, etc. Here too, a work area is optimized according to the "5S" method, standardized, and then compliance with the

[1] 5S stands for: Sort, Set in order, Shine, Standardize, Sustain.

standards is ensured. Based on a uniform evaluation method, audits can also be conducted, if necessary, with the explicit goal of improving resource efficiency and enabling comparability between work areas, including with regard to green topics.

Classic problem-solving methods, in turn, help to identify and eliminate the root causes of problems or deviations from target development. Typical methods include: "5-Why" method: A simple problem analysis technique in which repeated questioning of "Why?" is used to determine the root cause of a problem. The idea is to ask "Why?" at least five times and thus not be satisfied with merely describing the symptoms of a problem. Ishikawa diagram (fishbone diagram): Visualizes possible causes of a problem, grouped by categories such as machines, methods, materials, and people, to identify the main causes. A3 report: A structured problem-solving tool that documents problem analysis, objectives, solutions, and actions on a DIN A3 sheet. FMEA (Failure Mode and Effects Analysis): A systematic method for identifying and assessing potential failures in processes or products in order to minimize their impact.

Responsibility

A final and probably most essential point is that lean management fundamentally aims to anchor responsibility as deeply as possible within the hierarchy, thereby making it everyone's task. This is also an excellent target vision for the topic of sustainability. The more successfully the impact of each individual can be highlighted in relation to the sustainability strategy, the greater the enthusiasm and participation of employees in becoming co-creators of the transformation. The prerequisite, of course, is empowerment at all levels—for both lean and green topics. It is therefore particularly appealing to align qualification programs and provide integrated "Lean & Green" training. This not only makes synergies transparent, but can also motivate change in a completely different way.

The key advantage is that sustainability and green aspects are understood as a collective task and do not remain solely the responsibility of technical functions. This is particularly relevant at a time when many companies are unclear about how to further advance ecological sustainability. Many technical measures are obvious and have already been implemented in part—for example, installing photovoltaic (PV) systems on roofs, purchasing green electricity, well cooling, etc. However, true transformation requires far more solutions, which can no longer be driven solely by staff units such as environmental managers, energy managers, or sustainability managers. In the future, it will be much more about which products are developed, where we source our supplies, how we can produce, and of course, which products/services we offer and sell. This means that many more departments must be involved in the topic of sustainability, as the individual levers and opportunities for change depend on the departments and thus also on the know-how of the employees who manage the fundamental business processes as part of their daily work.

Just as it is not sustainable in the lean area for improvement processes to be permanently initiated and implemented by lean experts or consultants, the same applies in the green area: a sustainability strategy should be driven as broadly as possible. Only when sustainability is understood as a collective mission for the entire company will cross-functional solutions and innovations be developed that help achieve the necessary change. The integration of "green" into management systems then ensures that continuous and targeted improvement is also initiated with regard to sustainability.

3.4 Lean = Green and vice versa?

The fact that companies that are "lean" also tend to have better social and environmental performance on average can be explained, among other things, by systematic approaches and holistic management systems that help integrate sustainability issues into their own business processes or even the entire supply chain. However, engaging with ecological and social topics often also leads to further development of a company's own lean management approaches.

Sustainability goals are therefore a good starting point for examining process flows and procedures from a different perspective. It often becomes apparent that "looking through green-tinted glasses" offers a new approach to uncovering potential that would have remained hidden under the classic lean perspective. A concrete example is the analysis of packaging methods and processes. Avoiding environmentally harmful or unnecessary materials often leads to the discovery of alternative solutions that require less packaging material and, in turn, can also reduce handling and picking times. In this way, green can also be an innovation driver for process improvement, with positive effects on many levels (see also Sect. 2.5).

Likewise, green or sustainability topics offer the opportunity to generate a different or additional motivation for change and improvement processes. When an improvement measure aims to enhance the company's environmental or social performance, employees are often more likely to identify with the change than they would be if the goal were merely monetary savings. Since improving the "green" balance usually also involves avoiding waste and increasing process efficiency, monetary and environmental optimizations can often be achieved simultaneously. The only questions are which objectives are set and how achieved successes are reported and communicated. Especially in companies where lean is not yet part of the corporate culture and thus not "lived" by employees and managers, or where past implementation attempts have failed or not been carried out, green can be an additional motivator for employees to optimize processes.

Despite the many points of connection and synergies, it should be noted in conclusion that there can also be conflicts between lean and green objectives. One example is the ideal of just-in-time production: this concept calls for organizing material deliveries in shorter cycles to avoid unnecessary inventories. While this is certainly efficient from a lean perspective, from a green perspective it can have negative effects, as additional transport and truck traffic are required. The resulting increase in fuel consumption negatively impacts the environmental balance. In line with the three dimensions of sustainability, the aim in such cases should be to resolve goal conflicts as much as possible and strive for an overall optimum. One possible approach would be to review alternative transport options in addition to the increased transport frequency.

An even more pronounced effect is rooted in the fundamental idea of efficiency. If a process designed according to lean principles is particularly efficient, this can lead to more products being sold. While this makes both the customer and the company happy, it does not help the environment overall. With regard to such "rebound effects," it is therefore not enough to "simply" reduce waste in processes; rather, all the interrelationships outlined above must be addressed and sustainability considered as a separate objective.

References

Angerer, A. (2015). Die Lean-Philosophie in der Praxis. In D. Walker (Hrsg.), *Lean Hospital – Das Krankenhaus der Zukunft* (S. 49–76). MWV Medizinisch Wissenschaftliche Verlagsgesellschaft.

Brenner, J., & Matyas, K. (2018). *Lean Administration – Verschwendung erkennen, analysieren, beseitigen*. Hansa Fachbuch.

George, M. (2002). *Lean Six Sigma: Combining Six Sigma Quality with Lean Production Speed* (1. Aufl.). McGraw-Hill Education.

George, M., Rowlands, D., & Kastle, B. (2007). *Was ist Lean Six Sigma?* Springer.

Hammer, M., & Champy, J. (2003). *Reengineering the Corporation: A Manifesto for Business Revolution*. HarperBusiness.

Kovilage, M. P. (2021). Influence of lean – green practices on organizational sustainable performance. *Journal of Asian Business and Economic Studies 28*(2), 121–142.

Liker, J. (2004). *The Toyota way: 14 management principles from the world's greatest manufacturer*. McGraw-Hill.

Melnyk, et al. (2003). *Assessing the impact of environmental management systems on corporate and environmental performance*. Shingo Prize.

Müller, G. (2018). *TWI: Training Within Industry – Unterweisen, führen, verbessern*. Carl Hanser Verlag.

Nestor D'Alessio, N., & Oberbeck, H. (1994). *Lean Banking*. SOFI-Mitteilungen Nr. 21, Soziologisches Forschungsinstitut Göttingen (SOFI) e. V. an der Georg-August-Universität.

Rother, M. (2009). *Toyota Kata: Managing People for Improvement, Adaptiveness and Superior Results*. McGraw-Hill Education Ltd.

Scrum Guides. (2020). https://scrumguides.org/scrum-guide.html. Accessed 10. Sept 2024.

Womack, J. (1990). *The machine that change the world*. Rawson Associates.

Womack, J. (2003). *Lean is Green*. Lean Enterprise Institute. https://www.lean.org/the-lean-post/articles/is-lean-green/. Accessed 10. Sept 2024.

Womack, J., & Jones, D. (2003). *Lean Thinking*. Simon & Schuster.

Example methods for Industrial Companies

4

As outlined in the previous chapters, a holistic lean management approach facilitates the integration of sustainability aspects into business processes. Building on this, the following chapter will presenthow sustainability can be anchored in manufacturing companies, using specific areas of action. Starting from the definition of a sustainability strategy, three examples will illustrate how "lean" and "green" can be more closely intertwined.

4.1 Approaches to Strategic Anchoring

Numerous business studies show that the majority of strategies and change processes in companies fail to achieve their self-imposed goals. And this is already true for strategies in general, especially for economic approaches in which companies set the framework and direction for their own business models and seek to secure or develop fundamental profitability. It appears to be even more complicated when companies face the challenge of developing a new sustainability strategy. Often, this is designed in addition to existing strategies, and there is little experience on how to integrate concrete green objectives and—more importantly—how to operationalize them.

In the first edition of this book (2018), a structured approach was explained in detail at this point, outlining how sustainability strategies can be developed and operationalized. However, much has happened in this area, and with increasing regulation, mandatory standards for sustainability reporting have emerged (in particular CSRD-ESRS—see Chap. 2). Even though much is still evolving in the implementation of the new ESRS and all stakeholders are undergoing a learning process, these standards nevertheless provide a very consistent basis or framework for companies—not only to fulfill reporting obligations, but also to derive robust strategies. After all, a sustainability report without a strategy runs the risk of being ineffective and becoming a liability.

D. Reichert, *Lean & Green: Best Practice*, https://doi.org/10.1007/978-3-658-49880-1_4

(See also the fundamentals in Sect. 2.6.) More interestingly, the preparation of a sustainability report can help to deeply anchor sustainability within the organization by involving various corporate functions in the materiality analysis during the reporting process. This fosters greater awareness of sustainability issues at all levels. Each material topic requires specific policies, actions, objectives, and metrics, which means organizations need to develop an overarching strategy that should not be isolated from other strategic processes. As shown in Chap. 3, methods such as "Hoshin Kanri" and "OKR" enable this alignment and prioritization.

A concrete recommendation to avoid sustainability strategies developing separately from the actual strategy process is to define and make transparent a harmonized annual cycle for the key strategic processes. Strategic processes include, for example, the fundamental market and development strategy, the annual budgeting process, the personnel development process, and ideally also a continuous value stream process—as well as sustainability reporting. Each of these processes has specific dates throughout the year when it requires input and generates output. For example, it makes sense to conduct value stream analyses before the annual strategy workshops so that ideas for optimization potential can then be translated into strategic projects. Since these may also involve investments, it is equally sensible to consider when topics need to be available for the annual budget-setting and to schedule corresponding workshops early enough. The sustainability reporting process should also be harmonized with this, so that these topics receive equal attention in the company's strategic development. For example, an assessment of the impacts, opportunities, and risks of material topics should ideally also serve as input for strategy workshops and budget planning. It is also important that all strategic topics are subject to a regular review process, in which progress is evaluated and, if necessary, countermeasures or adjustments are made. This is also a way for sustainability to remain continuously on the agenda, so that information for the report does not have to be collected at the end of the year.

Another element from the lean environment can also help to keep these topics continuously on the company's radar. For a long time, target and ideal states in lean management have been mapped in maturity models in many companies, which outline a development path for the company (or for departments or sites) across many criteria and sub-criteria. This allows for a concrete description of what the ideal state for the company is and what gradations exist. This is usually depicted on a scale from 1 to 5, where 1 describes the absolute basics in this topic or criterion, and 5 describes an ideal state that is currently foreseeable and should be aimed for. Using such maturity levels, development progress (or regress) can be determined at certain intervals, and further actions can be derived accordingly. In the lean environment, this is a widely used tool to make the development of excellence systems measurable and understandable for everyone.[1] The aim is to make not only hard quantitative targets such as productivity or financial savings tangible, but

[1] Maturity models are also frequently used in process and quality management.

Tab. 4.1 Classic Steps of Change Management according to Kotter (2007)

Classic Steps according to Kotter (2007)		Description
1	Create urgency	Present the need for action as credibly as possible
2	Define change agents	Identify a group of people who will drive the change process
3	Develop vision	Develop a shared vision that explains why and where the journey is heading
4	Create structure	Establish an organizational structure to drive implementation
5	Communicate change	Set up a good communication strategy to involve the organization as broadly as possible in the initiative
6	Achieve short-term wins	Implement initial successes and flagship projects to convince and generate enthusiasm

also qualitative, enabling criteria. In some companies, this is now also used to describe and thus make measurable development paths in terms of sustainability. Ideally, these are considered in an integrated manner, and there is a maturity model that assesses both the level of lean excellence and green excellence.

It remains essential for the strategic anchoring of sustainability that the topic is treated as a top management priority and that leaders from all areas of the company understand the need for change and support it. In terms of the change process, it is therefore advantageous—beyond the reporting obligation—to create credible pressure to act and to identify the key group of people who can drive the implementation of the sustainability strategy (see Table 4.1).

To illustrate areas of responsibility and overlaps, these can be visualized in so-called "contribution" or "engagement maps." In such representations, each area is shown in terms of its influence on specific fields of action and where overlaps with other areas occur. This makes it possible to assign responsibility and identify where interdisciplinary approaches are necessary.

4.2 Machine Effectiveness

The optimal use of machines, equipment, and facilities is one of the key levers in manufacturing companies to make the business more resource-efficient. Through the consumption of energy, water, oils, and lubricants, as well as all auxiliary and operating materials in general, equipment has a direct impact on the environmental footprint of companies. In addition, problems with availability or quality lead to many additional activities, which in turn require the use of resources and thus make processes inefficient.

It is therefore not surprising that the topic of "green" should play a central role in the optimization and maintenance of equipment.

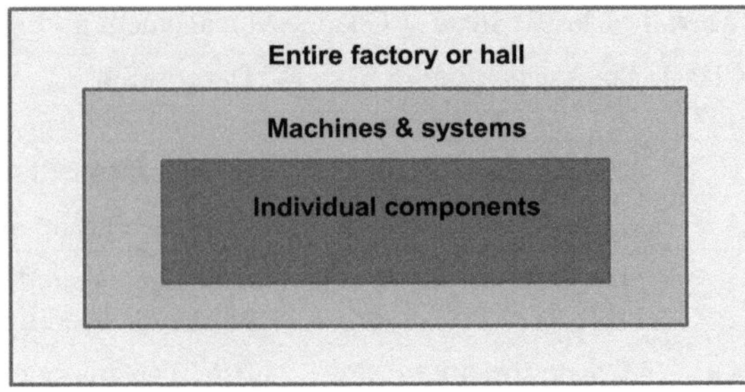

Fig. 4.1 Three levels of equipment effectiveness. (Own illustration)

Maintenance activities can be roughly divided into three levels. As part of the first level, the *entire factory or hall* is considered in terms of technical infrastructure. The focus here is on operating supply systems as efficiently as possible or making major adjustments to equipment and building technology. Solutions in this area include, for example, heat recovery, water treatment, and optimization of cooling circuits. Adjustments to building insulation and hall climate control are also key topics at this level. The second level relates to *machines and equipment* that are part of the production process and fall under the responsibility of production managers. Here, the main questions are when and in what states the equipment is running, whether consumption can be reduced in different operating states, or whether alternatives exist for the materials used. The third level goes a step further and focuses on the *individual components* of a system (see Fig. 4.1). Here, the way individual consumers within a system are controlled and their contribution to the overall consumption of the system is analyzed. A simple example is extraction systems, which in many facilities run continuously and contribute to the system's power consumption. Often, these can be switched so that extraction is only used when a workpiece is actually being processed. In this way, many individual components within a system can often be combined to achieve an overall optimum.

A decisive factor in optimizing equipment is how transparent consumption and environmental impact are. In terms of energy efficiency, an energy value stream can therefore be the first starting point to advance equipment effectiveness with regard to green topics. Here, energy consumption is recorded using mobile or installed measuring systems. The same applies to other media or consumables: consumption should be documented using measuring devices and sensor technology to identify potential levers and optimization approaches. Examples include ultrasonic measurements to identify compressed air leaks or thermal imaging to detect heat losses. In the simplest case, records such as lubricant consumption can be used to capture the environmental impact of a system.

In principle, for all types of equipment, the most environmentally friendly operation can be achieved especially when it is managed as part of classic maintenance management. Since, depending on the industry, between 15% and 40% of costs are directly influenced by maintenance, maintenance is one of the core processes in manufacturing companies. Existing organizations, processes, and methods can therefore be well adapted and improved from the perspective of resource efficiency.

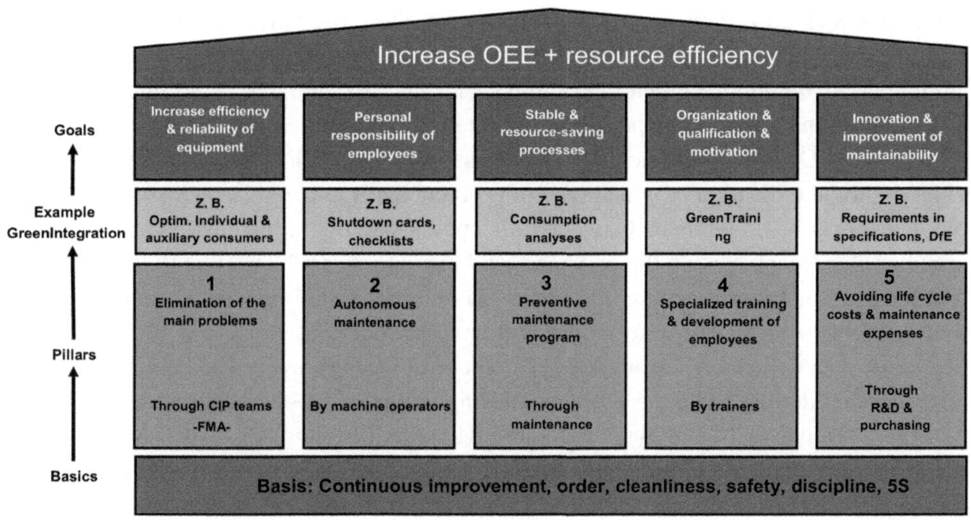

Fig. 4.2 "Total Productive Maintenance" house with "green" integration. DfE = Design for Environment; R&D = Research & Development; FMA = Failure Mode Analysis

A method closely linked to lean management, which aims to continuously improve equipment and avoid machine-related waste, is "Total Productive Maintenance" (TPM). Although TPM primarily focuses on production equipment, many aspects can also be applied to technical infrastructure systems. In any case, TPM offers several points of connection where resource efficiency can be integrated, allowing equipment effectiveness and resource efficiency to be optimized simultaneously (see Fig. 4.2).

As is generally the case in lean management, there is no uniform definition of TPM. In most approaches, TPM is understood as a program whose implementation follows individual steps or areas of action.

The number of individual areas of action varies between companies. However, a basic understanding of continuous improvement, safety, order and cleanliness, and the "5S" approach is always seen as the fundamental basis for any TPM activities. Environmental topics can be assigned to the subsequent areas of action, and actions can thus be linked to the respective TPM activities.

TPM Areas of Action

1. Elimination of Main Problems

A prerequisite for establishing a TPM organization is the structured recording of main problems with machines and equipment in order to eliminate them in a targeted manner. The goal is to increase the reliability and efficiency of the equipment. To determine which equipment should be prioritized, it is useful to define damage classes, as this allows both entire systems and components to be categorized and prioritized. Common categories include: “Impact of a malfunction on the customer,” “Internal impact of a malfunction,” “Probability of malfunction,” or “Replacement value of components or equipment.” To integrate green topics into such categorization, the environmental impact of a system can be used as an additional evaluation criterion.

If data on Overall Equipment Effectiveness (OEE) is collected and analyzed, it provides an initial indication of which type of problem leads to the greatest losses. For example, a distinction can be made between efficiency losses due to fluctuations in equipment speed or short stoppages on the one hand, and availability problems due to longer-lasting malfunctions or breakdowns on the other. To obtain detailed information about specific malfunctions, it is necessary to record and analyze root causes using written records or electronic data collection. Error codes can be used to categorize malfunctions, and Pareto analyses can identify the main problems. Using common problem-solving methods such as “7W,” “Ishikawa,” “5 Whys,” or Failure Mode and Effects Analysis (FMEA) can be identified and targeted optimizations derived. Defined key performance indicators help to measure results after implementation and ensure the effectiveness of measures.

To specifically improve equipment in terms of environmental performance, the main drivers should be determined and causes identified. In addition to efficiency gains from eliminating equipment malfunctions, this can also lead to improvements in the energy or media consumption of a system. For example, in addition to OEE targets, the energy efficiency of a system can be defined as a goal in equipment optimization. It should be noted in such optimization that a large proportion of consumption is usually caused by peripheral devices, so both main and auxiliary consumers should always be considered.

2. Autonomous Maintenance

A central aspect of TPM is that it is not solely the responsibility of a maintenance department, but rather an interfunctional approach that involves many departments. The focus is also on the employees and operators of a facility. In contrast to traditional approaches, which usually feature a clear, functional separation between operating and maintaining a facility, the TPM methodology strengthens the personal responsibility of employees. The goal of so-called “autonomous maintenance” is to transfer more responsibility to employees in order to enhance competencies, reduce response times, and relieve maintenance personnel. The responsibilities can range from standardized cleaning activities to simple repair tasks. Regular checking, refilling, or replacing of operating materials or filters can also be part of autonomous maintenance. Typically, these activities are summarized in checklists or visualizations on site, making their completion quickly visible and verifiable. Especially after optimizations and changes to equipment, autonomous maintenance helps to establish new standards and ensure their long-term adherence. Since the TPM philosophy also involves operators in optimization measures, it further strengthens the identification of all employees with the processes. This also means that operators do not simply have to wait for maintenance staff to fix malfunctions or carry out planned measures during equipment downtime, but can themselves perform simple, supportive tasks. As a result, downtime can be reduced and the maintenance team relieved.

Autonomous maintenance is a key element that can also improve the environmental performance of equipment and machinery. Efficiency potentials can often be realized by defining shutdown and standby guidelines. These cannot always be implemented economically through start-stop automation, so it is often the operators who are responsible for switching off equipment or peripheral devices when they are not needed. Simple visualizations (e.g., in the form of shutdown cards) can be used at the equipment to indicate when it should be in operation, on standby, or switched off. Monitoring and adjusting media consumption can also be part of checklists. An example here would be the regular inspection of compressed air leaks by the operator. Integrating "green" elements into autonomous maintenance not only enables rapid response and more efficient processes. It often becomes apparent that such integration raises awareness, leading to many additional suggestions and ideas that in turn help to operate machines and equipment more efficiently and effectively.

3. Preventive Maintenance

Another area within the TPM methodology encompasses "preventive maintenance." Unlike autonomous maintenance, these activities are usually carried out by specially trained and professional maintenance staff. The aim of preventive maintenance is to avoid or minimize failures by carrying out planned preventive maintenance measures. Such measures can be performed at set intervals or according to prescribed criteria. In the former case, the duration of use (either in time or production quantity) is usually decisive, while in "condition-based maintenance," intervention thresholds are defined that determine when an action becomes necessary. With ongoing developments in sensor technology, "predictive maintenance elements" are also increasingly being used in this area. In this form of maintenance, machines, equipment, and components are monitored according to specific parameters that enable a predictive assessment of the probability of failure, thus supporting more accurate planning of maintenance activities.

The intensity with which a facility is monitored and maintained preventively can be differentiated by categories. Building on the categorization of equipment and components described above, the appropriate maintenance strategy can be determined for each. Depending on the significance or damage class, a distinction is made as to whether equipment and components should be checked periodically or monitored based on condition. For very low damage classes (low probability of failure, impact, and replacement value), a "crash strategy" may sometimes be appropriate, in which maintenance activities are not performed at all or are reduced to a minimum. In contrast, for high damage classes, redundancies may be necessary to minimize the impact of a failure as much as possible.

To implement maintenance strategies as efficiently as possible and achieve professional maintenance management, many companies have found it effective to regularly analyze and evaluate their own processes. Classification using a maintenance excellence model makes it possible to identify optimization opportunities and compare one's own performance with that of other companies.

Such an assessment is also an ideal starting point for integrating green topics into the area of preventive maintenance. This allows for the definition of evaluation criteria that can measure how intensively resource efficiency and environmental considerations are being advanced as part of professional maintenance. A key aspect here is to define specific targets with regard to green aspects and resource efficiency. One possible metric is, for example, energy-efficient overall equipment effectiveness. For this metric, in addition to the OEE targets that apply to maintenance staff, energy efficiency is also considered. In the simplest case, this metric can be calculated by dividing the achieved OEE figures by the energy consumed. The resulting metric increases as OEE rises and energy consumption decreases. Based on such metrics, target values can be defined that ensure that environmental aspects are also considered in planned maintenance activities and that maintenance staff see themselves as responsible for optimizing equipment in this regard as well.

4. Training and Education

Central to the implementation of the TPM philosophy is building competencies and skills that correspond to the changed understanding of roles. In addition to purely technical skills, the ability to work in teams and problem-solving competence become important. In particular, the interplay between autonomous and professional preventive maintenance means that new areas of responsibility must be coordinated and traditional role divisions stop . This is not always entirely free of conflict, as experts may have to share their specialized knowledge and thus relinquish areas of responsibility. Especially in maintenance or repair work, tasks often need to be intelligently divided so that operators and maintenance staff complement each other as effectively as possible. Extensive maintenance and inspection plans can often be broken down into smaller steps and assigned according to competencies. However, this also means that not only skills must be developed, but coordination between areas must also function in order to ensure the smooth execution of maintenance activities.

Since a focus of TPM is the structured elimination of major problems, it must also be ensured that there is methodological competence in problem-solving and root cause analysis. The elimination of major problems and the optimization of equipment should be carried out in joint teamwork involving maintenance staff, production staff, as well as process developers and lean managers. This makes it possible to pool different skills and experiences, stimulates creative thinking, and strengthens the identification of all participants with the solutions found.

With regard to green aspects, it is important to train all involved functions and impart relevant competencies. Depending on the area of responsibility, the content can be deepened specifically. However, to ensure a common basic understanding and enable cross-functional workshops, many companies have developed training and communication strategies that provide basic knowledge on resource efficiency topics. One example is "energy experience worlds," where employees are given practical insights into the basics of energy waste and efficiency approaches. In principle, with regard to environmental and energy topics, the relevant functions, where available, should also be involved in equipment-specific optimizations. In this way, energy managers or environmental officers can contribute their expertise and knowledge to TPM workshops and help optimize the resource efficiency and environmental impact of machines and equipment.

5. Innovation and Improvement of Maintainability

In addition to optimizing existing equipment, TPM also focuses on the design and development of new equipment and processes. The aim is to transfer the experiences gained from operations, maintenance activities, and optimization measures into the development process, so that optimal workflows can be integrated at an early stage. Feedback from experience can be incorporated, on the one hand, by involving (process) developers in improvement initiatives. On the other hand, when redesigning processes and equipment, production employees should also be involved as early as possible to ensure that experiences gained with existing equipment in the daily production environment are taken into account. This type of input is difficult to replace with simulations or design programs and is therefore particularly valuable when redesigning workflows. By considering these aspects early on, many costs can usually be saved later in the process—costs that should be factored in when evaluating new equipment in order to achieve an overall optimum over the entire lifecycle of the equipment ("Total Cost Of Ownership"). Factors that play a role here include: accessibility for maintenance work, standardization of connector systems, improved ergonomics, good visibility for optical inspections, easy interchangeability of components, etc.

With regard to green aspects, requirements can be integrated, for example, concerning consumption values, the use of environmentally friendly materials, or "re-use" concepts for components. In addition, the insights gained from equipment optimization should be documented in detail and compiled in requirement specifications. This enables clear communication of the requirements for improved equipment to suppliers and helps define the prerequisites for procurement. An increasingly important aspect here is sensor technology, which can usually be implemented with little additional effort during early development, but is costly and less economical to retrofit later. Such technology enables both predictive maintenance elements and the collection of various consumption data, thereby optimizing the resource efficiency of the equipment.

4.3 Material Efficiency

Material efficiency has a major impact on both a company's environmental performance and its manufacturing costs. According to the German Federal Statistical Office, in the manufacturing industry, material costs account for an average of 42% of total manufacturing costs (Statistisches Bundesamt, 2017). One might assume that, for this reason, material and resource efficiency is already a top priority in many companies. However, many "Lean & Green" benchmark visits reveal that there is still significant potential for improvement in material efficiency. Only a few top companies had high transparency regarding resource waste and its associated costs. The fact that reduced resource use is better for the environment can be demonstrated with a simple equation: if fewer resources are needed, less energy is required for extraction, conversion, transport, or disposal of the respective resources, materials, or products. Another argument in favor of greater transparency is that better transparency ensures more reliable planning for material procurement and makes it easier to manage large fluctuations. As a result, only what is actually needed is ordered. As already mentioned in Chap. 3, high inventory levels are a perfect cover for potential inefficiencies or problems in the process. Having transparency over one's own consumption is the starting point for actually implementing "resource efficiency."

In recent years, the focus has often been on improving labor or personnel productivity. Workplaces have been streamlined, standard procedures defined, and training conducted, all with the aim of increasing labor productivity and thus reducing personnel costs. Similar efficiency programs for the even larger block of material costs are much rarer. Certainly, material efficiency is recognized by many companies as a key cost factor, but the levers for increasing efficiency are often underestimated. More often, it is the annual savings targets in purchasing that are used to reduce material costs. However, this is more of a reactive than a preventive action. The response to high material consumption is to reduce purchasing costs. At best, this only indirectly contributes to more efficient use of materials. A combined approach of material efficiency and purchasing cost reduction appears much more promising.

Approach to Increasing Material Efficiency

Early integration of material efficiency into the product development phase ensures that developers already receive clear guidelines. For example, life cycle assessments can be used during the development process to integrate improvements in material efficiency or substitutions of materials.

If production has already started, processes are analyzed for material waste in order to increase material efficiency (see Fig. 4.3). To gain transparency over waste, material flow analysis is particularly suitable. In material flow analysis, similar to value stream mapping, all material flows are recorded and, for each process step (material points), all material streams are considered (materials, raw materials, operating supplies, etc.). Due to its similarity to value stream mapping from lean management, it makes sense to adapt these methods and expand them to include material efficiency.

There are various methods of representation. An initial schematic representation on brown paper or in other IT programs (e.g., "Visio") is usually completely sufficient. Material flows can be made very transparent using Sankey diagrams (see Fig. 4.4).

Building on the material flow analysis, there is a method primarily used in Japan, which was implemented nationwide in manufacturing companies under government sponsorship: material flow cost accounting. This is a cost accounting system that serves as an internal basis for financially substantiating decision-making processes. The information obtained is then used for the operational planning of costs and revenues as well as for

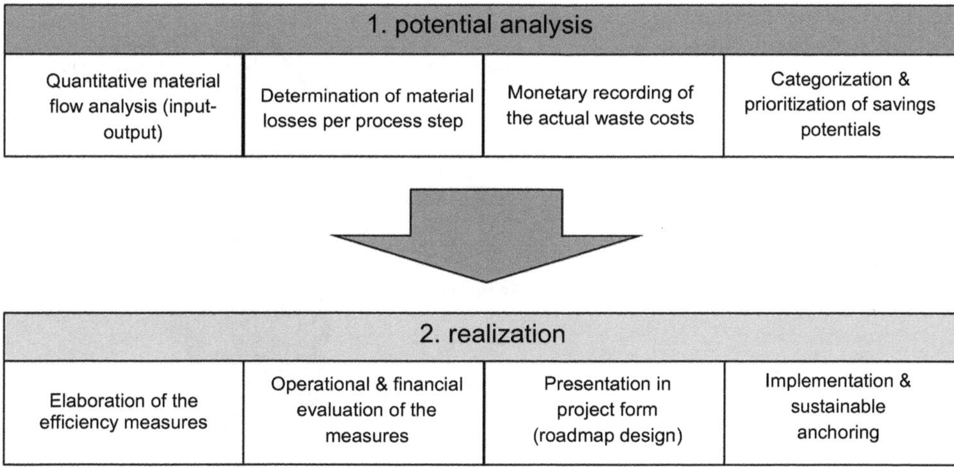

Fig. 4.3 Example approach for optimizing material efficiency. Roadmap design refers to the transfer of measures into a concrete implementation plan. (Source: own illustration)

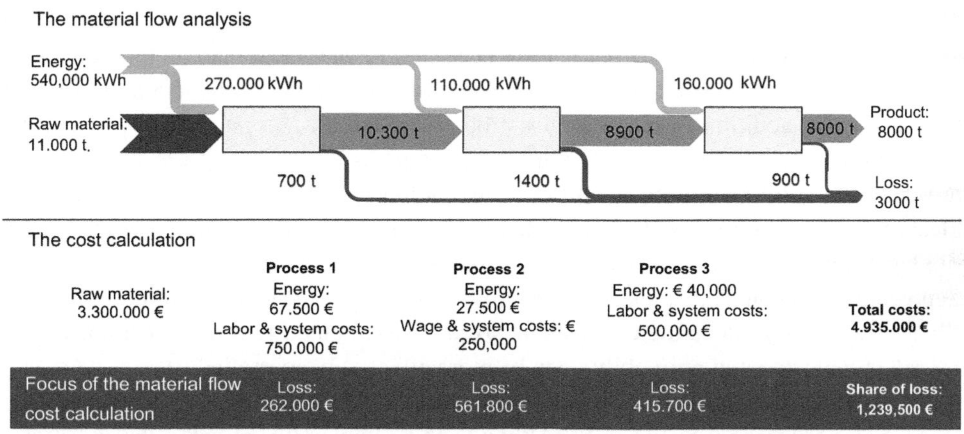

Fig. 4.4 Schematic example of a material flow analysis. (Source: own illustration)

deviations from actual target states. Unlike other cost accounting variants, material flow cost accounting focuses on the quantitative allocation of materials and all associated costs.

A key success factor in creating value stream maps—or, as in this case, in conducting material flow cost accounting—is having an interdisciplinary team from purchasing, logistics, production, quality, sales, etc. On the one hand, this helps to create a unified process understanding among all participants; on the other hand, questions or uncertainties can be communicated and resolved directly. Often, a simple schematic representation of the processes is enough to generate plenty of discussion and derive initial improvement approaches.

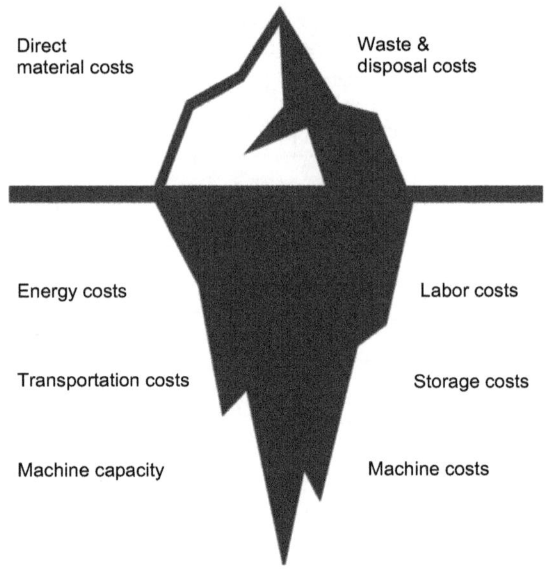

Fig. 4.5 Cost transparency of material efficiency. (Own illustration)

When conducting material flow cost accounting, the input and output quantities (usually in euros or kilograms) are presented for each process/production step (quantity center). In addition to material costs, other costs such as system, energy, and disposal costs are also calculated for each process step. As the name suggests, energy costs are determined by energy consumption. This includes energy sources such as oil, gas, electricity, fuels, compressed air, and steam. System costs, in turn, are costs incurred in the handling of processes. These include, for example, personnel costs, transport costs, depreciation, maintenance, and insurance. Disposal costs are incurred through the handling of waste. By allocating the costs incurred for each quantity center, cost objects can be better evaluated and profitability can be more effectively controlled.

It is often a challenge for companies to generate the data needed to calculate the identified material losses (see Fig. 4.5). Although this is generally possible through Enterprise Resource Planning (ERP) or Material Requirements Planning (MRP) systems, the effort involved is often very high and the potential of this data is frequently underestimated. However, once this data has been analyzed and evaluated, material loss data can be specifically used to uncover and optimize hidden material, energy, system, and waste costs, while simultaneously improving the ecological footprint.

In traditional cost accounting, material and manufacturing process costs are usually summed and reported as total product costs (see Fig. 4.6—Example A). For total product costs, it is rarely distinguished what portion of the incurred costs relates to waste. This makes it difficult to identify inefficiencies and potential improvements in the processes.

In material flow cost accounting, the costs for both product output and material losses are calculated and separated in detail for each quantity center. This makes it possible to

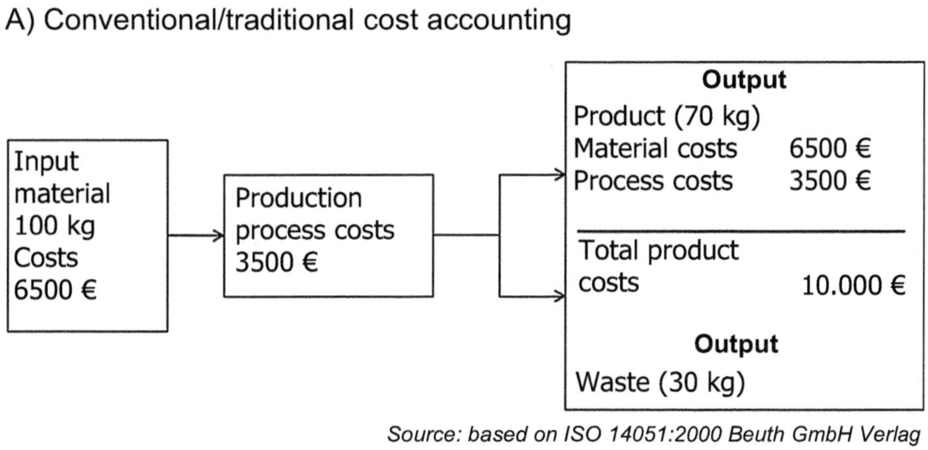

Fig. 4.6 Traditional cost accounting. (Own illustration based on ISO)

show which costs are ultimately contained in the product and which are material losses (see Fig. 4.7—Example B).

Methods and Approaches for Reducing Material Costs

The insights gained from material flow analysis and material flow cost accounting can now be addressed with selected optimization measures. Depending on the findings regarding which type of waste led to material losses, there is a wide range of methods and approaches that can be utilized. Most of these approaches can be derived from the Lean Management toolbox and adapted for material efficiency measures.

In regards to product and process design, "over-engineering" or poorly planned processes can be responsible for material losses. Stamping patterns are a good example here. Often, significant material losses occur with stamping patterns because the stamping is not optimally designed or simply because patterns that are too large are used.

Material costs can, of course, also be reduced in terms of quality aspects, such as poor material or scrap . If material flow cost accounting reveals that quality is a major cost driver, it is advisable to use targeted quality management tools to identify the root cause of quality problems. Suitable tools here would be "Quick-Response-Quality-Control" (QRQC) or "Genba Problem Solving" (GPS) — with the additional introduction of quality control loops. As the name suggests, the goal of QRQC is to enable an early response to deviations through rapid reaction. An effective means of direct intervention is the continuous comparison of actual and target values, the implementation of quality control loops, and empowering employees to actively participate in the quality improvement process.

Another starting point involves topics related to planning and control. Excessively purchased material or overproduced products have a significant negative impact on

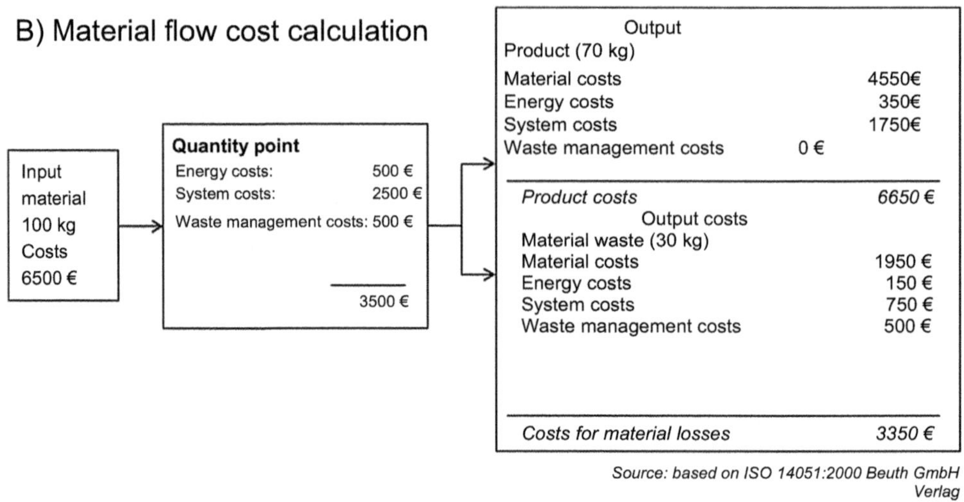

Fig. 4.7 Difference in material flow cost accounting. (Own illustration based on ISO)

material efficiency. Immature or incorrectly applied IT systems can also lead to control difficulties and booking errors. As a result, there is a risk that departments, teams, or individual employees have to act independently of systems, leading to a loss of transparency. For example, this can result in intermediate stocks not being recorded or scrap only being registered at the end of the booking chain, making material planning and control significantly more difficult. This often leads to incorrect inventories and necessitates adjustments, which in turn can cause material losses. Complicated logistics processes, such as different "labeling procedures," can also result in incorrect inventories.

If a material flow cost analysis reveals that many losses occur here, it is advisable to revise and optimize the control and booking systems. This can often be consistently complemented by improvements in complexity management, further reducing planning and control efforts. In particular, handling many variants with volatile demand makes planning and control extremely complex. Therefore, it is often worthwhile to deliberately minimize the variety of variants or, if possible, to decouple variant diversity using decoupling points (Table 4.2).

4.4 Energy Management

Since a company's energy consumption is one of the main drivers of CO_2 emissions and thus also of its climate footprint, it is one of the most important approaches to improving its environmental impact. In addition, it is a relevant cost factor, where every kilowatt hour (kWh) saved has a direct impact on results. In this context, energy primarily refers to the use and consumption of electricity, gas, oil, or district heating.

Tab. 4.2 The seven types of Lean waste in relation to material

Seven Lean Types of Waste	In relation to material losses	Solutions
Transport	Use of materials for transport and packaging	Alternative packaging and logistics concepts
Inventory	Losses due to storage, booking errors	Optimization of logistics and warehousing processes
Movement	Losses due to damage during handling	Improvements to area or cell layout/"5S method"
Waiting	Losses due to process flow, non-compliance with process times/shelf life	Adjustment of planning and control processes
Overproduction	Excessive use of material or operating and auxiliary materials	VA = Value Analysis VE = Value Engineering (functionality analysis + evaluation alternatives)
Incorrect Technology/Processes	Offcuts, start-up losses; waste resulting from the process	Material-efficient process design and recycling potential
Scrap	All materials used in the production of rejected parts	"Genba Problem Solving" and "Quick Response Quality Control"

The extent to which companies focus on optimizing energy consumption depends primarily on the relative share of energy costs in total manufacturing costs. While in process industry plants or foundries, energy consumption can quickly account for up to 50% of production costs, in pure assembly operations the share is often less than 1%. Accordingly, the pressure to act and the investment opportunities in companies vary. With relatively high energy costs, expensive technical solutions pay off comparatively quickly, whereas with low energy consumption, the focus must be on simpler solutions that do not require major investments.

If a company decides to improve its environmental performance with regard to energy consumption, there are several areas of action in which it can become active (Table 4.3).

One of the main tasks in companies is to promote the efficient use of energy. This repeatedly raises the question of what level of transparency regarding consumption is necessary in order to allocate and optimize it. For a long time, it was a trend to install as many online measuring devices as possible to achieve the highest possible level of transparency. However, networking all individual consumers in a company is only economically viable in rare cases, even though the installation of permanent measuring devices is becoming increasingly affordable. The objective when increasing transparency should be to make major consumers—and thus also key levers for improvement—visible and to assign responsibility for consumption. This clear allocation has the effect of making energy consumption controllable, allowing targets to be set and tracked. The prerequisite is that consumption can be assigned to its source and is influenceable. It is not absolutely

Tab. 4.3 Areas of influence with regard to energy

Improvement of the energy-related CO_2 balance	
Area of influence	Fields of action (selection)
Energy efficiency (Scope 1)	Process consumption
	Technical infrastructure
	Combined heat and power
Energy supply (Scope 2)	Energy flexibility
	In-house generation
	Renewable energy
	Energy storage
Value chain (Scope 3)	Reduce energy consumption of own products
	Energy optimization at suppliers
	Sustainability criteria in procurement
	Transport optimization
	Managing emissions from business travel
	Options for employee commuting and means of transport

necessary to connect every small consumer and piece of equipment individually to a measurement system; often, it is sufficient to increase transparency step by step.

A method that enables cost-effective transparency, allows direct improvement measures to be derived, and thus provides a good starting point for implementing a permanent operational energy management system is the "energy value stream method." The approach is similar to the classic value stream analysis, in which material and information flows are analyzed and which often serves as a basis for many lean activities. The aim of the energy value stream is, in addition to classic production data (such as machine cycle times, setup times, availability), to also record energy data for each process step and thus identify waste in the process.

Procedure for Creating an Energy Value Stream

a) Walkthrough and Scoping

The starting point for an energy value stream should be to clearly define which area or value stream is to be considered and which areas can potentially be excluded. The fundamental idea is to follow the material flow as closely as possible and to consider a product or product group. To do this, individual process steps that are necessary for processing a product must be defined. This is typically done by mapping the material flow from the starting point of the analysis (e.g., goods receipt) to the final processing step (e.g., shipping) and highlighting the individual processing steps. To ensure a shared understanding among all participants before starting an energy value stream project, it is advisable to walk through the selected area together and document the main processing steps in the form of a generic value stream.

b) Measurement Plan and Measurements

For an energy value stream in particular, it is important to gain an overview of where energy consumption is recorded and to which areas it can be assigned. On the one hand, the total values in the area under investigation should be known (e.g., the monthly electricity consumption of the entire hall). This subsequently enables statements to be made about the share of consumption considered by the energy value stream in relation to total consumption. On the other hand, it is important to define where mobile measurements are necessary and appropriate.

To determine which consumers should be included as part of the energy value stream, it is advisable to create a measurement plan. The starting point for such a plan is usually existing lists of installed machines, equipment, and devices. The rated capacities of the consumers, which are typically compiled in such lists, can serve as an indication of which equipment requires detailed measurement, but should not be the sole basis for the measurement plan. Actual consumption can differ significantly from rated capacity, and rated capacity does not provide information about total consumption. For example, a large motor that only runs a few days a year may have a high rated capacity but is likely to have only a minor impact in the overall assessment. In principle, it is important to distinguish between different types of energy. These are usually electricity, gas, oil, compressed air, and thermal energy.

The task of the measurement plan is to define what type of measurements should be carried out on each piece of equipment. A basic distinction is made between "spot measurements" and "load profile measurements." For some small consumers, a brief spot measurement during production is sufficient, while for all larger systems, it is necessary to conduct load profile measurements over a longer period. These allow conclusions to be drawn about consumption in different operating states and make it possible to identify patterns and optimization potential. Measurements should be taken during production, during breaks, and during non-production periods in order to later extrapolate losses during these times and make statements about annual costs. Especially with regard to break times or longer production shutdowns, there is often significant potential that can be tapped through "standby" and "shutdown management."

An energy value stream primarily focuses on the energy consumption of a value creation process. The main focus is on equipment required for processing a product. Nevertheless, it is also possible to include equipment and infrastructure that provide utilities or ensure basic production conditions. This includes, in particular, hall ventilation, air conditioning, lighting, cooling circuits, or compressed air supply. These types of consumption cannot always be precisely assigned to a process or value stream, but they can be included in a measurement plan and, as a first step, proportionally incorporated into the overall assessment.

c) Linking Data with Production Data

Once various measurements have been taken according to the plan and transferred into a database, the next step is to interpret the measurement results and link them with production data. To visualize this as clearly as possible, the representation used in the classic value stream method has proven to be highly effective. In this approach, all process steps of a value stream are recorded and the relevant process parameters are assigned. Process parameters include, among others, cycle times, scrap rates, OEE values, or availability indicators. To expand this classic view with energy data, the measured energy consumption is allocated to the individual process steps. The measured consumption during production, breaks, and non-production periods is then extrapolated according to the actual times (usually to an annual basis) to provide a tangible representation of each consumption. For example, the measured consumption during production times (in kWh) is multiplied by the number of hours actually produced. Together with the consumption during breaks and downtimes, this results in the total consumption, which, in relation to the quantity produced, provides information on the specific energy consumption per process step.

This approach enables not only the classic process data but also energy data (primarily electricity, gas, and oil consumption, as well as heat input) to be transparently displayed for each process step. This makes it easy to identify which process steps offer the greatest leverage for improvement and where energy waste is likely to occur (see Fig. 4.8). One easily identifiable type of waste, for example, is consumption during downtimes, for which there are often simple solutions.

If, in addition to consumption from production equipment, consumption from technical infrastructure systems has also been recorded, the measured power is also related to the operating hours. There are two options for displaying this in the energy value stream: either the consumption (such as hall ventilation, lighting, etc.) is shown as individual blocks alongside the actual value stream. This has the advantage that optimization and savings potentials can be more easily identified. Alternatively, the consumption can be allocated proportionally to the individual process steps (based on production volume). This allows for a more precise breakdown of specific consumption.

d) Targeted Improvements

The energy value stream that has now been created provides a transparent overview of the greatest levers for optimizing energy efficiency. By linking production data with consumption data, both consumption and costs are known for each area and process step. To develop targeted improvement measures, it is advisable to select several areas in an interdisciplinary manner in which to prioritize the search for potential improvements. Interdisciplinarity is a key success factor in process optimization. Many solutions require both technical know-how and a deep understanding of specific production processes, making the involvement of subject matter experts and production staff from the relevant areas essential. In addition, many organizational solutions can only be implemented across departments, and involving multiple areas can provide numerous approaches. Often, such solutions offer significant potential that can be implemented relatively easily and cost-effectively. Focused workshops on individual prioritized topics (e.g., 1–2 days) provide a good framework for identifying approaches and defining initial steps. For more

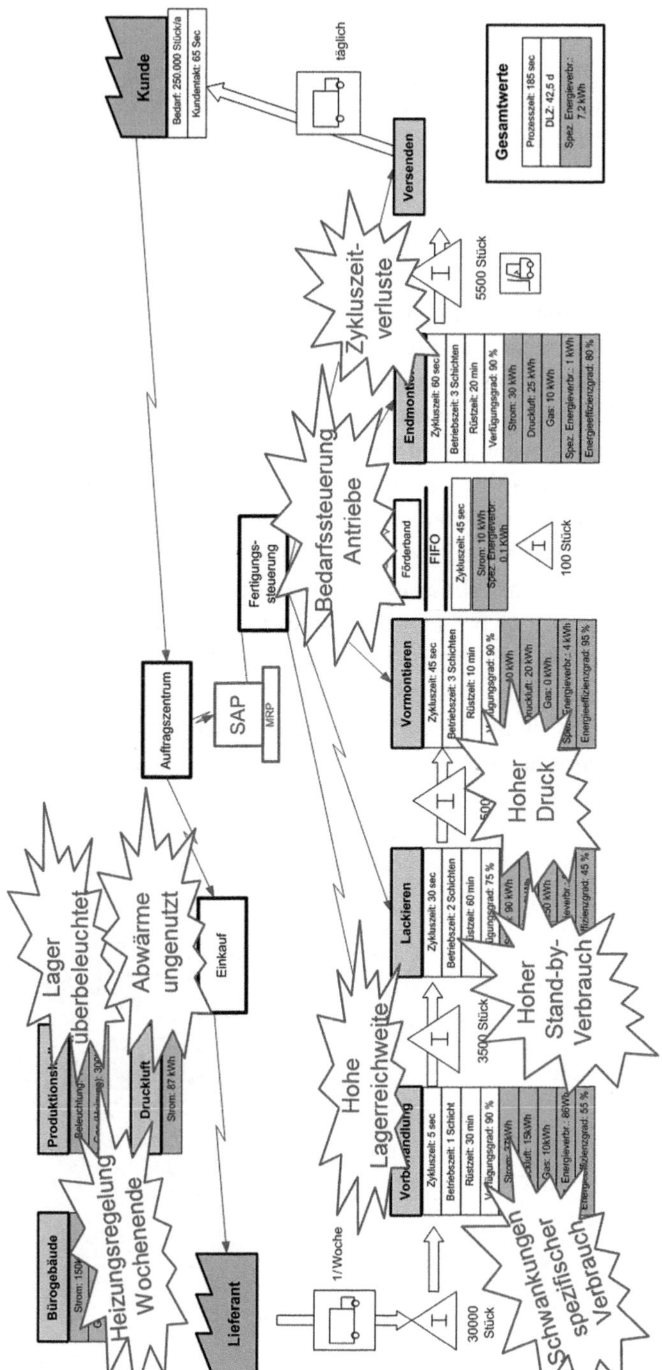

Abb. 4.8 Representation of the energy value stream. (Own illustration)

complex topics, it is also possible to involve specific subject matter experts in individual workshops.

A major advantage of an energy value stream is that ideas and approaches developed in such workshops can be directly evaluated in terms of their cost effects and thus their profitability—Return on Investment (ROI). Based on the results and findings from the measurement data, solution approaches can be discussed and their monetary benefits calculated in concrete terms. This quickly reveals which measures are worthwhile and which are likely to yield only minor savings.

e) Establishing Operational Energy Management

In addition to the improvement measures resulting from an energy value stream project, it also serves as an ideal starting point for establishing or further enhancing operational energy management (see Fig. 4.9). On the one hand, the measurement data reveal where continuous monitoring of consumption is worthwhile, and on the other hand, consumption can be assigned to areas of responsibility, allowing for the definition of performance indicators and targets. If consumption is allocated according to the source, not only can the implementation of identified measures be ensured, but daily energy consumption can also be assigned to the responsibilities of production managers. The implementation of new ideas and the assurance of behavioral changes then become part of the continuous improvement process (CIP), helping to achieve energy efficiency targets. As with other key performance indicators, departments are required to identify and activate potential. The targets to be achieved should follow a holistic logic, aligned with a defined strategy, and relate department-specific goals to the overall plant or company direction.

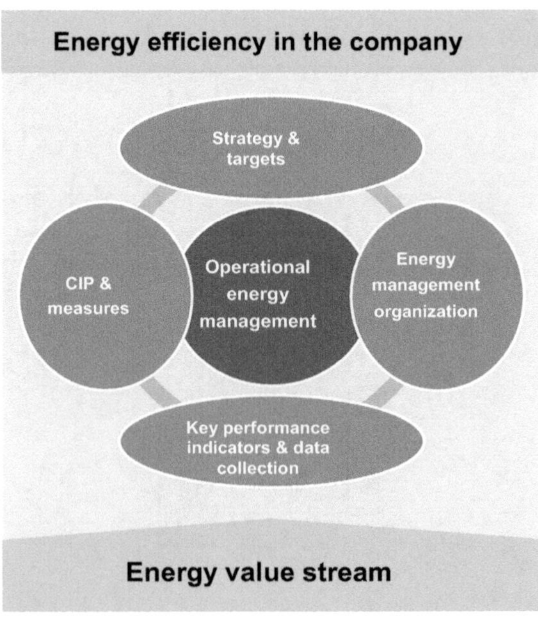

Abb. 4.9 Representation of operational energy management. (Own illustration)

To embed energy topics methodically and professionally within the organization, it makes sense to establish an energy management organization within the company, which is also a mandatory requirement for ISO certification. By appointing an energy manager who reports directly to top management, it is ensured that these topics receive the necessary importance and attention. In addition, a regularly convening energy team can promote exchange between departments and provide support through team experts. Sponsorship or multiplier approaches have also proven effective, in which selected individuals from various departments are trained, involved in the work of energy teams, and thus can disseminate know-how and successful approaches across the organization.

References

Kotter, J. P. (2007). Leading change: Why transformation efforts fail. *Harvard Business Review Classics*. https://hbr.org/1995/05/leading-change-why-transformation-efforts-fail-2. Accessed 15. Dec 2024.

Statistisches Bundesamt. (2017). *Produzierendes Gewerbe Kostenstruktur der Unternehmen des Verarbeitenden Gewerbes sowie des Bergbaus und der Gewinnung von Steinen und Erden*. Fachserie 4, Reihe 4.3, 2015.

5 Lean & Green Management Award

Since 2012, the "Lean & Green Management Award" has been held annually, organized primarily by the consulting firm "T&O Group." The award recognizes companies for their achievements in process and resource efficiency.

The Lean & Green Management Award is unique in its kind. Unlike many other awards, it is both cross-industry and international. Most other environmental prizes or excellence competitions are organized nationally or focus on specific industries or subject areas. Cross-industry and cross-border awards are relatively rare. What truly sets the Lean & Green Management Award apart is that it evaluates not only a company's performance in the area of lean management, but also environmental and sustainability aspects. To date, more than 300 companies from 18 countries and a wide range of industries have participated in the competition and have been thoroughly analyzed (Fig. 5.1).

The central motivation behind the Lean & Green Management Award is to facilitate the exchange of best practices, specifically focusing on how sustainability and lean approaches are embedded in management systems. The evaluation process explicitly considers not only technical individual solutions, but rather examines the company's processes as a whole. The key question is how companies succeed in integrating sustainability, lean management, and resource efficiency into their corporate culture and strategies. Both the award participants and the organizers benefit from this international and cross-industry knowledge transfer, as it allows them to track over the years which approaches are promising, which have already proven practical, and which have fallen short of expectations.

A significant part of the entire award process is the feedback culture between participants and assessors. Participants and assessors are in close contact even during the completion of the questionnaire. This intensive exchange allows participants to ask questions and raise uncertainties at any time. The focus of the Lean & Green Management Award is on learning with and, above all, from each other.

D. Reichert, *Lean & Green: Best Practice*, https://doi.org/10.1007/978-3-658-49880-1_5

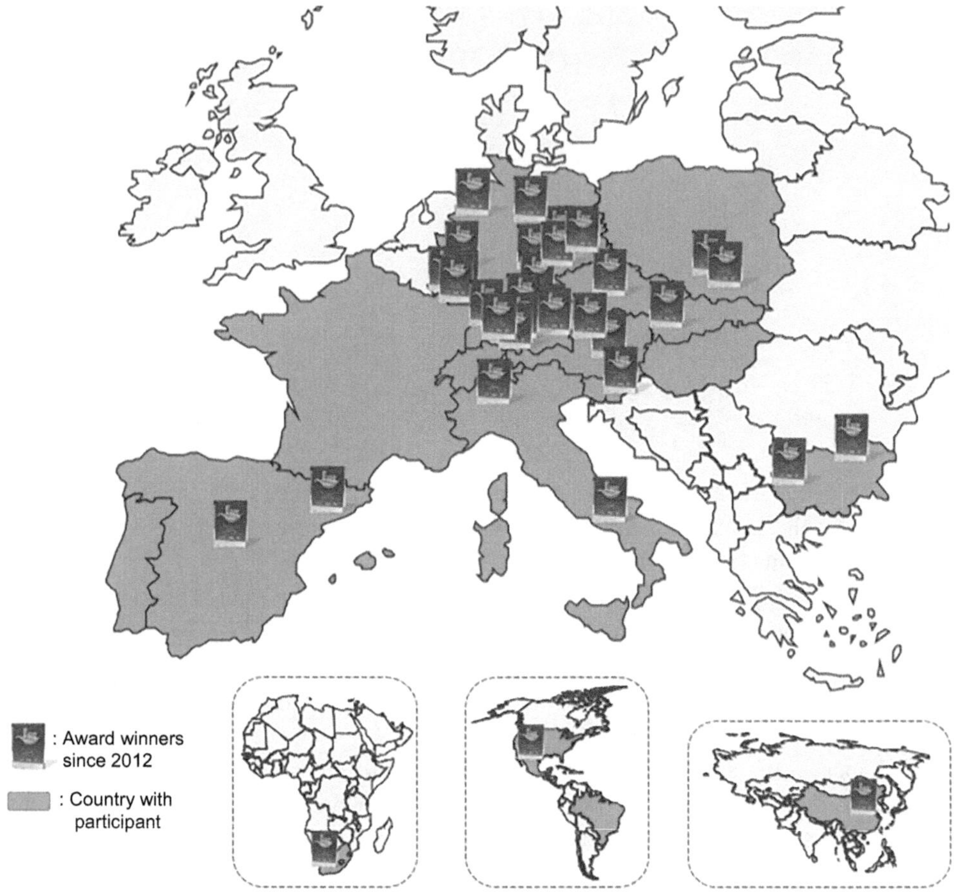

Fig. 5.1 Countries with participants and winners

5.1 Award Process

The Lean & Green Award is presented in two rounds.

In the first round, all participants submit a self-assessment using a standardized questionnaire. For many participants, completing the questionnaire already leads to initial insights and ideas. The detailed questionnaire is based on a comprehensive maturity model that has been developed over many years through numerous assessments and projects. Based on the self-assessments in the questionnaire, experts can classify the

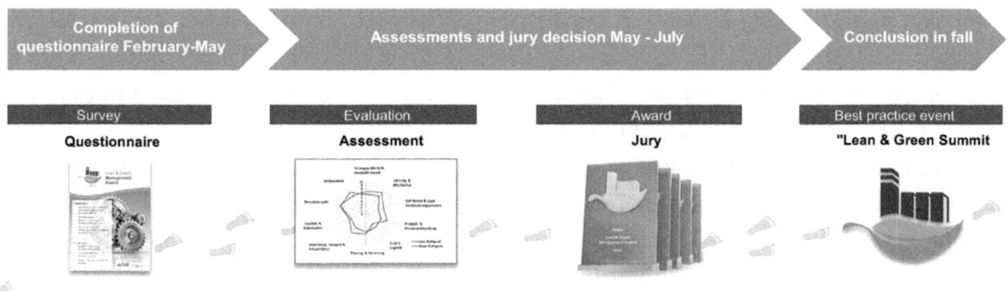

Fig. 5.2 The award process. (Own illustration)

company using more than 100 criteria from the maturity model and compare the results of the participants. Afterwards, all participants receive detailed feedback and a well-founded company benchmark, showing each company how it rates itself compared to its competitors.

The aim of the first round is to use the companies' responses to make a preliminary selection based on their self-assessment in the area of "Lean & Green," thereby qualifying participants for the second round (Fig. 5.2).

In the second round, an assessment of the qualified companies takes place. During a transitional phase since the onset of the pandemic, these assessments have been conducted as multi-hour online assessments up to 2024. Before 2020 and after 2024, companies were and will be evaluated through a one-day on-site assessment. In this standardized process, all main processes of the company are analyzed. Again, the detailed maturity model serves as the basis. Depending on the size of the company, the visit is conducted by 2 to 4 experts who, following a standardized agenda, evaluate over 100 individual criteria in the area of "Lean & Green." In addition to interviews and discussions with management and staff, the core of the visit is an extensive plant tour, during which all criteria are discussed directly on site, allowing for targeted follow-up on relevant aspects. Besides validating the information from the questionnaire, this brief evaluation is primarily intended to help understand and discuss how the company deals with specific challenges. Since each company faces different challenges, it is important for the expert team to understand and assess the relevance of each company's achievements and solutions. The maturity model then allows the qualitative assessments to be converted into point scores, which, together with actual results from various company key figures, enable an overall evaluation.

The visit explicitly emphasizes discussion and exchange. Companies are not only evaluated based on their achieved key figures, but also on the meaningful and effective implementation of lean principles and sustainability strategies. This approach enables cross-sector and cross-industry comparisons and—more importantly—allows all participants to benefit from discussion and direct best-practice exchange. Throughout the assessment, the expert team provides feedback or possible solutions and improvement suggestions that can be implemented on site.

After consolidating all results and transferring them into a standardized feedback format, the on-site assessment concludes with a presentation of the findings. The experts present the results in detail, highlighting identified strengths and weaknesses, and provide practical suggestions for individual measures and improvement steps that could help the company reach the next stage of development. Here, too, the aim is to allow as much room for discussion as possible, in order to maximize the benefit for all involved and to fulfill the award's goal of enabling best-practice transfer.

After all visits, the results of each company are presented to a jury consisting of equal representatives from academia, media partners, and consulting firms. Based on the evaluations, the jury decides who the award winners are for each year.

Following the jury's decision, all companies receive a detailed report with benchmark comparisons to all participants and a strengths-weaknesses profile based on the main criteria. For many companies, this feedback is a motivation to participate in the award in subsequent years, in order to receive external feedback on the measures implemented and the achievements attained. Each year, the award thus provides an opportunity to measure progress and also offers input on current trends and developments.

The annual award concludes with the "Lean & Green" Summit. As part of this event, the prizes are presented to the winners during a formal award ceremony, and each winning company shares insights into its individual success factors in the area of Lean & Green through presentations. All current and former participants of the award are invited to the "Lean & Green" Summit. In addition to the practical presentations, the focus of the entire event is again on the exchange between companies.

This is further supported by the accompanying plant tour hosted by the previous year's winning company. Here, the host company provides exclusive insights into its solutions and approaches, and success factors are discussed with the participants. The exchange and personal contact among all participants mark the conclusion of the award. The award and the summit have developed to a network of Lean & Green experts and leading companies who continuously exchange ideas on lean and green topics (see Tab. 5.1).

Tab. 5.1 Lean & Green Management Award winners and previous event locations. (As of 2018)

Year	Summit Host	Winning Companies				
2024	fischer Group of Companies, Waldachtal	Festo Production EOOD, Bulgaria	Witte Automotive Bulgaria	Walter AG, Münsingen	Vitesco Technologies GmbH, Limbach-Oberfrohna	Ideal Standard (Villeroy & Boch) Produktions-GmbH, Wittlich
2023	DMG MORI, Pfronten	Volkswagen South Africa Kariega (ZA)	TE Connectivity, Wört/ Dinkelsbühl	BSH Hausgeräte, Nazarje, Slovenia	Südpack, Ochsenhausen	
2022	Porsche Leipzig GmbH—Leipzig	Volkswagen de México S. A. de C. V., Puebla	DMG MORI, Pfronten	Festo SE & Co. KG, Ostfildern	fischer Group of Companies, Waldachtal	Schaltbau GmbH, Velden
2021	Award Ceremony in Berlin	Porsche Leipzig GmbH—Leipzig	Siemens AG—Gerätewerk Erlangen	Welbilt Deutschland GmbH—Eglfing	Bosch—Blaichach/ Immenstadt	elobau GmbH & Co. KG—Leutkirch & Hammerer Aluminium Industries—Ranshofen
2019	Continental Automotive GmbH—Regensburg Plant	Volkswagen AG—Wolfsburg Plant	Festo Production EOOD—Sofia Plant (BGR)	Bosch Diesel s. r. o.—Jihlava Plant (CZ)	Iveco España S. L.—Madrid Plant (ESP)	FCA Italy SpA—Bielsko-Biała Plant (PL)
2018	ASM Assembly Systems GmbH & Co. KG—Munich	Continental Automotive GmbH—Regensburg Plant	Lohmann & Rauscher GmbH & Co. KG—Neuwied Plant	Kaercher Cleaning Technology Co. Ltd—Changshu/ China		
2017	Rohde & Schwarz—Munich/ Memmingen	FCA Italy SPA—Verrone Transmission Plant	Bühler Motor GmbH—Monheim	ASM Assembly Systems GmbH & Co. KG—Munich	Convotherm Elektrogeräte GmbH—Eglfing	MAN Truck & Bus AG—Munich
2016	Robert Bosch—Blaichach	BMW—Munich Plant	Bolta Werke—Leinburg/ Diepersdorf	Rohde & Schwarz Messgerätebau—Memmingen	Neuenhauser Maschinenbau—Geeste-Dalum	Festo—Scharnhausen Technology Factory

(continued)

Tab. 5.1 (continued)

Year	Summit Host	Winning Companies				
2015	Siemens—Erlangen	SEAT—Martorell Plant	AGC Glass Germany GmbH—Wegberg Plant	Siemens Digital Factory Motion Control—Erlangen Plant	W.O.M. World of Medicine GmbH—Ludwigsstadt Plant	Robert Bosch GmbH—Blaichach Plant
2014	BMW—Leipzig	BMW Leipzig Plant	Bühler Motor GmbH—Monheim	AT&S, Leoben	Rational, Landsberg	Elobau -Leutkirch & FCA Italy SPA—Pomigliano D'Arco
2013	Bosch—Stuttgart	Bosch Diesel Systems, Feuerbach and Homburg Plants	Stanztechnik & Werkzeugbau Wolfgang Loch e. K.	SKF, Schweinfurt Plant	Schreiner Group, Oberschleißheim Plant	Volkswagen Sachsen, Zwickau Plant & Fiat, Tychy Plant (Poland)
2012	Award Ceremony in Nuremberg	Volkswagen Slovakia	Griwe Umformtechnik			BMW Light Metal Foundry Landshut

5.2 Dynamic Maturity Model and Benchmark

The methodological foundation for the entire award is the "Lean & Green" maturity model. It serves as the basis for evaluating the questionnaires, the on-site assessments, and the final benchmark. The maturity model defines over 100 individual criteria that encompass most business processes and are grouped into ten main criteria. Table 5.2 lists the main criteria and some sample questions used to assess individual criteria.

Each main criterion is assessed based on individual evaluations of 10–15 sub-criteria, each rated on a scale from 1 ("not or only partially evident") to 5 ("highly innovative and effective"). For each intermediate step on the scale, the model defines indicators specifying what a company must have achieved or implemented to receive a higher maturity rating. This allows a kind of development path to be mapped for each criterion, enabling the precise classification of a company's status and making the next individual development steps clear.

Tab. 5.2 Sample Questions for the "Lean & Green" Assessment

Main Criterion	Sample Questions	
	LEAN	GREEN
Strategy, Market, and Business Model	What role does Lean play in achieving the company/site strategy? Are Lean methods applied in marketing/sales?	What is the site's Green strategy? Are there quantified targets related to Green? What role does this play for the customer?
Leadership and Employees	What is the process and content of leadership development? Are elements of Lean leadership implemented? How are team-based organizational structures designed?	Which functions have which sustainability targets? What training and communication methods are used?
Process Orientation and Transparency	Which methods are used for process analysis? What routines are in place? How are interfaces managed?	How transparent is resource consumption? Are greenhouse gas emissions recorded? How transparent are supply chain risks?
Planning and Control	How does bottleneck and capacity planning work? Is production leveled/smoothed? Are there self-regulating systems?	Which sustainability indicators are relevant? What reporting structures exist? How are stand-by and shutdown management handled? How are peak and base loads managed?
SCM (Supply Chain Management) and Logistics	How are suppliers developed? How are inventories managed? How are procurement processes optimized? How does internal material supply work?	What Green requirements exist for suppliers? What optimizations have been made in external and internal transport? How is Green advanced in the supply chain?
Machinery, Equipment, and Infrastructure	How is the production layout designed? What is the maturity level of the TPM organization (TPM = Total Productive Maintenance)? How are setup times reduced? To what extent do OEE analyses enable improvement (OEE = Overall Equipment Effectiveness)?	How are resource efficiency indicators considered in equipment procurement? What improvements have been made to machinery and building infrastructure?
Quality, Workplace, and Management Systems	What quality control loops exist? What problem-solving methods are used? How are response systems structured?	What indicators exist regarding occupational safety? What ergonomic measures have been implemented?

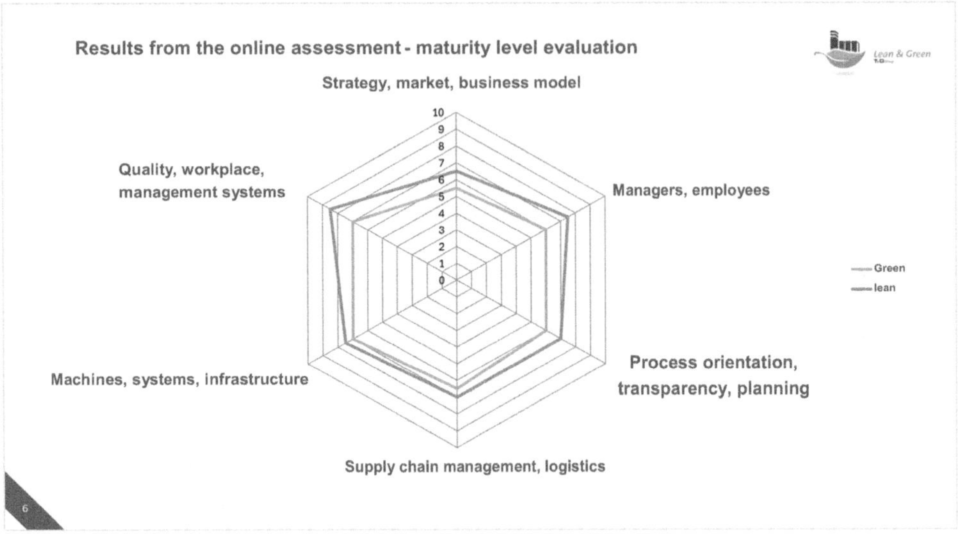

Fig. 5.3 Representation in a Radar Chart

The individual criteria are then aggregated into an overall score. Grouping individual criteria into main criteria enables structured feedback that can be visualized for relevant discussions and comparisons. For example, the result of the on-site assessment is a representation of the respective "Lean & Green" performance in a radar chart. This is accompanied by concrete, written recommendations indicating, for example, which steps are necessary in areas with weak performance, providing all participating companies with direct and practical benefits (Fig. 5.3).

For the final comparison among all participants, the results are consolidated in the form of a benchmark. This allows companies to determine their position and see how they compare to others in each category (Fig. 5.4).

In order to continuously reflect best-practice approaches and innovative developments within the maturity model, the model is further developed in phases. Each year, the results and approaches from the assessments of award participants are compared with project experiences from consulting firms and academic studies, and approaches for further development of the maturity model are defined. In this process, each criterion is analyzed to determine what currently constitutes a top score in terms of innovative "best practice" and what may have evolved over time into an industry standard. This approach ensures that the maturity model evolves dynamically and is able to continuously represent best practices and practical innovations. One example of this is the many "Industry 4.0" applications, which initially appeared as innovative standalone solutions but are now firmly established in many companies, as their practical benefits have been proven. Ultimately, it is also an explicit goal of the Lean & Green Award to help disseminate good approaches among industrial companies.

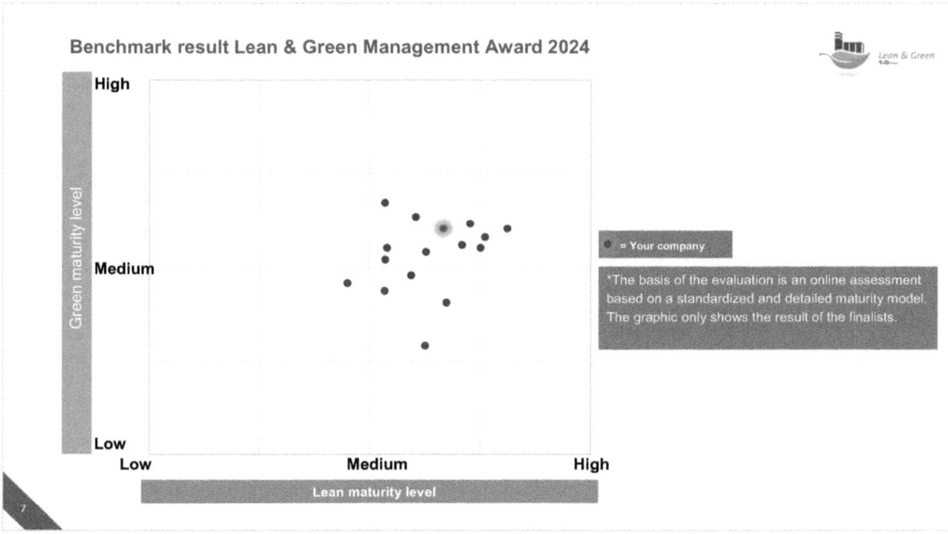

Fig. 5.4 Benchmark Compared to Other Companies (Example)

To ensure comparability over the years despite this dynamic development, companies that participate in the award multiple times receive, in addition to their current assessment, a comparative evaluation based on the previous version of the maturity model. These assessments give companies the opportunity to identify possible trends and developments compared to the previous year. This is particularly relevant for companies that regularly participate in the award, either to evaluate their own performance or to assess the performance of different plants or suppliers. Through this dynamic approach, these companies benefit directly, as they continuously receive input on the latest developments and can also compare the performance of sites or suppliers through external and independent expert evaluations.

The annual results from the Lean & Green Award have demonstrated for years that a high level of lean maturity correlates with a high level of green maturity. This not only confirms the causal relationships outlined in Chap. 3, but is also supported by the discussions and findings from on-site visits. The companies that are leaders in resource efficiency— some will be presented in the following chapter—are characterized by a high level of lean excellence. They succeed in implementing "Lean & Green" best-practice approaches and embedding them sustainably within their organizations.

Best-practice examples from industry 6

How "Lean & Green" can be embedded and advanced within companies is demonstrated each year by the companies participating in the "Lean & Green Management Award." These organizations provide insights into best-practice examples in both lean management and resource efficiency, where "Lean & Green" is either considered as an integrated approach or where both topics positively reinforce each other. In the following chapter, some of the top award participants present their recipes for success and describe their implementation strategies.

The contribution from the **fischer Group of Companies** clearly illustrates how the company succeeds in establishing an integrated sustainability management system that is not separate from the corporate strategy, but rather deeply embedded within it.

The example of the **SÜDPACK Group** explains how combining the two originally independent concepts of "Lean" and "Green" within an excellent business system can contribute to a deeper integration of these topics.

DMG MORI Pfronten GmbH provides a practical explanation of how "Lean & Green" can be implemented both along the entire value chain and within the company's own value creation processes.

The contribution from **BSH Hausgeräte** in Slovenia discusses how a culture of continuous improvement enables flexibility, competitiveness, and resilience.

At **ASM Assembly Systems** in Munich, it becomes clear that "Lean & Green" represents a consistent concept to further develop the "Lean" approach , and that a shared focus on waste reduction helps achieve both economic and ecological optimization of the supply chain.

The **Siemens Electronics Factory Erlangen (GWE)** explains in an initial example how Synchronized Value Chain Design enables the company to be both "lean" and "agile," thereby also improving the environmental performance of the entire value chain.

D. Reichert, *Lean & Green: Best Practice*, https://doi.org/10.1007/978-3-658-49880-1_6

The contribution from the **Festo plant in Sofia (Bulgaria)** focuses on how operational excellence can be elevated to the next level through the intelligent use of digital tools.

Hammerer Aluminium Industries, on the other hand, describes how the company has embarked on the path toward climate neutrality and a circular economy, and how these efforts are also reflected in its continuous improvement process (CIP) system.

Schaltbau describes how the company is setting a new standard for green production with a direct current factory (the NExT Factory).

The **Festo Technology Factory in Scharnhausen** demonstrates the opportunities a new factory building offers in terms of lean management, sustainability, and resource efficiency, and how resource efficiency can be sustainably anchored in management systems and control loops.

The second example from the **Siemens Electronics Factory Erlangen (GWE)** explains how the adaptation of Lean, Scrum, and Kata helps make administrative processes more efficient, thereby also reducing resource consumption.

The brief contribution from **TE Connectivity** discusses how a consistent structure can make the continuous improvement process transparent and measurable, thus ensuring the achievement of strategy and sustainability goals.

At **Welbit Deutschland (Convotherm)**, resource efficiency in the company's own production processes is continuously improved using lean management methods. Through numerous projects and initiatives, the Eglfing site succeeds in making its products and business processes more efficient and environmentally friendly.

Witte Automotive Bulgaria describes how continuous efficiency improvements at the site can be achieved through targeted lean projects and intelligent system integration.

Volkswagen de México presents how the Puebla plant uses "Lean & Green" best practices to improve resource efficiency across all areas.

6.1 Fischer: Implementing Sustainability Management

- Name: **fischer** Group of Companies
- Location: Waldachtal
- Employees at site: approx. 1200
- Industry: Construction/Trades/DIY
- Production processes: Plastic injection molding, cold forging of steel, friction welding, hardening, chemical mixing, filling systems for mortar cartridges and capsules, assembly/packaging (manual and automated)

Assuming responsibility for people and the environment is not at odds with a company's economic success. This realization has now become established in many German industrial enterprises. But how exactly can companies anchor sustainability in their strategy and make it part of their daily operations? A best-practice example from the **fischer** Group of Companies provides an answer.

Sustainability is no longer a niche topic in business, but is being standardized for companies at the EU level. For fischer, sustainability means ensuring the company's future viability. Fischer aligns long-term economic success with ecological responsibility and social justice. The challenge is to integrate sustainability management with proven elements of corporate culture and processes. To this end, fischer has developed the fischer Sustainability Compass. This tool captures the company's mission statement, process system, and strategic sustainability objectives, and, together with controlling, transfers them into a monitoring system. As a result, sustainability activities become transparent, measurable, and manageable. Strategic integration is represented by the TIGER acronym (see below). The TIGER serves as the "umbrella" and "eye-catcher" for the 2030 strategy, including sustainability, and provides an overview of the company's key strategic challenges in direct connection with the relevant UN SDGs.

Initial Situation for fischer Sustainability Management

Over the past 75 years, the fischer Group of Companies, headquartered in the northern Black Forest, has established itself as a global market leader in key areas of fastening technology. Stable growth and active environmental protection have not been mutually exclusive. In 2015, this family-owned company began to engage more intensively with the topic of sustainability. It quickly became clear that the company's guiding principles and the values they communicate already describe a sustainability-oriented approach that goes far beyond environmental protection. Further analysis focused on areas within the dimensions of *ecology*, *economy*, and *social responsibility* that required even greater attention. With a clear commitment from management to a concrete sustainability concept, the project "Implementation of a Sustainability Management System at fischer" was officially launched. After one year, a continuous improvement process was developed and established as an outcome of the project. In the meantime, a dedicated department for sustainability, environment, and energy has been created. To date, fischer is not yet subject to mandatory sustainability reporting under the CSR reporting obligation. Nevertheless, fischer already describes and documents measures in the form of a sustainability report, through which it ensures its sustainable business practices via a continuous improvement process. By joining the WIN Charter (see below) of the state of Baden-Württemberg in 2015, the fischer Group of Companies reaffirmed its commitment to economic, ecological, and social responsibility. The project team's vision: corporate strategy and sustainability strategy must be congruent. As a consequence, the company's strategic challenges and key performance indicators are assigned to the respective sustainability dimensions and supplemented by specific sustainability objectives.

Implementation and Instruments of Sustainability in the Company

Numerous elements and success factors that form the foundation for a sustainable orientation have been present and established at fischer from the outset. The corresponding values are enshrined in the company's mission statement and are lived out daily: innovative, responsible, reliable. The *fischer Process System (fPS)* is designed to eliminate waste and, through its defined processes, has always ensured customer satisfaction as well as resource and energy efficiency. The quality of these processes has a positive impact on growth, ultimately increasing both revenue and the number of employees. To secure the company's future viability in terms of sustainability, ongoing innovative product development and process optimization are particularly essential.

Success Factors and Enablers Educational research shows that information we have merely read tends to remain only superficially in our memory. In contrast, real-life experiences are retained much more effectively. Active and hands-on engagement with specific topics is a prerequisite for developing competencies. This is especially true for sustainability—a term that is often used indiscriminately today—where it is crucial to demonstrate to employees what sustainability actually means within the company. For this purpose, fischer has introduced the "Blue Path" (Fig. 6.1).

The Blue Path represents the connection between several sustainability stations within the company. At each station, real-life examples of sustainability can be observed, preferably in production and logistics, but also in administration. The elements of the Blue Path are the results of successful projects arising from the culture of continuous improvement and the fPS. Relevant projects and examples that are both economically viable and environmentally friendly are visualized on site, making them visible and comprehensible to all. The resulting savings simultaneously enhance the company's social performance.

The social dimension also extends beyond the company's boundaries to include society at large. In this area, fischer has already achieved a great deal. The Klaus Fischer Foundation, with numerous projects in education, training, and welfare, serves as a key pillar.

The strategic orientation of a sustainable company requires a consistent focus on the three dimensions of ecology, economy, and social responsibility. Accordingly, fischer's

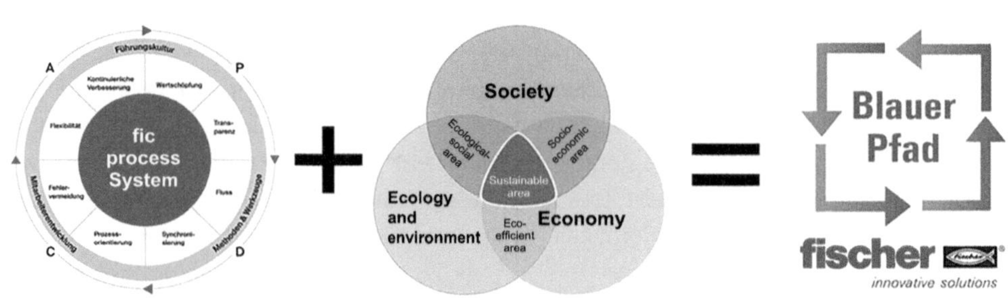

Fig. 6.1 The Blue Path at fischer. *Source:* fischer

sustainability management encompasses innovative products, active market development and customer satisfaction, resource conservation and environmental protection, optimized and efficient processes, occupational health and safety, as well as motivated and well-trained employees.

fischer initiated its strategic entry into sustainability management with the help of the WIN Charter. The *Business Initiative for Sustainability* (WIN) of the state of Baden-Württemberg was launched in 2010 with the aim of pooling the experience and knowledge of sustainably committed companies from all sectors and promoting sustainable business practices. For many years, the WIN Charter has fulfilled the EU directive on mandatory sustainability reporting. fischer follows the pragmatic WIN method and its twelve guiding principles for sustainability. The company places particular emphasis on the areas of *Resources*, *Energy and Emissions*, *Business Success and Employment*, *Sustainable Innovation*, and *Regional Value Creation*.

Ambitious goals have been defined within these WIN Charter principles and are supported by specific key performance indicators. Their qualitative and quantitative documentation is provided in the annually published *fischer Sustainability Report*.

The relevant goals and key figures of the guiding principles have been aligned and synchronized with the SDGs, and highlighted according to their relevance for the company. fischer focuses on eight of the 17 SDGs. In this way, the fischer strategy also aligns with the UN's objectives, which are intended to ensure sustainable development worldwide on economic, social, and environmental levels.

In addition, the goals and key figures of the fischer sustainability strategy have been harmonized with the overarching strategic objectives of the company. The acronym TIGER represents the key strategic challenges in *Technology*, *Innovation*, *Globalisation*, *Ecology*, and *Responsibility* through to 2030 (Fig. 6.2). The strategic orientation aims to combine resilience, competitiveness, and climate protection. As a manufacturing company, the focus is on decoupling resource consumption from growth. From fischer's perspective, the greatest potential lies in innovation and technological progress.

This iterative process has led to the development of the *fischer Sustainability Compass*. This is an integrative framework that maps the strategy of the fischer group and incorporates the specific sustainability goals that are aligned with the fischer mission statement, the fPS, the SDGs, and the WIN principles (Fig. 6.3).

The goals and their respective achievement levels are monitored using the sutainablity radar. This tool is fed with data from controlling and is thus able to depict the current status and verify whether the measures taken are effective. In addition, developments are reviewed and discussed quarterly in a joint meeting with the management board.

Development of Sustainablity in the Company: Future Requirements and Strategies
Over time, what began as a well-intentioned initiative has increasingly become an obligation. Companies are confronted with a wide range of requirements and expectations in the area of sustainability. Regulatory mandates, market demands, and internal expectations all influence the design of sustainable business models.

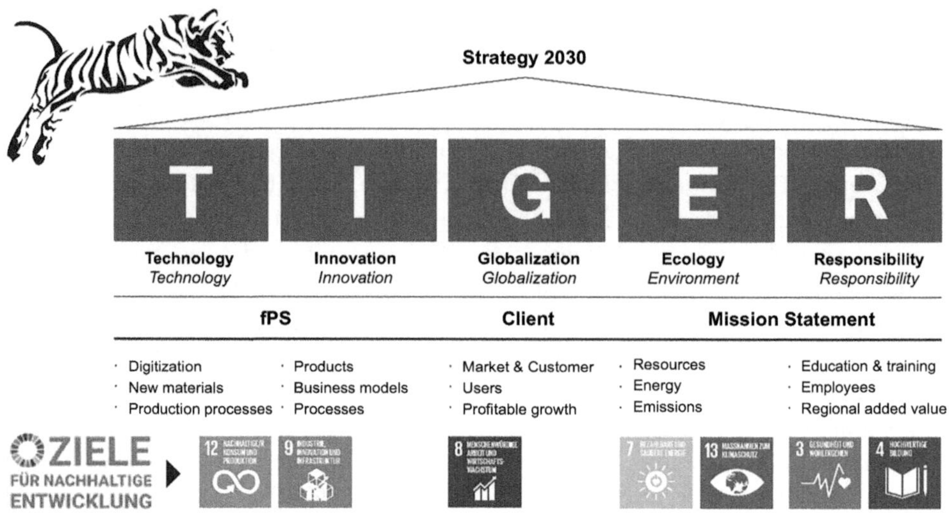

Fig. 6.2 fischer Sustainability Strategy. *Source:* fischer

Regulatory Pressure EU directives and national laws are increasing the pressure on companies to integrate sustainability aspects. The CSRD, which comes into effect in 2025, requires companies such as fischer to prepare detailed sustainability reports if they meet at least two of the following criteria: more than 250 employees, over €40 million in revenue, or a balance sheet total exceeding €20 million.

The implementation of the CSRD will specifically lead to an expansion of current sustainability reporting, covering both qualitative and quantitative data points. This will further enhance transparency. The topics to be reported under the CSRD are determined by a double materiality analysis, representing an extension of the previous materiality assessment. At the fischer Group, the key topics are closely aligned and harmonized with the existing sustainability compass management tool (Note Okt. 2025: This is currently under discussion, and it remains to be seen what the final regulation will look like).

Financial Markets and Investors Investors and financial markets are placing increasing importance on sustainability metrics. Transparent and credible data on *environmental*, *social*, and *governance-related* (ESG) performance are critical for investment decisions and can lead to more favorable financing conditions.

Customers and Competition Customers expect sustainable products and services. Industry initiatives and certifications set standards that companies must meet to remain competitive. The performance of competitors increases the pressure to proactively implement sustainable practices.

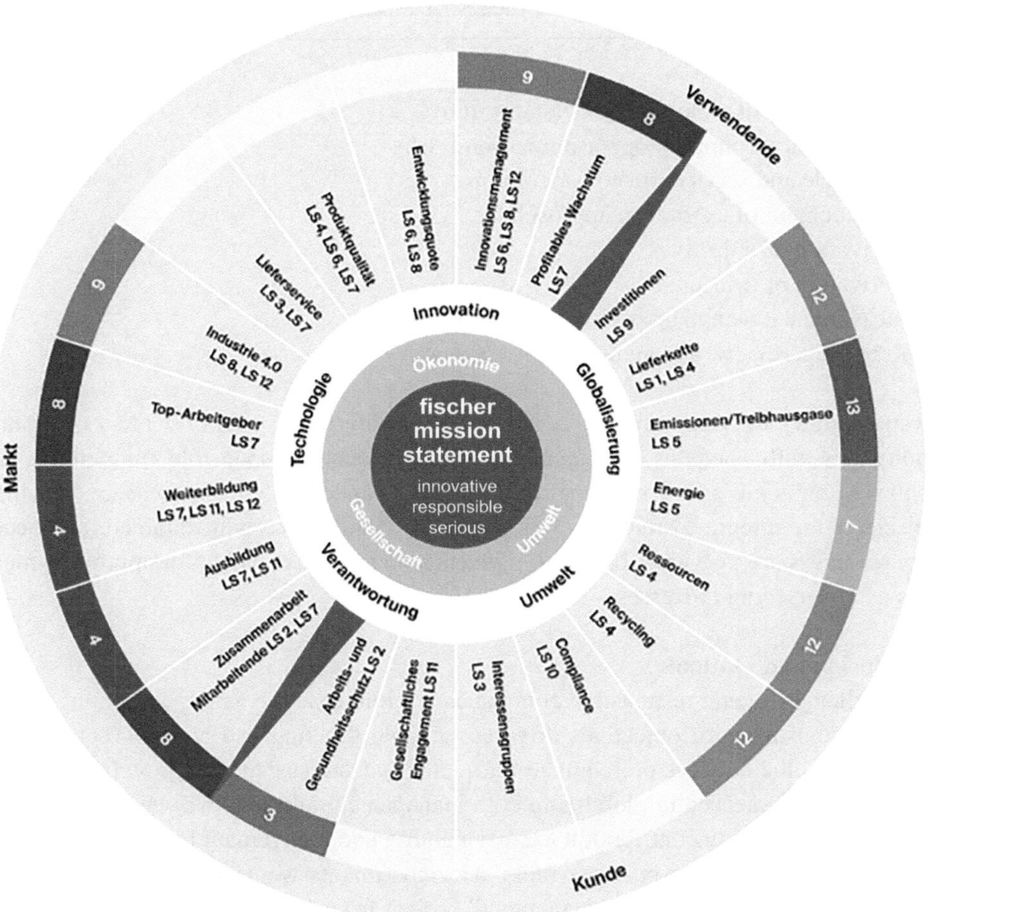

Fig. 6.3 The fischer Mission Statement. *Source:* fischer

Public and Consumers The trend toward sustainable consumption is growing. Consumers demand transparency and sustainability in the products they purchase. Clear and comprehensible communication of sustainability measures is essential to earn public trust.

Internal Requirements Employees expect responsible corporate governance. Individual departments have specific needs that must be integrated into the sustainability strategy. This requires close collaboration and coordination within the company.

Process Steps Toward Sustainability The sustainability strategy must build on existing elements. The sustainability management is tasked with harmonizing topics, designing streamlined processes, and closing existing gaps. Harmonization is primarily about making the topic manageable. Many pieces of information are based on the same core data and standardized process steps:

1. Identification of material topics (status quo)
2. Assessment of impacts, opportunities, and risks
3. Life cycle and service life considerations
4. Development of a strategic approach
5. Derivation of objectives
6. Derivation of measures
7. Measurement using key performance indicators
8. Reporting, review, and audits

Responsibility of Management A key responsibility in the overall context of sustainability lies with company management. Management is responsible for defining and achieving strategic and operational sustainability objectives. It must ensure that these objectives are integrated into business processes, compliance is maintained, and necessary resources are provided. In addition, management is responsible for approving measures and overseeing processes.

Conclusion and Outlook

The challenges facing responsible companies are immense. Dynamic conditions and the ongoing adjustment of objectives drive sustainable thinking and action. Technological innovation is the decisive prerequisite for qualitative and sustainable growth. Only those companies that succeed in mobilizing both management and staff will be able to make a significant and lasting contribution to sustainability and thus remain fit for the future.

At **fischer**, numerous business units and departments were involved in the "Implementation of a sustainability management" project from the outset. fischer established a cross-functional sustainability team whose members address the topic directly with the responsible parties. At the same time, the company succeeded in breaking down the relevance of the topic to the respective levels of action and areas of responsibility, enabling individuals to become aware of their own responsibilities.

Among other achievements, the company's outstanding performance earned it first place in the "Large Enterprises" category at the *German Sustainability Award* (DNP) in 2020. In addition to successes in product and production responsibility, fischer's holistic and integrative NHM sustainability management was explicitly recognized.

The fischer Group aims to take responsibility and share its sustainability experience as an inspiring role model. At the newly established *fischer Sustainability Campus*, other companies or organizations, as well as suppliers and partners, can request support and thus participate in introductory or advanced training on sustainability and sustainability management. With its own coaches, the company supports the development of individual sustainability strategies or the implementation of sustainability projects. The focus is on creating a network for collaboration and exchange, enabling challenges to be addressed collectively. This objective is in line with "SDG 17: Partnerships for the Goals."

fischer sees itself as a learning organization that always acts ambitiously, but is not free from shortcomings that can still be addressed. At every opportunity, the company has sought feedback on its sustainability concept and, where possible, implemented adjustments. There can be no final sustainability goal. The environment is and will remain dynamic. Therefore, the guiding principle must be: The journey is the destination!

Author: Christian Ziegler, Head of Sustainability, Environment, and Energy

6.2 Südpack: Lean Management as a Fundamental Building Block for Sustainability

- Name: SÜDPACK Group
- Location: all sites of the SÜDPACK Group
- Employees in the group: 1800
- Industry: High-performance films and packaging materials for the food industry, as well as the medical and technical industries
- Production processes: Blown film and cast film extrusion, bag converting, compounding, gravure, flexographic and digital printing, lamination

Sustainability has always been of essential importance to **SÜDPACK**. It lies at the heart of the company's philosophy—and is the strongest driving force in the pursuit of *excellence* and *sustainable leadership* across the three key areas of *ecology*, *economy*, and *social responsibility*. As such, sustainability is firmly embedded in operational processes. It enjoys broad acceptance throughout the organization and is increasingly recognized by the public: for example, in 2023, *WirtschaftsWoche* included SÜDPACK for the second consecutive year among the top 50 most sustainable medium-sized companies in Germany in its Sustainability Ranking.

To consistently implement its sustainability strategy, SÜDPACK has deliberately chosen a holistic, systemic approach—making Lean & Green the central pillars of the SÜDPACK Business System. Within Lean Management, the company primarily relies on four main categories: Policy Deployment, Shopfloor Management, Project Management Office (PMO), and Six Sigma. Through its Green initiatives, SÜDPACK places energy, materials, and environmental management at the center of its activities. At the same time, with its pioneering product portfolio and investments in advanced recycling technologies, SÜDPACK has positioned itself as a key driver of circular economy, resource efficiency, and CO_2 reduction within its industry. In addition, occupational safety, employee health, and responsibility for people are fixed points in the sustainability strategy framework.

The combination of the two originally independent concepts, "Lean" and "Green," is consistently aimed at implementing and managing economic, ecological, and social corporate objectives. The guiding principle: to achieve consciously goals together as a team with maximum transparency.

Systems Thinking as the Core of "Lean & Green" (Fig. 6.4)

The systemic approach primarily ensures that a wide range of requirements in an increasingly volatile market environment can be quickly communicated to and addressed within the organization. This applies regardless of whether the requirements are driven by customers, politics, legislation, or arise from ISO management systems. Lean enables

- a focus on strategic and operational objectives,
- the decentralization of objectives to key stakeholders,
- a clear view of the current status of goal achievement, and
- the assessment of key driver projects to ensure targets are met.

Structure of the SÜDPACK Strategy

The development of the corporate strategy takes place within the executive management team of the SÜDPACK Group, which consists of the management board, business unit managers, and the heads of all central functions. Taking into account the business environment as well as the company's vision and mission, the team first develops the corporate strategy, which forms the basis for defining the central corporate objectives. Implementation planning for various initiatives and projects that contribute to achieving the 2030 strategy is also carried out.

Measuring Strategy Implementation Using a Group-wide Corporate Objectives Table

In a second step, a corporate objectives table is created, whose primary purpose is to visualize and monitor the implementation of the strategy. This is done on a monthly basis

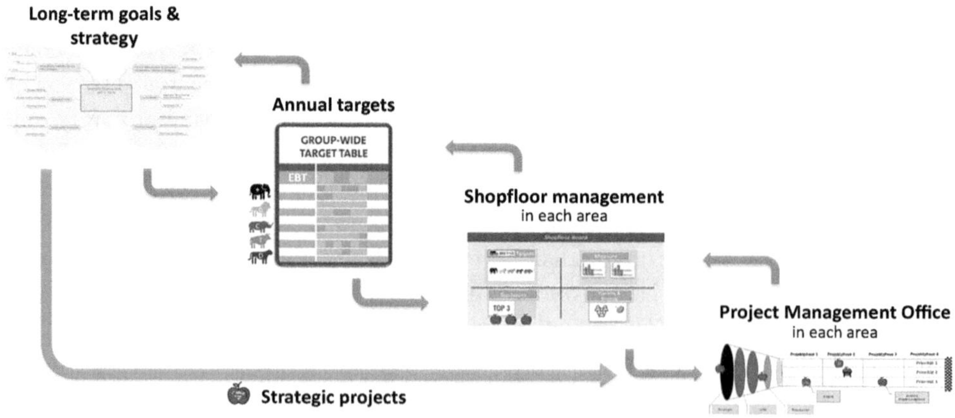

Fig. 6.4 SÜDPACK Business System. *Source:* SÜDPACK Group

by consistently measuring and closely tracking the annual targets derived from the corporate strategy. At SÜDPACK, the key performance framework of the corporate objectives table consists of the following five target categories—internally referred to as the "Big Five":

- Safety, Health, Environment
- Quality
- Costs
- Delivery Time
- Throughput

A necessary tool for the goal-oriented, cross-hierarchical management of the corporate objectives table is *Policy Deployment*. Policy Deployment enables the systematic translation and communication of overarching goals and strategies to the various organizational levels, departments, and employees. It is crucial that the defined objectives reach the key stakeholders.

The main advantage of Policy Deployment is that each key stakeholder is made aware of both the overarching group objectives and their own role-specific goals, and is effectively supported in achieving the group's targets.

Decentralized Target Management via Shopfloor Management

With Shopfloor Management, SÜDPACK employs an effective method for managing the aforementioned decentralized objectives—specifically through the active presence of managers at the point of action. As with the corporate objectives table, the decentralized goals are always listed within the "Big Five" performance framework.

This tool is implemented in every area at SÜDPACK. It serves both to anchor and to visualize and measure the objectives required to achieve both operational and strategic corporate goals. Shopfloor Management is therefore a key enabler of a constructive and positive error culture. Ultimately, it allows focus on the levers that contribute to achieving targets.

The current status of goal achievement is regularly reviewed and communicated at different organizational levels and in all functional areas during shopfloor meetings. In these meetings, the target management teams, as well as each individual team member, are proactively encouraged to propose necessary actions based on their detailed process knowledge to achieve the objectives. This can ultimately lead to project-related topics or smaller to-dos.

Decentralized Project Visualization and Management via Multi-Project Management

A third important step is the visualization of strategic projects and the necessary key driver projects arising from shopfloor management activities. At SÜDPACK, these projects are presented within the multi-project management platform in a standardized format.

A key aspect here is that each person responsible in the central functions, business units, plants, or individual departments has access to their own project management board. This makes it easy to generate views of the projects relevant to each target owner, which must be managed independently to achieve their objectives. In addition, individual projects can be easily linked with all other areas, enabling cross-functional project work.

Before a project officially begins, its contribution to the overall corporate objective is always carefully considered—not just its impact on individual "silos." This is particularly important, for example, when shared resources such as IT need to be utilized.

Strategic projects such as the SPQ technology, digitalization, production investments, or the implementation of a stage-gate process for new product development are mapped on the PMO platform and are always addressed proactively and with priority. For SÜDPACK, the PMO is an effective tool for pursuing strategic objectives in a dynamic environment, maintaining an overview as project volume and complexity increase, managing capacities efficiently, setting priorities, and at the same time meeting high quality standards.

Application of Tools for Project Implementation/Problem Solving

Agile project management methods or "Six Sigma" approaches are used to handle selected projects. Six Sigma, for example, is applied to complex issues that can be resolved more efficiently using statistical tools.

Within both project management approaches, "classic lean tools" such as "5S" or "Single-Minute Exchange of Die (SMED)" can be utilized as needed. Ultimately, every project is accessible to all participants via the PMO, with a simple traffic light logic indicating the current project status. This status is briefly presented in regular PMO meetings. In addition, critical projects can be escalated to higher organizational levels through a structured escalation process, allowing targeted countermeasures to be initiated.

In summary, "Lean & Green" stands for

- the intelligent integration of economic, ecological, and social action,
- the reduction of costs, resources, energy, and unnecessary work steps,
- the optimization of collaboration along the value chain,
- and thus ultimately for the future viability and profitable growth of the organization.

Rapid adaptation of market and customer requirements into internal targets is achieved through our intelligent business system, which is embedded in all areas of the company and consistently applied. This ensures that the increasing green requirements are quickly communicated to the main stakeholders and can be consciously managed in a decentralized manner.

Employee development at **SÜDPACK** is therefore aimed at ensuring that this overall system can be operated in its current form and continuously developed further. The declared goal is a smart symbiosis of lean management, sustainability, digitalization, automation, and social responsibility, which is now considered the gold standard or optimum. SÜDPACK is therefore working intensively to ensure that all activities are balanced in terms of economic efficiency, social responsibility, and environmental compatibility.

6.3 DMG MORI: Sustainable Business = Successful Business

- Name: DMG MORI Pfronten GmbH
- Location: Pfronten in the Allgäu region
- Employees: approx. 1500 at the Pfronten site
- Industry: Mechanical engineering
- Production processes: Assembly; machining production

DMG MORI is a globally leading manufacturer of high-precision machine tools, represented in 43 countries with 116 sales and service locations, including 17 production plants. In the "Global One Company," more than 13,000 employees drive the development of holistic solutions in the manufacturing environment. The group's parent company is DMG MORI COMPANY LIMITED, with its global headquarters in Tokyo, Japan, and its European headquarters in Munich. DMG MORI AG is listed on the German stock exchange in the "Prime Standard" and has its registered office in Bielefeld.

Our portfolio includes sustainable manufacturing solutions based on technologies such as turning, milling, grinding, drilling, as well as ultrasonic, laser technology, and additive manufacturing. Through technology integration and comprehensive automation and digitalization solutions, we enable increased productivity and resource efficiency at the same time.

With around 1500 employees and a total area of 149,000 m^2, the Pfronten site is one of the most important development and largest production plants in Europe. As a milling specialist, the plant manufactures over 50 different machine types, ranging from the versatile monoBLOCK series to XXL machines.

From raw materials to recycling, from employees to customers—DMG MORI AG assumes responsibility along the entire value chain. We structure our areas of action along the entire value chain (see Fig. 6.5). Topics over which we have direct influence—such as through internal and external information, measures, or concepts—are highlighted in black.

Sustainability at DMG MORI

With clearly defined goals and concrete measures, we contribute to achieving the Paris Climate Agreement. Since September 2021, DMG MORI AG has committed itself to

Fig. 6.5 Value chain of DMG MORI AG. *Source:* DMG MORI

the goals of the "Science Based Targets" initiative, which aims to limit global warming to a maximum of 1.5 °C. To this end, we aim to reduce our Scope 1 and 2 emissions by 46.2% and Scope 3 emissions by at least 27.5% by 2030 (base year: 2019).

To achieve our goals, DMG MORI AG operates an energy and environmental management system. This system records, among other things, energy consumption, environmentally relevant data, and key performance indicators for monitoring. Based on this data, appropriate measures can be implemented to achieve the targets.

The consumption data is mainly obtained from our energy monitoring software, which we have implemented group-wide at all production sites.

For example, in 2023, DMG MORI Pfronten GmbH was able to equip all suitable roof surfaces with PV modules and expand the existing system from 2022, which had 740 kWp and over 2000 modules, by an additional nearly 3 MWp and over 7000 modules. With a total capacity of over 3.7 MWp, the site achieves an electrical self-sufficiency rate of over 30%.

Starting in May 2024, group-wide waste management will be introduced at the Pfronten site. New recyclable waste fractions will be created to improve the waste sorting process. In addition to establishing a new central recycling center, single-use containers in the company restaurant will be replaced with reusable containers, including a deposit system and dishwashing service. New disposal processes will be introduced in close cooperation with a regional service provider.

GREENMODE: 13 Measures for Energy Efficiency

With the "GREENMODE measures," DMG MORI is systematically increasing the energy and resource efficiency of its machines (Scope 3: "Downstream"). At "EMO 2023" in Hanover, the company demonstrated that the use of innovative hardware and software components can achieve energy savings of over 30% in the operation of machine tools. Examples of GREENMODE measures presented include demand-driven operation of machine components, the use of highly efficient cooling units, and adaptive supply of cooling lubricant (Fig. 6.6).

As a result, DMG MORI products also help conserve the environment and resources during customer operation. For example, the energy efficiency of the newly introduced DMU 65 FDS monoBLOCK 2nd Generation was increased by 36% in the reporting year through the GREENMODE measures. The effectiveness of these energy efficiency measures and the calculation methods used have also been confirmed by the renowned TÜV SÜD Industrie Service GmbH: In January 2023, DMG MORI became the first machine tool manufacturer in Germany to be awarded the *TÜV SÜD EME Certificate* for its GREENMODE management system. DMG MORI further enhances resource efficiency through a high degree of technology integration as well as the highest quality and precision of its machines, ensuring maximum service life and minimal scrap. With comprehensive automation and digitalization solutions, machining centers can operate around the clock at maximum efficiency—enabling customers to save even more resources. One example is the "Digital Twin," which allows components to be tested virtually so that the desired result is achieved on the first attempt during actual production.

The machines and their components are also designed for easy repair and selective replacement of wear parts. In the event of service, support is provided quickly, efficiently, and in an environmentally friendly manner—wherever possible, 100% remotely—using digital solutions such as *NETservice*, the new knowledge management platform *DMG MORI weKNOW*, and the customer portal *my DMG MORI*.

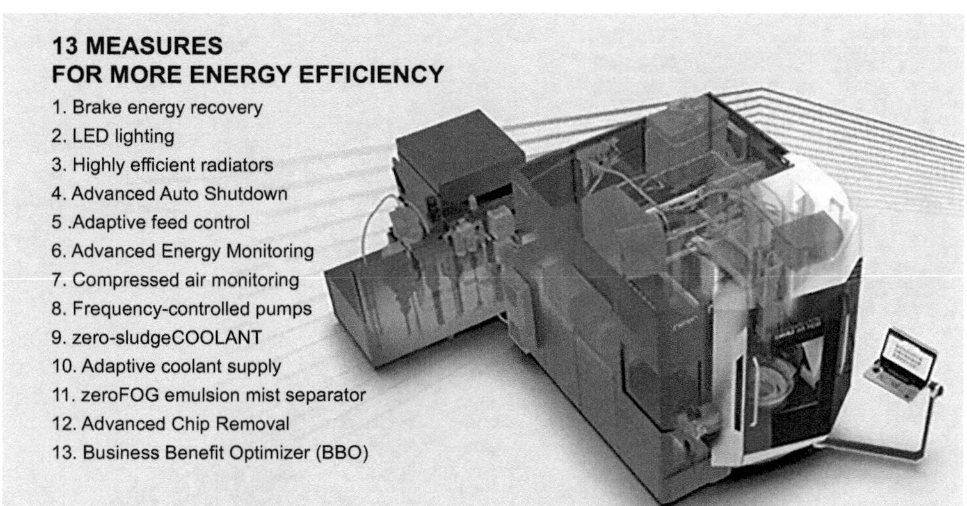

Fig. 6.6 13 measures (including "Business Benefit Optimizer") for greater energy efficiency. *Source:* DMG MORI

"Pull" and "Flow"—A Success Concept for Flow Assembly

Since August 2020, the entire model mix of the monoBLOCK series—including all models with pallet changers (DMC) and mill-turn pallets (FD)—has been assembled in a flow production process in 34 cycles at the 4000 m^2 "Excellence Factory" in Pfronten. This process starts with basic assembly, followed by geometry, control cabinet installation, and ends with final inspection. The machines are assembled on automated guided vehicles (AGVs). With a cycle time of two and a half hours, this enables a machine throughput time of 12 days in the current single-shift operation. This innovative manufacturing concept has significantly reduced throughput time and greatly increased capacity. As a result, production is more sustainable and costs are lower, allowing DMG MORI to pass on savings to customers through price reductions (Fig. 6.7).

To make the processes for this assembly concept "leaner," DMG MORI relies on so-called *Production Dojos*. These manufacturability studies identify potential waste in the value chain, enabling new production chains to be optimized for sustainability and cost-effectiveness.

The Production Dojos for the *Excellence Factory* were conducted in a laboratory environment in a separate assembly hall. In addition to the required material supply, the necessary personnel and their occupational safety were analyzed and documented. This study enabled the development of a concept for flow assembly. Pre-assembly was

Fig. 6.7 Excellence Factory monoBLOCK of DMG MORI Pfronten GmbH. *Source:* DMG MORI

expanded from 4 to 15 work areas, making it possible to adapt certain machine types for flow production. In addition, materials are delivered to the main production line already unpacked, following the "fishbone principle." As a result, there is no packaging waste in flow production. Furthermore, single-use wooden transport racks have been replaced by sustainable metal racks, which shuttle back and forth with suppliers. Pre-assembly is scheduled one day in advance, allowing for quick responses to short-term logistics issues and providing internal logistics with more lead time. The entire process runs more smoothly, ensuring a sustainable and cost-effective production base.

Lean Excellence

With regard to Lean Excellence, DMG MORI has established the so-called "TAKT—Improve-Together Organization" (TAKT ITO). The core idea is the continuous improvement of processes, the implementation of uniform group-wide standards, the global exchange of best practices, and a shared understanding of improvement approaches, methods, and tools. In addition, TAKT ITO, through the "TAKT Academy," provides group-wide standards for the training of "Digital Lean Six Sigma" (DLSS) and the DLSS improvement toolkit. The aim is for a large proportion of employees (20% of all employees with a Green Belt certification, 2% with a Black Belt certification) to have a fundamental understanding of Lean, be familiar with DLSS, and implement projects to drive the continuous improvement of the company.

Within the framework of TAKT ITO, there are four core activities at the company level to drive improvement, enabling improvement measures at the site through the active involvement of all employees. Specifically, these are idea management with employee CIP and the company suggestion scheme, as well as TAKT CIP with CIP workshops and CIP projects, and DLSS projects.

Through these activities under TAKT ITO, DMG MORI implemented 16,845 ideas in the 2023 fiscal year, generating a calculated first-year benefit of €3.9 million. The calculated first-year benefit resulting from the completed CIP projects amounts to approximately €1.6 million, and the calculated savings, net of relevant costs, from the DLSS projects totaled around €2.5 million in the 2023 fiscal year (Fig. 6.8).

Shopfloor Management

For shopfloor management, DMG MORI uses a standardized *Balanced Scorecard* across the group, comprising a total of 16 KPIs, such as assembly time productivity and on-time delivery performance. Based on these KPIs, which are cascaded through the assembly areas—station-based and line assembly—as well as the individual production units, production can be managed in a targeted manner.

This is digitally supported by a proprietary digital shopfloor management system and production cockpit with interfaces to SAP S/4HANA. In this system, shopfloor employees, who log in with their employee badges, can digitally confirm the completion of tasks and processes or document additional assembly times. Materials or fixtures can

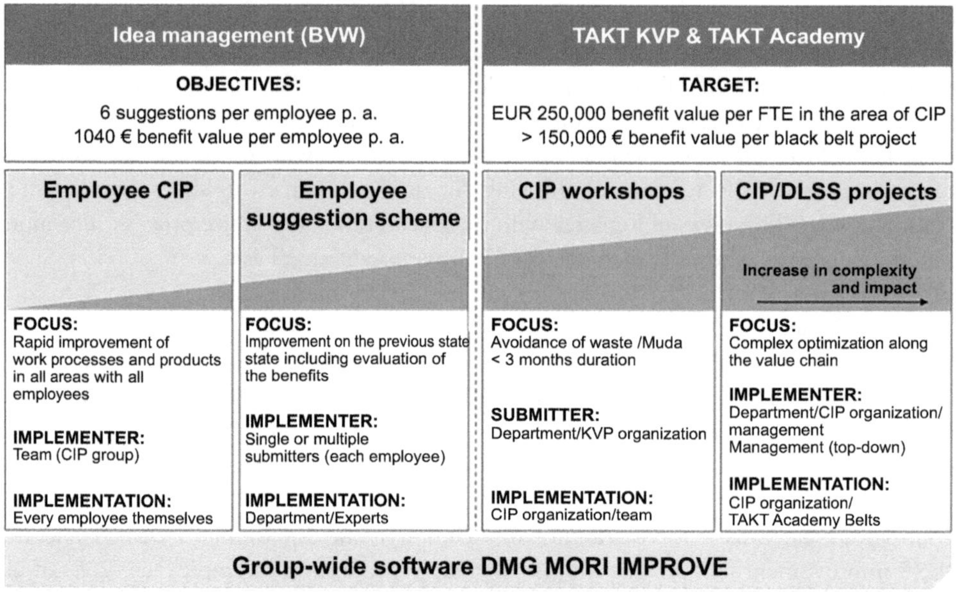

Fig. 6.8 TAKT ITO—Idea management and continuous improvement process. *Source:* DMG MORI

also be requested in this way. The current progress of the machine thus becomes transparent, and key figures such as productivity can be derived from this data.

Disruptions or missing parts can be entered into the system with minimal effort, and in the event of an error, the responsible supervisors are digitally notified. Depending on the urgency and extent of the disruption, the appropriate escalation level is triggered. The system distinguishes between *Low*, *Middle*, and *High*. For minor issues, supervisors and technologists are informed; for "Middle," the relevant department heads are additionally notified of the need for action. At the highest escalation level, executive management is also informed. This paves the way for rapid problem resolution. The shopfloor monitor and production cockpit are therefore central to the company's lean excellence—not only to provide a live overview of the entire production process, but also to accelerate and prioritize processes (Fig. 6.9).

6.4 BSH Slovenia: How a Culture of Continuous Improvement Enables Flexibility, Competitiveness, and Resilience

- Name: BSH Hausgeräte GmbH
- Location: Nazarje—Slovenia
- Employees at site: approx. 1600

Fig. 6.9 Shopfloor management system and production cockpit with integrated interface to SAP S/4HANA. *Source:* DMG MORI

- Industry: Consumer goods/Electrical appliances
- Production processes: Assembly including testing, motor production, plastics, logistics

The **BSH Home Appliances Factory** in Slovenia is the largest production site for small home appliances in Europe and the sixth largest of BSH's 39 factories worldwide. This outstanding position is the result of a consistent strategy focused on flexibility, scalability, and sustainability, as well as a strong corporate culture that enables BSH Slovenia to integrate these strategic principles into its own processes.

To make the strategy and value stream orientation tangible for everyone, BSH made use of visual language. Together with its employees, BSH visualized its corporate strategy. With the support of a children's book author, an appealing illustration was developed that not only communicates the company's goals and values, but also serves as a communication tool within the workforce. This concept was further extended at Christmas, when employees' children received this "hidden object picture" as a puzzle, thereby fostering understanding and identification with the corporate strategy at home as well (Fig. 6.10).

Three central strategic elements conveyed through this visualization are the consistent focus on flexibility, the emphasis on cost efficiency, and the culture of continuous improvement in the context of ongoing digitalization.

Fig. 6.10 Strategy and values of BSH Slovenia visualized. *Source:* BSH Slovenia

The factory produces up to 10 million devices annually and offers a broad portfolio ranging from affordable hand blenders to high-end built-in fully automatic coffee machines. During periods of high demand, such as the COVID-19 pandemic, production was increased by 35% within a short time. This impressive flexibility is crucial for remaining successful in a highly competitive market. In addition, production in Europe is subject to significant cost pressures. For this reason, BSH continuously optimizes its processes, material costs, and structures to stay competitive. Despite intense competition, especially from Asia, BSH has so far won every benchmark competition and leverages its strengths in flexibility and delivery capability.

A key factor in the success of the BSH factory in Slovenia is the implementation of a value stream-oriented organizational structure in 2018. This structure dissolves traditional departmental boundaries and puts the product at the center. Each value stream has its own manager who brings together all the functions required for the production and optimization of the product. These managers make entrepreneurial decisions for their value stream, ensuring faster decision-making processes (Fig. 6.11).

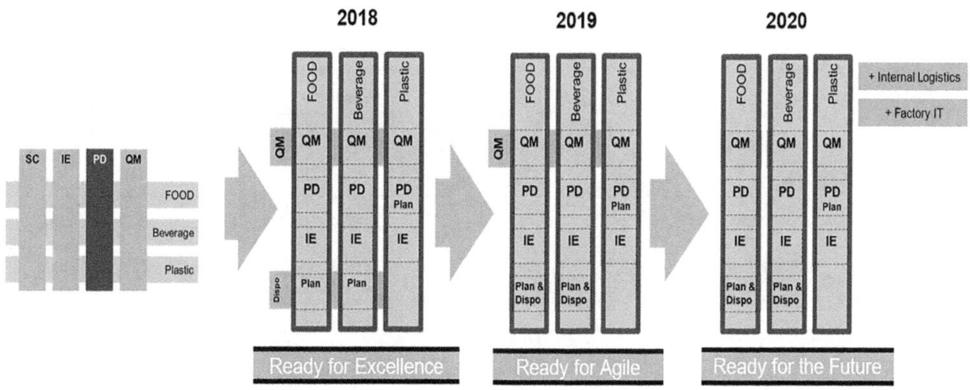

Fig. 6.11 Development of the value stream organization at BSH Slovenia. *Source:* BSH Slovenia

The value stream-oriented structure offers several advantages:

Speed	Decisions can be made directly within the value stream without having to wait for coordination between different departments
Focus	Each value stream focuses on its specific product and can drive targeted improvements
Responsibility	Value stream managers have full responsibility for their areas, leading to stronger identification and motivation

This structural change enabled BSH to further increase its flexibility and efficiency by minimizing conflicts between departments and maximizing synergies. It also led to greater employee identification with the company and its organizational structures, which in turn strengthened the company's adaptability.

A particularly challenging event that required team spirit and adaptability was the flooding in Slovenia in August 2023. This flood, which can be directly attributed to ongoing climate change, hit the factory hard. Despite significant damage, BSH quickly began reconstruction and was able to resume initial production after just four weeks. The value stream-oriented organization played a key role in ramping up production quickly, implementing necessary process adjustments, and setting the right priorities.

This resilience demonstrates the strength of the corporate culture and the ability to successfully overcome crises.

However, BSH has been committed to sustainability issues long before this disaster. The factory has set itself the goal of achieving CO_2-free production by the end of 2025. Even today, heating and cooling are provided exclusively by geothermal energy and waste heat from injection molding, eliminating the need for fossil fuels. Photovoltaic systems and other projects also contribute to reducing the CO_2 footprint (Fig. 6.12).

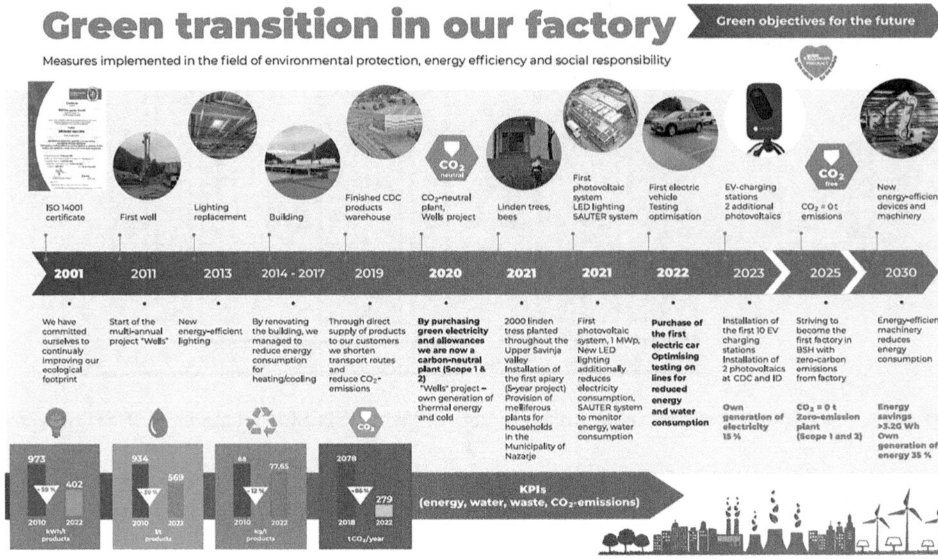

Fig. 6.12 The sustainability roadmap of BSH Slovenia. *Source:* BSH Slovenia

As the largest employer in a small valley, BSH also assumes responsibility for the local community. Supporting beekeepers, planting trees, and purchasing pianos for the music school are just a few examples of the factory's engagement. These activities not only foster local ties but also strengthen cohesion within the workforce.

6.5 ASMPT SMT Solutions: Value Stream-Oriented Lean Management—Achieving Economic and Environmental Excellence in Tandem

- Name: ASMPT GmbH & Co. KG
- Location: Rupert-Mayer-Str. 48, 81379 Munich
- Employees at site: approx. 1000
- Industry: Mechanical engineering for the electronics industry
- Production processes: Assembly and electronics manufacturing

ASMPT SMT Solutions, a segment of the **ASMPT Group**, is a global leader in supporting, implementing, and realizing smart factories for electronics manufacturers. ASMPT solutions support both line and factory levels with hardware, software, and services. The product portfolio includes hardware and software such as SIPLACE placement machines, DEK printers, inspection and material storage solutions, as well as the WORKS software suite. ASMPT's intelligent manufacturing solutions not only set new global standards for electronics manufacturers, but the placement machine production in Munich is also considered an industry leader thanks to its consistent focus on digital lean principles—as evidenced by repeated recognition as Factory of the Year.

In 2008, ASMPT SMT Solutions faced the challenges of the global economic crisis and restructured its supply chain. The stated goal was to introduce comprehensive and intensive lean management with an exclusive focus on value-adding activities. Processes were to be streamlined and throughput times reduced. This was implemented quickly and successfully, in large part because management recognized from the outset that this ambitious goal and the associated radical organizational change could only be achieved with consensus across the entire team, a coherent vision and strategy, and deep integration into the corporate philosophy. A positive side effect: consistent application of lean principles quickly revealed that ASMPT's resource efficiency and sustainability—in short, its environmental performance—had also improved significantly. Today, for ASMPT, "Lean" is inseparably linked with "Green."

Foundation: The ASMPT SMT Solutions SCM Strategy Development

The ASMPT SMT Solutions SCM strategy cycle is set for four years. For this four-year period, an overarching objective is defined, which relates to a maximum of ten strategic initiatives. Over the course of the four-year cycle, two to three of these strategic initiatives are addressed each year, and the resulting objectives are implemented as projects. The individual project phases are regularly reviewed, shared, and approved by management in global reviews. As part of this strategy development, ASMPT defined the alignment of the supply chain with lean management in 2008 (Fig. 6.13).

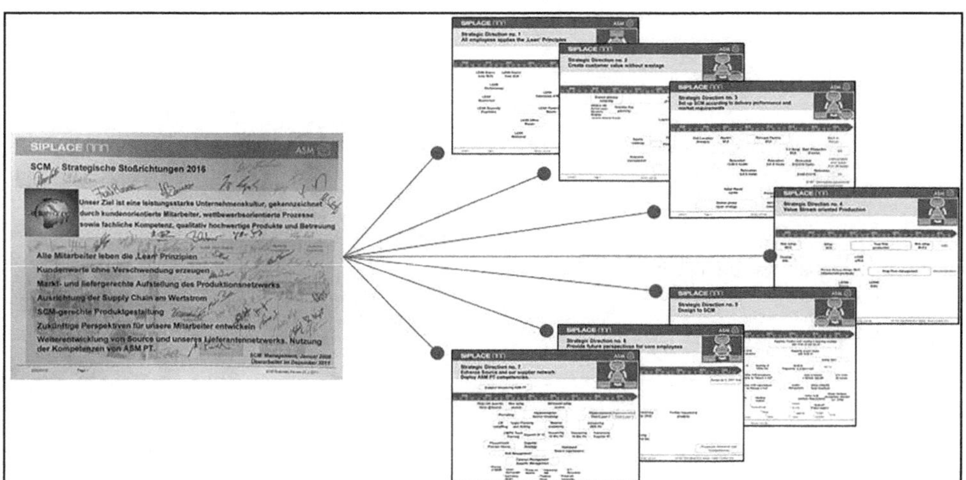

Fig. 6.13 Project roadmaps for each strategic initiative. *Source:* ASMPT GmbH & Co. KG

Achieving Success with Lean Management

Based on the lean concept, the ASMPT SMT Solutions Supply Chain team established a completely new SIPLACE machine factory in Munich within just four months. The consistent focus on value stream orientation and the rigorous application of lean principles—such as order-based flow production, the pull principle, the "lot size 1" method, and the elimination of waste in production—quickly led to initial successes (Fig. 6.14). Thanks to this radically new approach and the team's commitment and willingness to embrace change, outstanding results were achieved in a short period of time (Fig. 6.15), including:

- an 80% reduction in lead time
- an 80% reduction in manufacturing floor space

Key Success Factors of Value Stream-Oriented Lean Management

One of the most important success factors in radical change is the workforce, which is why the focus from the outset was on the consistent involvement of the team. As part of the project, all employees first received training to acquire the necessary methodological knowledge of lean processes and were supported in making their own workstations more efficient through value stream analysis workshops and the use of cardboard models. This personal involvement was very positively received by all employees, significantly increasing their willingness to embrace change. It also enabled major restructuring

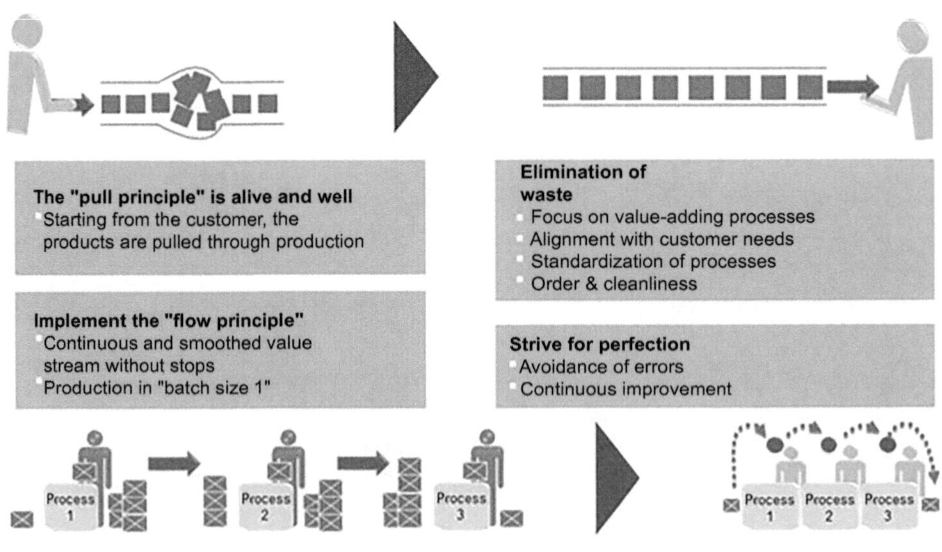

Fig. 6.14 Siplace SCM lean principles. *Source:* ASMPT GmbH & Co. KG

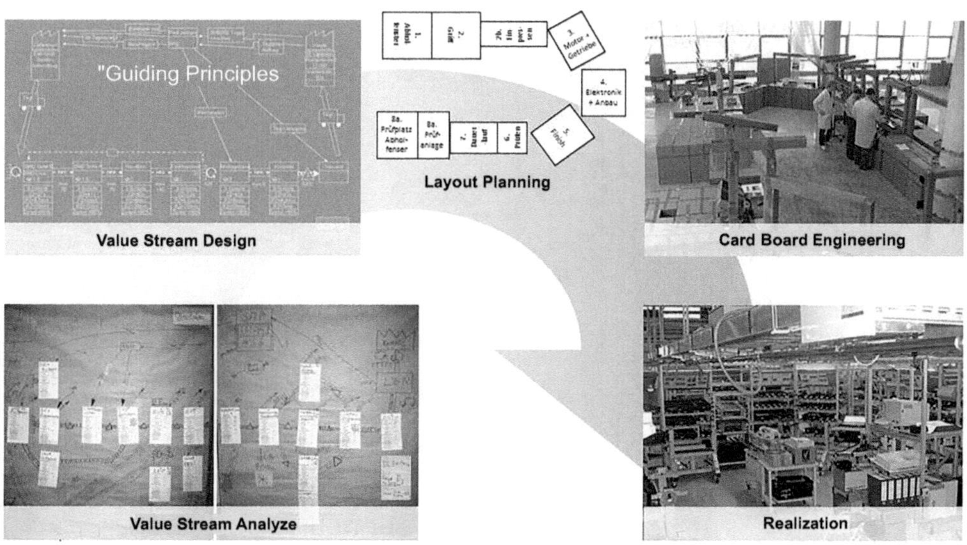

Fig. 6.15 From value stream to realization. *Source:* ASMPT GmbH & Co. KG

measures in production—such as integrating additional manufacturing cells or doubling the cycle rate—to be carried out more quickly, efficiently, and at regular intervals. To ensure that improvements were sustained, consolidation phases were also introduced, during which new processes and changes were optimized and adapted as part of continuous improvement (CIP) (Fig. 6.16).

Another key success factor is undoubtedly the integration of procurement into the SCM organization. ASMPT now refers to this as the Source organization. Here, all functions—from strategic and operational procurement to supplier quality and inbound logistics—are consolidated. This ensures end-to-end process responsibility up to the supplier.

"Lean" and "Green"—an ideal combination

What does "Lean & Green" mean? Essentially, it is the consistent further development of the lean concept. The lean concept, with its already well-known and established "seven types of waste," provides the ideal foundation to include an additional type of waste: "waste associated with all forms of environmental impact." To implement this as systematically as possible, this "new" type of waste is divided into seven factors. The selection of these factors is based on the ecological reporting criteria of the *Global Reporting Initiative* (GRI).

By mapping energy, water, material, waste, transport, emissions, and biodiversity along the value stream, consumption becomes transparent and measurable—an essential prerequisite for subsequent optimization (Fig. 6.17).

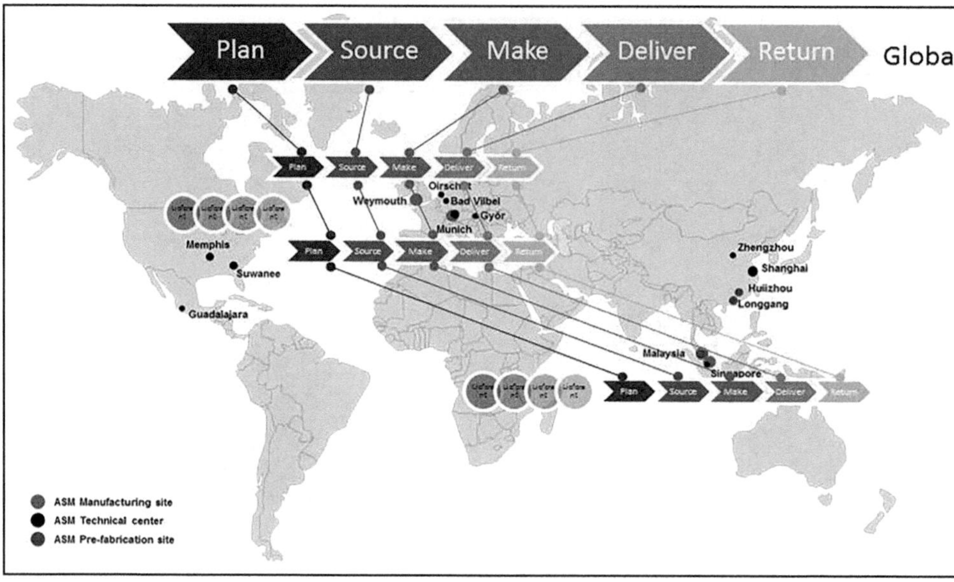

Fig. 6.16 Fundamental companion: consistent process organization. *Source:* ASMPT GmbH & Co. KG

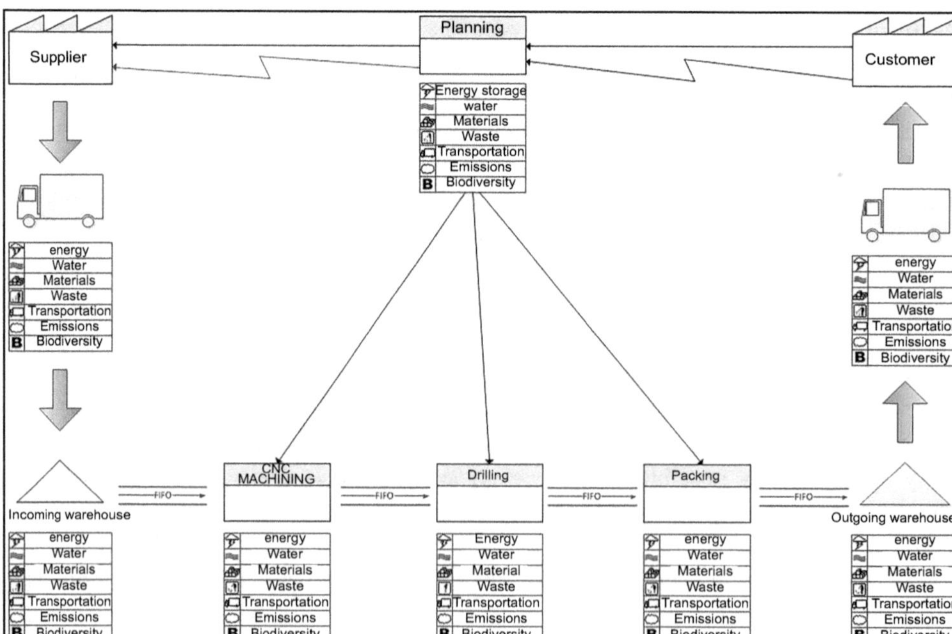

Fig. 6.17 Value stream illustrating the environmental factor. (Adapted from Wills, 2009)

"Lean & Green" at ASMPT: Shared Successes and Results

Companies that establish this comprehensive approach will quickly realize that some of the original lean methods also deliver significant green benefits.

Space Consolidation/Insourcing

Through annual reviews of its production layout, ASMPT continuously improves its value stream. Achievements include increased space productivity, reduced lead times, and, above all, a high willingness to embrace change among employees. In terms of "Green," this means that every square meter saved in production reduces the impact on our ecosystem and thus supports existing biodiversity.

Expansion of Repair Centers and Increase in Repair Rate

By expanding global repair centers, improving customers' ability to carry out their own repairs, and increasing the in-house repair rate, not only are external failure and logistics costs reduced, but CO_2 emissions from transporting defective parts and waste from scrapped materials are also minimized.

Kanban Optimization and Returnable Packaging

Continuous optimization and adjustment of Kanban quantities is necessary not only to avoid excess inventory in production, but also as a method to reduce unnecessary internal transport. This has a direct impact on CO_2 emissions, which can thus be significantly reduced.

Returnable packaging is an excellent way to transport demanding, high-quality, and sensitive parts safely. Custom inlays protect materials from damage, thereby preventing unnecessary scrap, which in turn can lead to unplanned production downtime. In addition, returnable packaging offers an optimal way to reduce packaging waste. From an ecological perspective, however, the use of returnable packaging is not always unproblematic. Suppliers should be located as close as possible to the production site, and the return or delivery of packaging should ideally be handled via a milk run.

Measurability of Consumption

Moreover, mapping environmental waste along the value stream brings another significant advantage: consumption becomes measurable.

In this context, "measurable" does not necessarily mean a fully integrated digital metering system at the outset. For example, in the case of energy consumption, initial estimates can be made using nameplates, or temporary flexible meters can be connected to individual devices (e.g., Fluke Energy Logger 1730). These meters make it easy and quick to record standby consumption, which is often significantly underestimated.

In summary, lean principles have proven to be an excellent method for identifying the economic optimum of a supply chain. Furthermore, by extending the perspective to include the seven common types of environmental waste, the ecological optimum is also promoted.

6.6 Siemens: Synchronized Value Chain Design Lean vs. Agile Across the Entire Value Chain

- Name: Siemens AG—Digital Industries, Motion Control, Electronics Factory Erlangen.
- Plant: Electronics Factory Erlangen (GWE), Frauenauracher Straße 80, 91056 Erlangen
- Employees at the plant: approx. 1000
- Industry: Drive and control technology
- Production processes: Assembly of printed circuit boards—SMT assembly (Surface-Mounting Technology), THT assembly (Through-Hole Technology), coating process for printed circuit boards, and final product assembly.

Changing customer requirements, price fluctuations, bottleneck issues, and safety stocks all make managing the value chain extremely complex. Frequently, the so-called "bull-whip" effect occurs, where order fluctuations increase the further one moves "upstream" from the end customer in the value chain. Many companies have long since learned that not only individual company performance leads to competitive advantage, but above all, a synchronized, harmonized value chain can unlock significant potential in terms of cost, quality, and lead times. The literature refers to this as strategic partnerships, maximum transparency through data exchange, or perfectly tailored planning algorithms. What sounds logical and self-explanatory in theory, however, is not always so easy to implement in practice.

The **Siemens AG—in the Digital Industries, Business Unit Motion Control, Electronics Factory Erlangen**—hereafter referred to as **Electronics Factory Erlangen (GWE)**—also faced the challenge of synchronizing its value chain. The main objective was to reduce the discrepancy between lead times in the supply chain and the short-cycle, volatile order frequencies of customers. This resulted in so-called "lead time gaps," where the delivery time to the customer is too long: the customer wants the product within a certain timeframe, but production, including procurement of individual components, takes longer than the customer desires (Fig. 6.18).

Electronics Factory Erlangen (GWE) set itself the task of counteracting these problems. The plan was to align the entire value chain, starting from the customer and moving "upstream," according to a holistic approach. The goal was to synchronize the complex structures of suppliers, plants, service providers, and customers.

The first step in implementation was to define a common goal with suppliers and customers across the entire value chain. To keep the project manageable, the focus was on synchronizing call-off frequencies and lead times through decoupling points (strategic inventories). The definition of shared objectives was crucial to avoid conflicting goals among individual functional units (functional silos).

A key success factor was the early involvement of second-, third-, and fourth-tier suppliers. Only in this way could cross-functional collaboration between suppliers, procurement, production, logistics, sales, and customers be established across the entire value chain. It was essential that the primary goal was not cost reduction, but rather that by

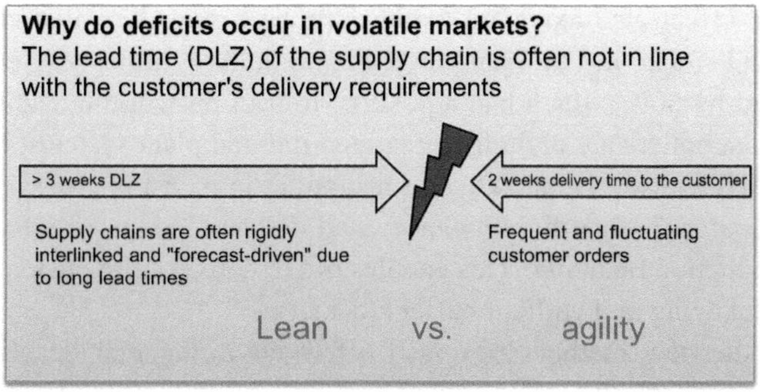

Fig. 6.18 Lead time of the supply chain vs. delivery time to the customer. *Source:* Electronics Factory Erlangen (GWE)

initially focusing on improving lead times, cost effects would follow automatically. A central prerequisite for the close integration of suppliers is digital connectivity, which enables direct delivery to production cells without buffer stocks. At Electronics Factory Erlangen (GWE), almost 100% of suppliers are electronically connected and have direct access to current demand data.

Based on the jointly defined objectives, specific customer requirements such as ordering behavior and desired delivery times were analyzed and systematically simulated "upstream" along the value chain directly with the customer on site. This made it possible to identify lead time fluctuations in upstream processes. Subsequently, it was determined where strategic inventories should best be placed within the value chain to enable more flexible responses to order fluctuations and short delivery deadlines (Fig. 6.19).

The increased flexibility enabled by the decoupling points allowed Electronics Factory Erlangen (GWE) to synchronize the entire value chain to a certain extent. By increasing delivery capability by 30%, both customer satisfaction and loyalty improved, which in turn led to a medium-term increase in order volume.

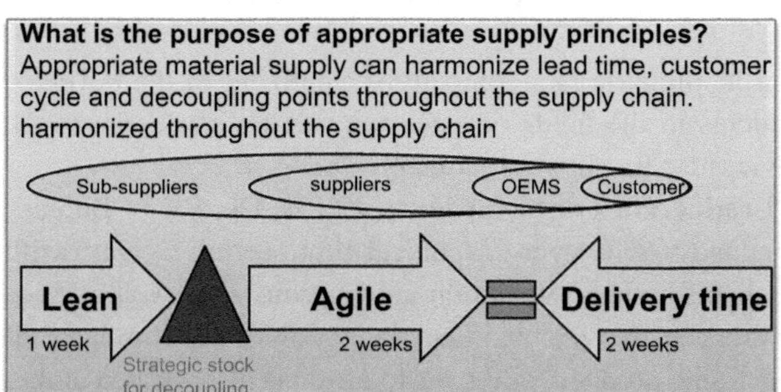

Fig. 6.19 Strategic decoupling points. *Source:* Electronics Factory Erlangen (GWE)

This positive effect also extended to other processes in the value chain, creating a classic "win-win" situation. For example, lead and delivery times as well as inventories could be reduced by 50%, which had a positive impact on working capital and freed up capacity. Just as suppliers are digitally integrated into the plant systems, Electronics Factory Erlangen (GWE) itself is integrated as a supplier into customers' systems, providing immediate transparency regarding inventory and demand, which is automatically incorporated into production planning. This enables direct deliveries to customers' production lines without packaging and without buffer stocks.

In addition, the new methodology also offers environmental benefits. Harmonized production processes in the value chain make it possible to utilize resources more evenly. This helps, for example, to avoid electricity peaks and reduce the effort required for storage and handling of inventories. "Milkruns" to customers and suppliers also eliminate empty runs, thereby reducing CO_2 emissions. Furthermore, agreements were reached on the use of unpackaged modules and returnable packaging to avoid waste.

This approach was also applied by Electronics Factory Erlangen (GWE) to optimize resource flows in production. For example, **Electronics Factory Erlangen (GWE)** maps energy consumption using value streams, enabling it to define energy measures in line with the existing production strategy and continuously improve energy productivity by 30%.

In addition to the improvements already achieved in all lean and green areas, end-to-end digitalization creates transparency, provides an overview of the entire system, and thus facilitates the sustainable optimization of further processes in the future.

6.7 Festo Production EOOD: Operational Excellence through Digital Tools

- Name: Festo Production EOOD
- Location: Sofia, Bulgaria, Christopher Columbus Blvd. 7
- Employees: 1000
- Industry: Electronics
- Manufacturing Processes: Electronics, SMT assembly, assembly

Festo Production in Bulgaria is a company specializing in the development and manufacturing of products in the fields of electronics and electric drives, as well as control modules and devices for the medical industry.

The **Global Production Center of Festo KG & Co. SE** in Bulgaria employs more than 1000 people and has its own "Technical Engineering Center" with over 150 engineers from various disciplines developing new products, as well as an engineering team of 100 engineers responsible for the industrialization of new products. The global prototype shop for electronic products of the Festo group is also located at the Sofia facility.

Effective management of all processes in both direct and indirect areas is of paramount importance for the success of any manufacturing enterprise.

We have been developing our Lean system for over 15 years. In 2013, we introduced our first production system, "Festo Value Production" (FVP), which consisted of 10 pillars (Fig. 6.20).

The excellence concept is, of course, not static but evolves continuously. In 2018, we established our "OPEX" organization and began our transformation into "Value Streams" (VS), significantly changing the traditional departmental structure (Fig. 6.21).

"Make Things happen @ FESTO"
One year later, in 2019, we successfully implemented all "Quality, Cost, Delivery" (QCD) functions in the VS organization, achieving the so-called "Small Factories within the Factory" with the aim of empowering our people and increasing the speed and efficiency of the organization (Fig. 6.22). In the same year, we won our first "Lean & Green Management Award" in the "General Manufacturing" category.

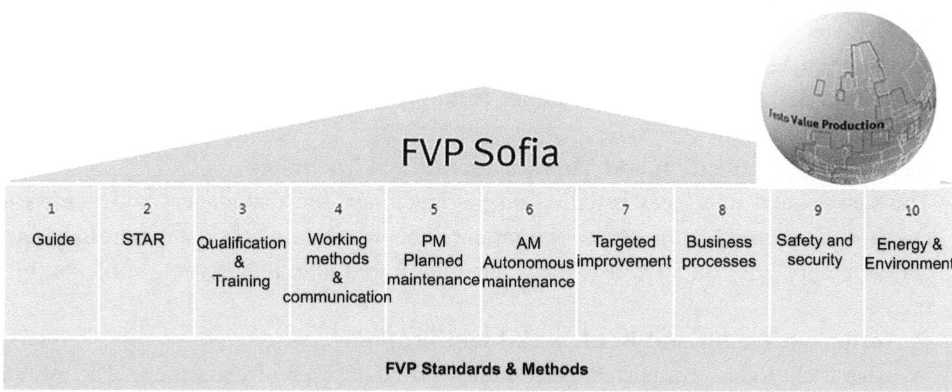

Fig. 6.20 Festo Value Production. *Source:* Festo Production EOOD

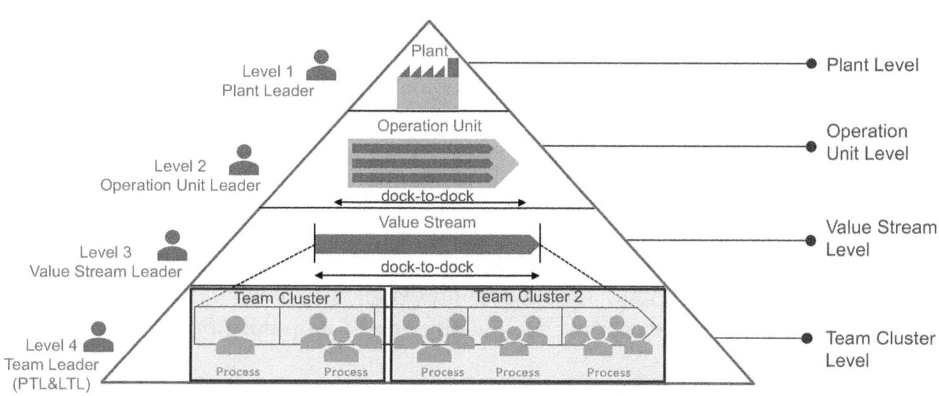

Fig. 6.21 Festo Improvement Levels. *Source:* Festo Production EOOD

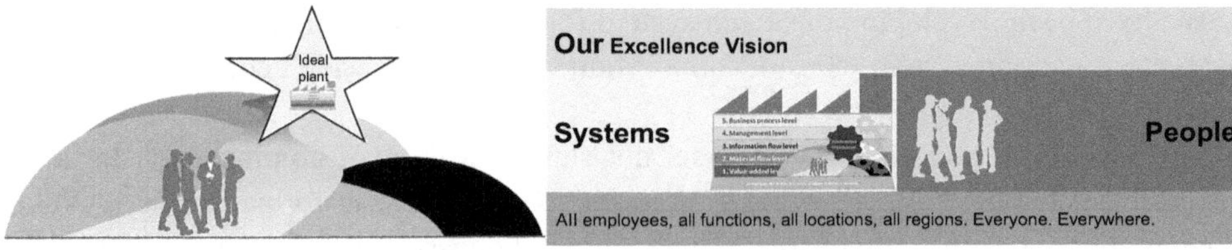

Fig. 6.22 Festo Excellence Vision. *Source:* Festo Production EOOD

We continued to enhance our VS organization and established a "Synchronized Production System," standardizing plant structures within the "Festo network" and thereby elevating many of the best practices developed over the years to a global standard.

Over these years, we have trained the organization in data collection and analysis, as well as systematic problem-solving, with the goal of fostering strong ownership and a culture of continuous improvement.

A key step in modernizing production processes was the implementation of the "Plants Unified Manufacturing Assistant" (PUMA).

This innovative digital solution enables us to manage data more effectively. Some of the system's key features include:

- **Real-Time Visualization and Monitoring of Each Machine**
  The sensors and interfaces installed on the machines allow managers and experts to monitor the current status of the equipment. The system collects data from machines and assembly lines on an hourly basis, enabling rapid identification of problems (Fig. 6.23).
- **Performance Trends and Bottleneck Identification**
  We also track long-term performance trends for each piece of equipment. The system analyzes the data and automatically identifies bottlenecks in the production process, enabling us to take timely measures for optimization and improvement (Fig. 6.24).
- **Metrics and Reports**
  It generates daily, weekly, and monthly reports that include KPIs (Fig. 6.25).
- **Integrated Incident Reporting System**
  Enables quick and easy documentation of problems and incidents (Fig. 6.26).
- **Integrated Digital Problem Solving**
  The system monitors the QCD status of each machine and provides real-time information through a user-friendly dashboard (Fig. 6.27).

- **Continuous Improvement and Maintenance**
  PUMA supports a strategy of continuous improvement by enabling the organization to easily and regularly analyze data and identify areas for optimization.
- **Training and Support**
  Successful implementation of any tool also requires staff training. Regular training sessions and user manuals ensure that all employees can use the system effectively.

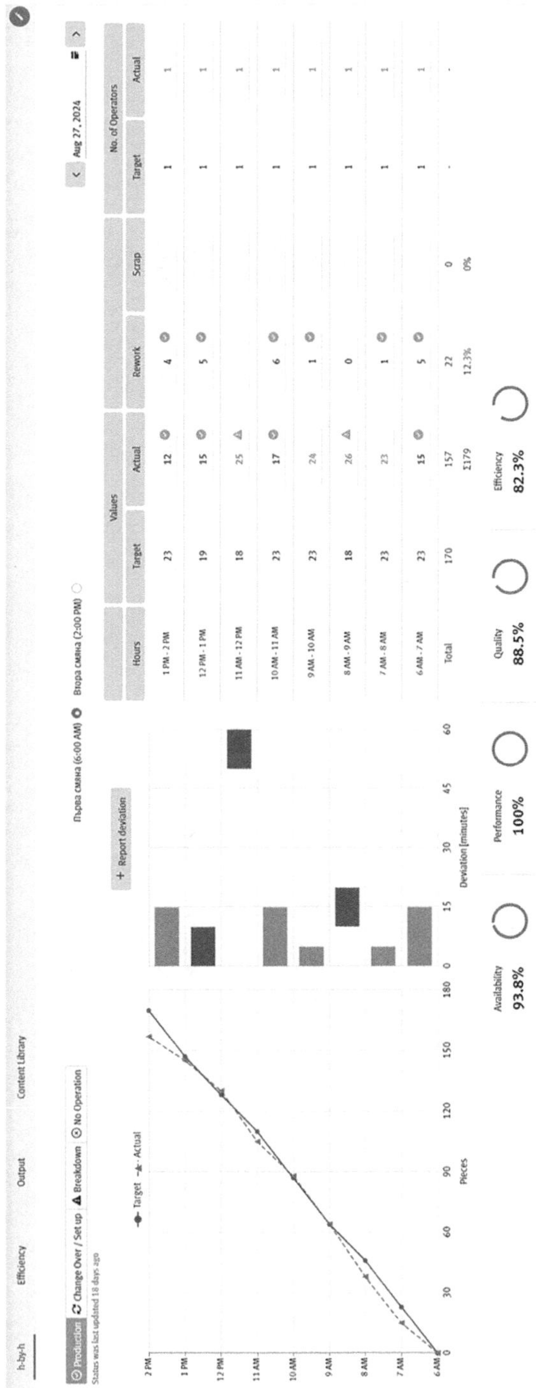

Fig. 6.23 Visualization in real time. *Source:* Festo Production EOOD

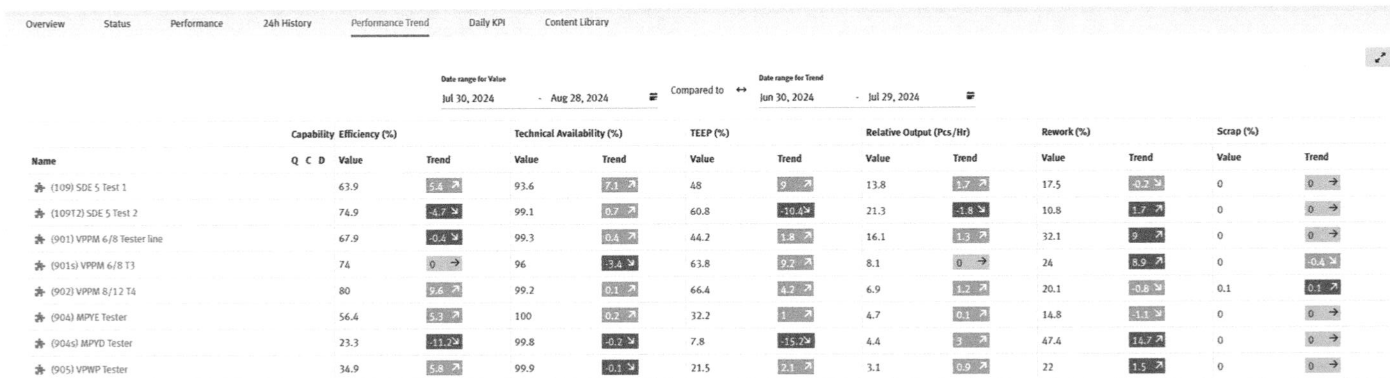

Name	Q C D	Capability Efficiency (%) Value	Trend	Technical Availability (%) Value	Trend	TEEP (%) Value	Trend	Relative Output (Pcs/Hr) Value	Trend	Rework (%) Value	Trend	Scrap (%) Value	Trend
(109) SDE 5 Test 1		63.9	5.4 ↗	93.6	7.1 ↗	48	9 ↗	13.8	1.7 ↗	17.5	-0.2 ↘	0	0 →
(109T2) SDE 5 Test 2		74.9	-4.7 ↘	99.1	0.7 ↗	60.8	-10.4 ↘	21.3	-1.8 ↘	10.8	1.7 ↗	0	0 →
(901) VPPM 6/8 Tester line		67.9	-0.4 ↘	99.3	0.4 ↗	44.2	1.8 ↗	16.1	1.3 ↗	32.1	9 ↗	0	0 →
(901s) VPPM 6/8 T3		74	0 →	96	-3.4 ↘	63.8	9.2 ↗	8.1	0 →	24	8.9 ↗	0	-0.4 ↘
(902) VPPM 8/12 T4		80	9.6 ↗	99.2	0.1 ↗	66.4	4.2 ↗	6.9	1.2 ↗	20.1	-0.8 ↘	0.1	0.1 ↗
(904) MPYE Tester		56.4	5.3 ↗	100	0.2 ↗	32.2	1 ↗	4.7	0.1 ↗	14.8	-1.1 ↘	0	0 →
(904s) MPYD Tester		23.3	-11.2 ↘	99.8	-0.2 ↘	7.8	-15.2 ↘	4.4	3 ↗	47.4	14.7 ↗	0	0 →
(905) VPWP Tester		34.9	5.8 ↗	99.9	-0.1 ↘	21.5	2.1 ↗	3.1	0.9 ↗	22	1.5 ↗	0	0 →

Fig. 6.24 "Performance Trends" and "Bottleneck Identification". *Source:* Festo Production EOOD

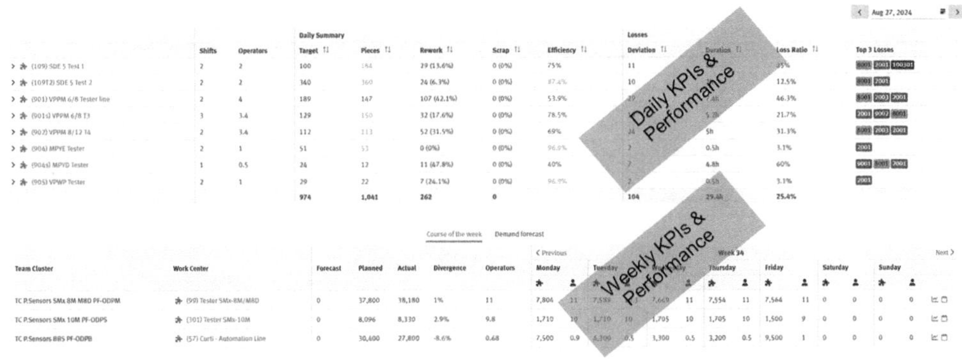

Fig. 6.25 Daily and weekly reports. *Source:* Festo Production EOOD

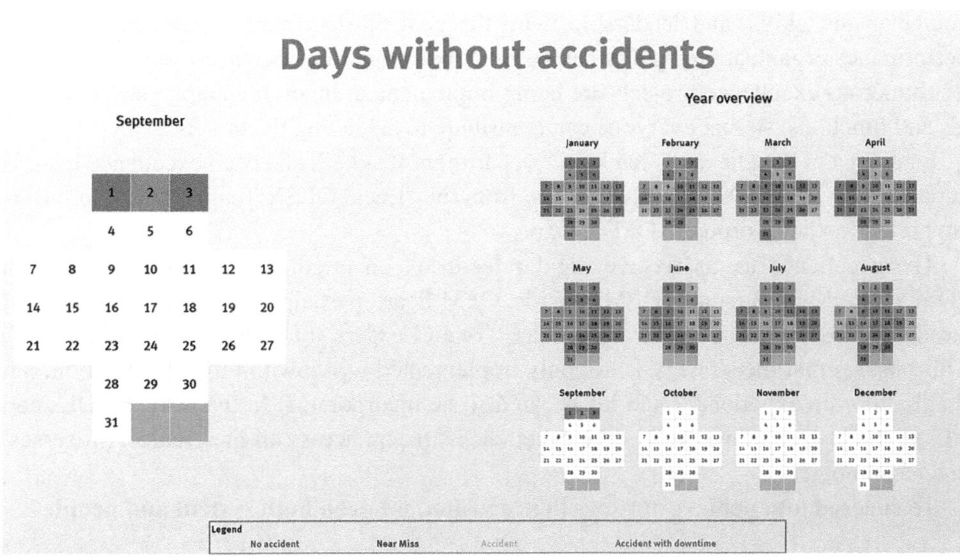

Fig. 6.26 Incident Reporting System. *Source:* Festo Production EOOD

Reliable technical support provides quick resolution of any issues that arise. This system is used daily at all levels, from operators to general management, thereby fostering active, open, and effective communication within the organization.

"Administrative Excellence" (ADEX) The next logical step in the continuous improvement of our processes was the implementation of ADEX—tools and methods designed to sustainably eliminate waste in administrative or indirect processes. This concept addresses strategic, organizational, and process-related issues as well as

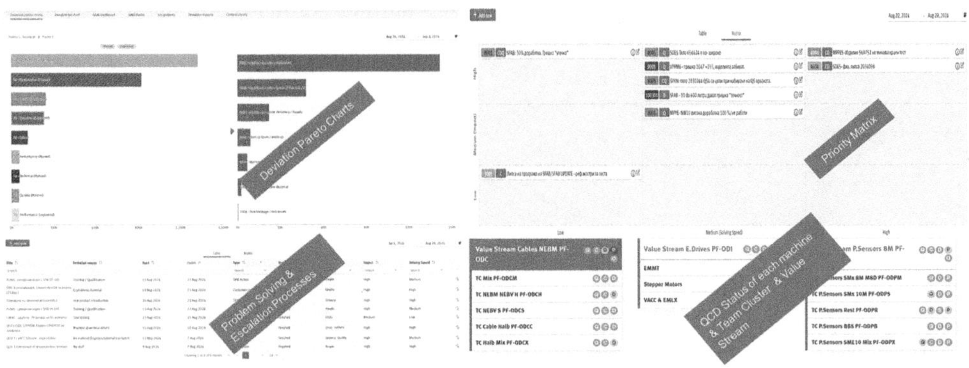

Fig. 6.27 Digital Problem Solving. *Source:* Festo Production EOOD

competencies, skills, and leadership, with the goal of sustainably establishing a high-performance organization. ADEX can be described from three perspectives (Fig. 6.28).

Numerous excellence projects are being implemented, involving employees at all levels and functions, so that everyone can contribute to achieving the targets.

Each area of excellence is led by a "Department Leader", and each excellence team is supported by an OPEX/ADEX employee from the "Local OPEX Team", which in turn is supported by the "Corporate OPEX Team".

The excellence teams receive regular feedback on ongoing projects and ideas via "Officefloor Management" (OFM) boards. OFM board participants include "Department Leaders" (DL) of the administrative areas, "Team Leaders" (TL), and "Team Members". This ensures that the strategy is not only implemented top-down in the organization, but that bottom-up experiences and ideas can also be incorporated. In this way, all DLs and TLs in the plant are involved in the excellence concept across all hierarchies, processes, and technologies.

To succeed and achieve our excellence vision, we need both system and people.

- ADEX maps both the system side and the people side (Fig. 6.29).

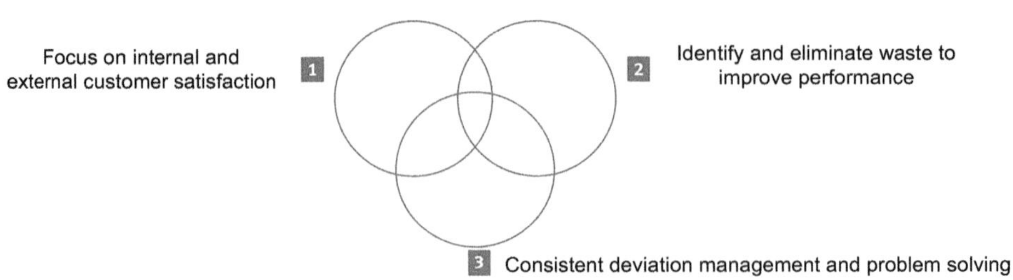

Fig. 6.28 Three perspectives of ADEX. *Source:* Festo Production EOOD

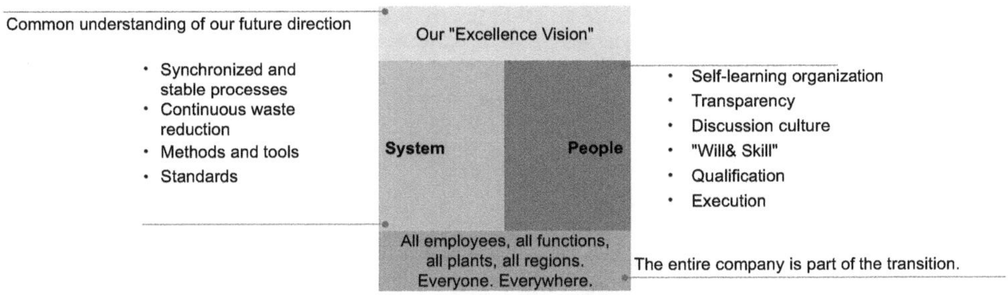

Fig. 6.29 ADEX focus on people and system. *Source:* Festo Production EOOD

Examples for the people side

- The sustainable implementation of ADEX requires an introduction to the concept. The first training module is ADEX Basics, covering the following main topics:
  - Why? What? How?
  - "5 S" training;
  - "7 Types of Waste" training;
  - "Awareness" training (Fig. 6.30)
- The OFM board serves the following purposes (Fig. 6.31):
  - Transparency
  - Culture of discussion
  - Qualification
  - Will & Skill
  - Execution.

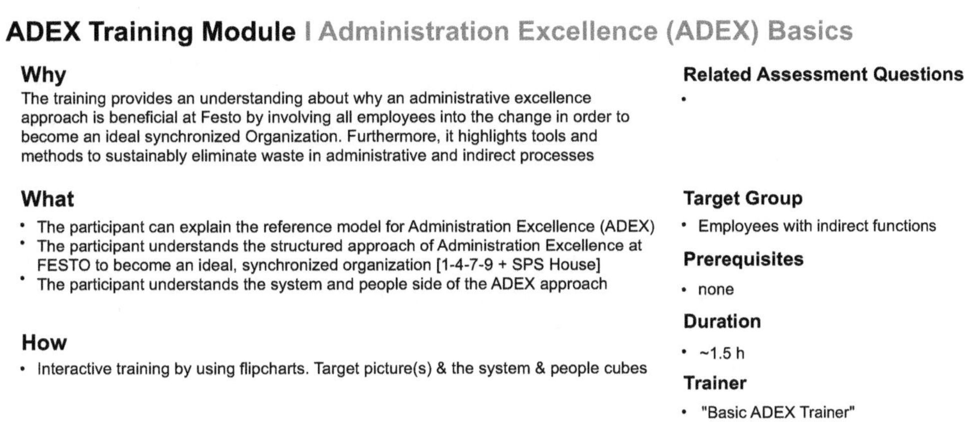

Fig. 6.30 ADEX training. *Source:* Festo Production EOOD

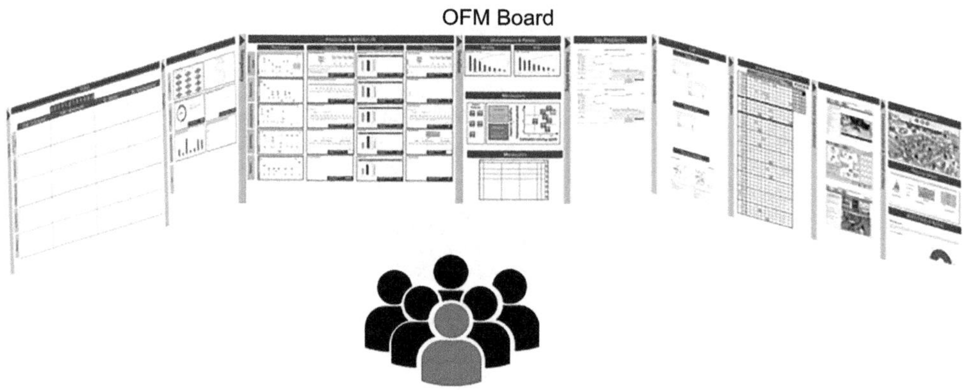

Fig. 6.31 Officefloor Management Board. *Source:* Festo Production EOOD

- Methods and Standards—"Go&See":
  - We encourage "Go&See" or sharing experiences, both those gained internally within the company and externally.
  - Sharing best practices among departments and teams on a "Monthly Review" platform, where everyone can view, evaluate, and, if applicable, try them out.

Examples for the system side

- The sustainable implementation of ADEX follows the PDCA methodology, simply referred to as the "One Approach Cycle". The main components are:
  - Self-assessment—showing the current status;
  - Four steps of implementation—to achieve a continuous improvement process;
  - External ADEX assessment—with recommendations for improvement from the assessors;
  - Lessons learned—identifying the next steps in the improvement process.
- Located in an easily accessible area or in digital form, the OFM board provides an overview of how departments and teams are progressing toward the process vision. It displays information and the progress of strategic initiatives across all processes, KPIs, deviations, and tasks.
- Methods and Standards:

  "5 S"—A logical and transparent workplace organization provides a solid foundation for reducing search times and achieving faster orientation;

  "Swimlane" analysis and "Waste Hunting"—"7 types of waste" based on analysis of core processes with a focus on losses;

  "Problem Solving Process";

  "GoTo" office ("Gemba")—The DL regularly conduct this coaching.

Festo Production in Bulgaria has undergone significant transformation over the past year and has become one of the most modern electronics production sites in Bulgaria and Eastern Europe.

Through continuous process improvement and the implementation of sustainability goals, we not only increase effectiveness and cost efficiency, but also make a significant contribution to enhancing the competitiveness of the **Festo Group** and its overall strategic development.

6.8 Hammerer Aluminium Industries: on the path to climate neutrality and circular economy

- Name: Hammerer Aluminium Industries Holding GmbH
- Employees: Approximately 2100 in Austria, Germany, Romania, Poland, and South Korea
- Industry: Metal processing industry
- Production processes: Casting (foundry for aluminum billets), extrusion (production of high-quality aluminum profiles with special requirements for surface finish and profile geometry), and processing (mechanical further processing of profiles: sawing, drilling, milling, cutting, punching, bending, welding)

The "Hammerer Aluminium Industries" (HAI) Group produces complete aluminum solutions (profiles and further processed products) for the construction, transportation, electrical engineering, and mechanical and plant engineering sectors. HAI has existed in its current form since 2007 and has achieved extremely rapid, dynamic, and at the same time healthy growth in recent years. In the 17 years since its founding, the company has expanded from one to nine locations in five countries, more than tripled its annual processed tonnage to 250,000 t, increased its revenue from €110 million to €890 million in 2023, and grown its team from 350 to over 2000 employees.

HAI offers innovative aluminum solutions and covers the entire value chain—from recycled raw materials to sophisticated profiles and complex components—while taking all aspects of sustainability into account. To achieve this, the company relies on state-of-the-art production facilities, comprehensive research and development, especially with regard to new alloys, and sustainable development partnerships. These partnerships benefit from HAI's unique manufacturing depth and integrated value chain (see Fig. 6.32).

The mission is to build trustworthy, long-term partnerships with customers and to drive dynamic joint development. This means that innovative solutions are brought to market quickly, technologically advanced products are manufactured to the highest quality standards, and reliable delivery is ensured at all times. Special attention is also paid to occupational safety, environmental protection, and sustainability.

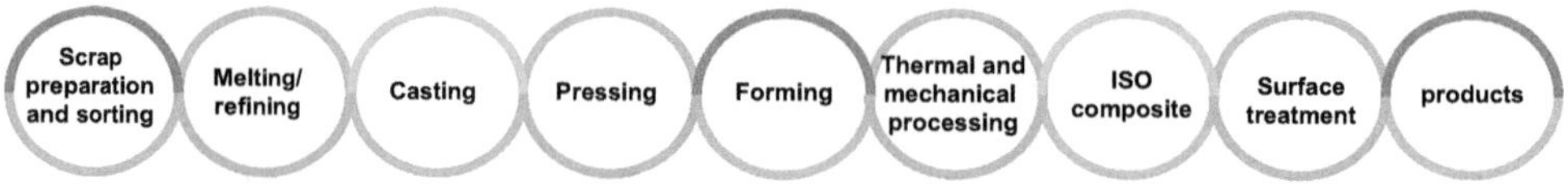

Fig. 6.32 HAI value chain. *Source:* Hammerer Aluminium Industries Holding GmbH

A declared goal of the HAI Group is to continuously increase the sustainability of aluminum products through ongoing innovation. The aim is to make aluminum as a raw material for products even more sustainable and high-performing, as well as to open up new fields of application.

Recycling and the associated sustainable production of goods have become key topics for the future. For HAI, it is essential to ensure that aluminum scrap from all product segments is efficiently recycled in order to increase recycling rates and thus contribute to climate neutrality and the circular economy (see Fig. 6.33).

HAI achieves a recycling rate of 80%. Such a high scrap rate requires optimal infrastructure. At HAI, sales planning and scrap purchasing are combined in a single department. This ensures a reliable supply of suitable scrap for production. It is also very helpful that the facilities can process different qualities and that certain types of scrap can be prepared in-house.

Fig. 6.33 HAI aluminum cycle. *Source:* Hammerer Aluminium Industries Holding GmbH

Recycling scrap significantly reduces the CO_2 footprint and also lowers energy consumption. Compared to primary metals, using recycled aluminum can reduce energy consumption by up to 95% and CO_2 emissions by up to 80%. However, the preparation process is highly complex and requires extensive expertise to achieve the highest quality.

The use of scrap can be described as follows: The ability to use a wide variety of scrap types makes procurement much more flexible. A special furnace technology allows even contaminated scrap to be used. This enables highly flexible scrap purchasing. Prerequisites for this are the separate storage of different types and careful incoming inspection. Since HAI was founded, the company's expertise and infrastructure in this area have been systematically developed and expanded. HAI is continuously working to increase the scrap ratio. Incoming inspection plays a crucial role in recycling, with highly experienced employees checking the delivered scrap. Since random sampling is required, a great deal of experience is needed to obtain reliable test results. The scope of inspection is adapted to the quality standards of the suppliers to combine efficiency with quality.

In 2021, HAI launched particularly sustainable aluminum products on the market. This is only possible by using significantly high proportions of recycled material. As a result, the CO_2 footprint is reduced by up to 80% and energy consumption drops by 95%. In addition, aluminum can be recycled indefinitely without any loss of quality. These alloys have one of the lowest footprints worldwide (see Fig. 6.34).

In addition to the high recycling rate, other factors are also important to enable sustainable business development. Sustainable corporate management, "green sourcing" and

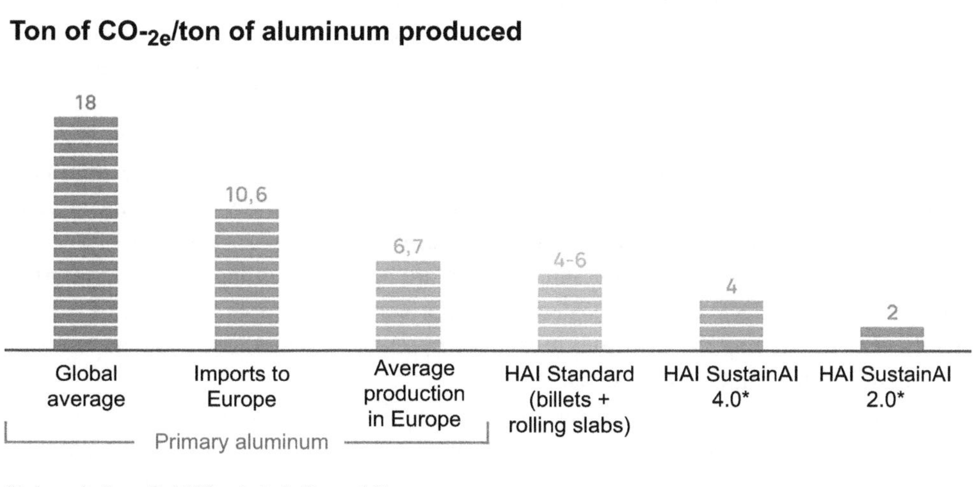

Fig. 6.34 The CO_2 footprint in the aluminum industry. *Source:* Hammerer Aluminium Industries Holding GmbH

"green energy," as well as environmentally friendly processes, are further key pillars. Ultimately, it is the small things that lead to major changes.

HAI pursues a consistent green electricity strategy and has thus significantly improved its CO_2 footprint. In addition, there is strong investment in photovoltaics: In Ranshofen, a 9300 m^2 photovoltaic system for solar power has been installed on the company's rooftops. This system produces almost 5% of the Ranshofen site's energy consumption. In 2023, a photovoltaic system was also installed at the Soest site, and additional systems are planned for the Romanian production sites in 2024.

Within the framework of the CIP, all employees have the opportunity to take responsibility for their own workplace. Employees can contribute ideas in two ways: on the one hand, through the company suggestion scheme, which allows suggestions to be submitted online via a dedicated system (currently around 4000 suggestions per year), and on the other hand, through CIP groups, where recommendations are developed collaboratively. Suggestions that originate from a group are often particularly valuable, as they are supported and endorsed by several employees from the outset. As a principle of success, the CIP is thus a central component of corporate policy. By regularly reviewing and optimizing processes, the company strives for continuous and sustainable improvements—efficiency is increased and quality is ensured.

The CIP also takes sustainability goals into account, which are included in the evaluation process. Employees who successfully implement sustainability-related improvement measures receive a bonus. A recent example is an improvement suggestion affecting one of the presses. Previously, after each pressing of a production order (= production length), a front and end cut was made. By optimizing the production length, it was possible to save 25% of the pre-saw lengths per production order. This allows the entire extraction length of a billet to be used more efficiently. With 53 pressings per order, more than 1 kg of scrap can be saved. Over the course of a year, this amounts to 26.7 tons. This not only reduces scrap but also saves energy (Fig. 6.35).

By conducting *Lifecycle Assessments* (LCAs) according to ISO 14040/44 for HAI products, not only was a solid data foundation and transparency regarding emissions established, but also opportunities for improvement were identified, enabling targeted action on factors with the greatest impact. This also facilitates communication with our customers, as emissions from their supply chain are becoming an increasingly important factor in product selection. HAI is a competent partner with in-depth expertise in sustainability issues, enabling the company to provide optimal advice to its customers and support them in reducing CO_2 emissions.

HAI continuously invests in retrofitting existing facilities as well as in new installations to improve environmental performance. When specifying new equipment, environmental and sustainability criteria are considered as an integral part of the requirements, so that energy consumption or emissions such as dust, smoke, or exhaust gases are minimized, or production by-products can be returned to the cycle even more efficiently. Among other things, HAI has invested in modern heat recovery technologies, which are

Fig. 6.35 Recycling at HAI. *Source:* Hammerer Aluminium Industries Holding GmbH

now used to heat production halls, and has implemented a process in which aluminum chips are separated from emulsion, allowing the aluminum chips to be remelted more efficiently and the emulsion to be reused.

6.9 Schaltbau: DC NExT Factory Sets a New Standard for Green Production

- Name: Schaltbau GmbH
- Location: Velden
- Employees at site: approx. 300
- Industry: Rail, Industry, Renewable Energy, Automotive
- Production processes: manual assembly, semi-automated linked assembly, automated assembly, logistics, test laboratory

Is it possible to build a factory for which there is no blueprint? One that enables CO_2-neutral production based on direct current technology? And in which the very products are used that the factory itself manufactures for customers around the world? The answer from Schaltbau's engineers: "Yes!" With the *NExT Factory* in Velden near Landshut, the world's first direct current factory went into operation in September 2023 after two and a half years of construction. The new production facility sets a benchmark for resource-efficient and CO_2-free manufacturing and is "Lean" and "Green" in the truest sense.

DC specialist **Schaltbau**, which received the Lean & Green Award for the NExT Factory in 2022 and the German Innovation Award as well as the German Award for Sustainability Projects in 2024, is a globally leading industrial company specializing in direct current and offering products and solutions that enable electrification. With a broad portfolio of contactors, connectors, switches, and safety components, Schaltbau supports partners and customers in solving complex challenges in the rail, energy, and e-mobility sectors.

Direct Current—The Power of the Future

While direct current has so far been used primarily in rail transport, it is experiencing a significant upswing with the energy transition, as it enables efficient electricity storage. Unlike alternating current technology, disconnecting direct current connections can generate dangerous electric arcs with a high risk of fire, making contactors—switches for high electrical loads—a crucial contribution to the safety of people and machinery.

Schaltbau contactors are used in inverters for solar systems, battery storage units, and test benches, as well as in electric vehicles of all kinds. Another area of application is charging stations, as charging with direct current enables electric vehicles to achieve long ranges with relatively short charging times.

When the production facility in Velden, which has existed since 1973, reached its capacity limits, Schaltbau faced the question of where to produce in the future in light of cost and efficiency pressures. The company also considered how the need for skilled workers, political risks, and supply chain dependencies would develop. The decision: no relocation to Eastern Europe or Asia, but to remain in Bavaria.

Greener and Economically Efficient Supply Chains

To remain competitive, however, it was clear that the factory had to be not only highly automated but also energy efficient. Schaltbau's new flagship facility was intended to set new standards for the production and logistics of electromechanical switching devices. At the same time, the NExT Factory was to demonstrate the company's strong identification with the growth markets of energy and e-mobility.

Internally, the aim was to achieve maximum transparency between individual functions with the NExT Factory and to establish short communication and coordination channels between development and production. In addition, a modern and functional factory design was intended to increase employee satisfaction and further streamline and improve process flows and key performance indicators such as on-time delivery.

On this basis, planning for the €60 million project began in 2019. Shortly thereafter, the coronavirus pandemic disrupted the economy and society. Nevertheless, Schaltbau stuck to its construction plans, broke ground in spring 2021 in the midst of the pandemic, and even managed to deal with delivery times of up to 50 weeks.

The NExT Factory: A New Standard for Green Production

The climate-friendly design of the new production facility starts on the roof, where a photovoltaic system generates around 1,600 MWh of energy per year. The electricity produced is fed directly into operations via a direct current (DC) network, without the need for conversion to alternating current (AC) as is typically required. This alone results in annual energy savings of up to 15%. Surplus energy from the PV system can, once the facility is fully developed, be stored either in a battery system with a storage capacity of 1 MWh or in a thermal storage unit. The innovative idea of using two fire water tanks in the building's basement as a thermal storage system with nearly 10 MWh of capacity was also implemented (Fig. 6.36).

The lean concept of minimizing waste is applied in the NExT Factory not only to goods and material flows, but also to energy efficiency and energy management. The goal was and is to achieve a high utilization rate of self-generated electricity, to store energy—instead of losing it as heat during AC to DC conversion—and to reduce the required connection capacity to the conventional AC power grid. By transmitting high power levels, which is possible in a DC microgrid, up to 25% of the wiring material in the DC infrastructure, such as copper due to smaller cable cross-sections, was saved during the factory's construction.

These efforts pay off both ecologically and economically. Combined with intelligent energy management, the factory's energy costs were reduced by around 35% annually at launch compared to a conventional energy concept with heat generation from fossil fuels. In addition, the new plant produces zero CO_2 emissions and, once fully developed, will achieve an average annual energy self-sufficiency rate of 70% from the regional

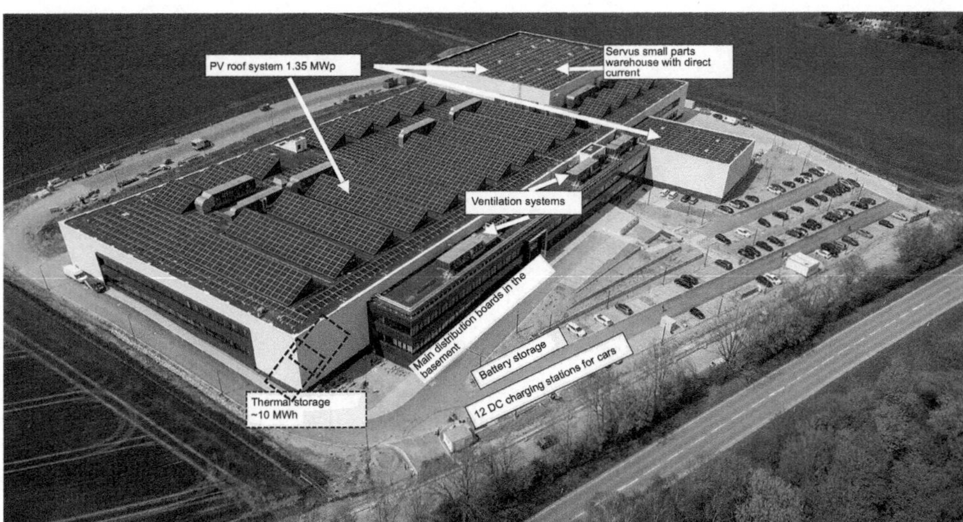

Fig. 6.36 The CO_2-neutral NExT Factory by Schaltbau. (Image: Schaltbau)

power grid. The functionality and reliability of the DC network are ensured, among other things, by numerous in-house Schaltbau DC contactors of types C320 and C295, which were installed throughout the facility (Fig. 6.37).

The DC network of the NExT Factory functions as a kind of circular economy for energy. It connects the DC-generating photovoltaic system on the roof directly, without conversion losses, to DC consumers such as the warehouse and storage systems within the production facility. Only in the event of an energy shortfall is green electricity sourced from the grid. Considering the number of production, storage, and logistics facilities in Germany, the potential of DC networks for the energy transition becomes clear.

Diverse Challenges

To realize the NExT Factory with more than 22,000 m² of usable space within two and a half years required close collaboration with authorities, academia, grid operators, and partners willing to engage in this pioneering project. Several hurdles had to be overcome, ranging from finding suitable service providers and available DC components to the lack of DIN standards in the field of direct current.

Even the search for a suitable specialist planner proved challenging: after contacting more than 80 electrical planners and engineering firms, a planning office was finally found that was fundamentally open to designing and planning the DC network. Finding a suitable craft and installation company for the implementation of the factory's DC network was no less difficult, as binding standards for the construction, securing, and operation of electrical DC installations are still lacking.

The absence of standards also explains the current lack of mass-produced and certified DC components. Protective elements, in particular, are essential for the safe operation of

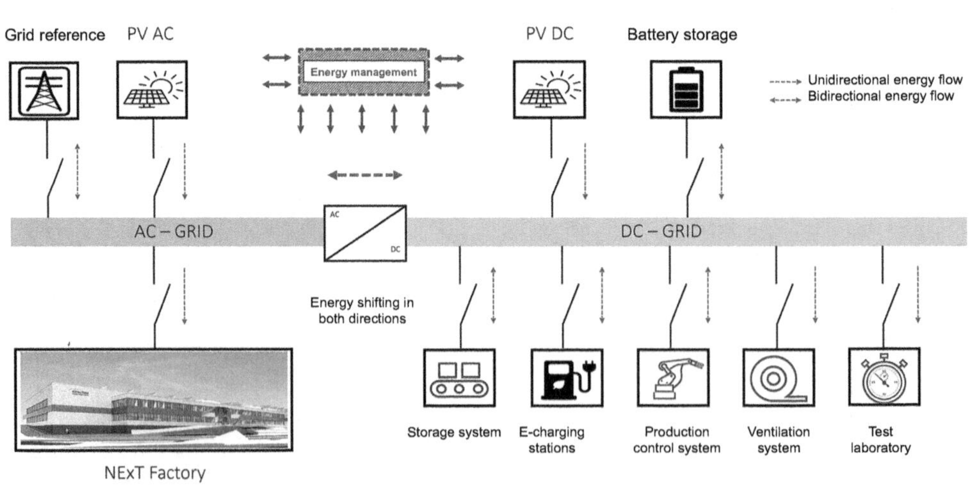

Fig. 6.37 Schematic overview of the energy concept for the new production site. (Image: Schaltbau)

DC networks. Compared to AC, a DC network can transmit higher power at the same or even smaller cable cross-sections. At the same time, the network has high capacities, and especially in machine circuits, it is essential to protect employees from potential hazards such as electric arcs. In a DC microgrid, much faster shutdown and response times—sometimes in the microsecond range—must also be ensured.

Additionally, public institutions, authorities, and distribution network operators had no prior experience with such innovative concepts as that of the NExT Factory and therefore acted very cautiously during inspections, approvals, and decision-making processes. For this reason, Schaltbau decided to plan the DC factory in stages, with the aim of realizing the vision of a fully DC-powered factory by 2028 (Fig. 6.38).

Green Production and Economic Success through Direct Current: The Warehouse
Could a conventional factory have been built with less hassle? Very likely. But as an expert in direct current technology, Schaltbau deliberately ventured into new territory and took a risk to demonstrate the potential of direct current in industrial manufacturing.

One of the direct current consumers in the NExT Factory is an automated warehouse system that supplies the entire production and shipping operations with the necessary materials. The system is ideally suited for operation with direct current, as it is

Fig. 6.38 Production with DC power: Interior view of the NExT Factory. (Image: Schaltbau)

a dynamic application in which up to 80 ceiling-guided swarm robots travel on rails to handle the NExT Factory's material flow at high speed.

The greatest savings effect is achieved through recuperation within the system: countless times per minute, transport boxes are accelerated or moved from one height level to another in the seven storage aisles and the system, which is over 19 meters high. This is where the system's approach comes into play: with every lowering movement of a swarm robot, kinetic or braking energy is generated, which in conventional applications is usually converted into heat via resistors and largely dissipated unused.

Not so in the NExT Factory: by connecting to the in-house direct current microgrid and installing double-layer capacitors, the company recovers energy with every braking process. This energy is then fed back into the warehouse system to lift transport boxes to higher storage levels or temporarily stored in the capacitors. By recovering energy, the peak load in the logistics warehouse system is reduced by up to 85%.

Savings Potential Exceeding Expectations

In other words, the simple principle of recuperation—as used in every electric car—ensures that almost all the supplied energy remains within the warehouse system. In Schaltbau's case, this amounts to up to 800 MWh annually. The average peak load of the warehouse system, which has over 55,000 storage locations, is below 20 kW. According to calculations, a conventional connection to an alternating current grid would have resulted in peak loads of up to 150 kW. With this knowledge, peak and connection loads can already be reduced during the planning and design of microgrid systems, significantly lowering the associated power charges per kW of peak load (Fig. 6.39).

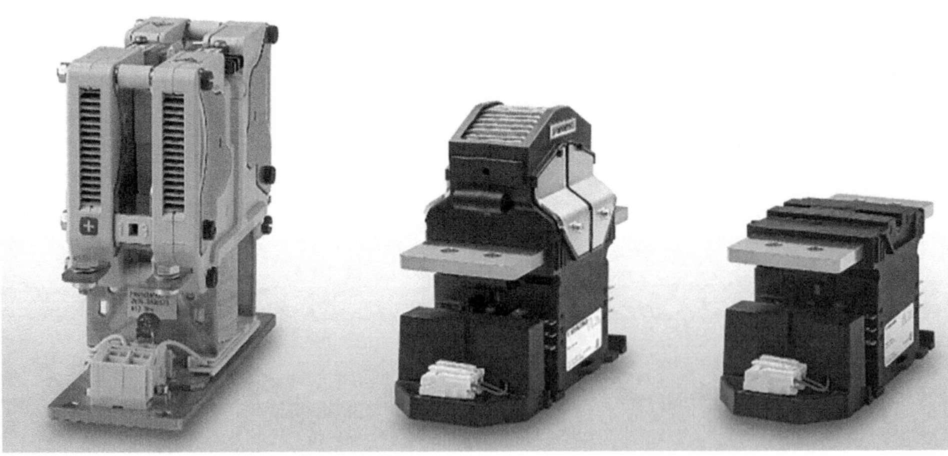

Fig. 6.39 Contactors that ensure the safe operation of direct current in the NExT Factory. (Image: Schaltbau)

The questions Schaltbau asked itself in 2019 at the start of planning the NExT Factory have since become increasingly urgent for all companies. Whether Germany is facing deindustrialization due to high energy costs or whether the energy transition is progressing quickly enough is a concern for politics, business, and society alike. But talk alone is not enough. With the NExT Factory, Schaltbau demonstrates that cost-effective and climate-neutral production using direct current is both possible and safe for people and machines.

In doing so, Schaltbau commits to economically efficient, green supply chains and to Germany as a production location. The company also hopes that its example will inspire many imitators in the industry, as local industrial companies are particularly well positioned to drive sustainability improvements and fully leverage the economic and ecological benefits of electrification with direct current technology.

6.10 Festo: Resource Efficiency in the Construction of the Scharnhausen Technology Plant

- Name: Festo AG & Co. KG
- Location: Scharnhausen near Stuttgart
- Employees: approx. 1600
- Industry: Control and automation technology
- Production processes: Assembly; machining; electronics; surface technology

(The following project description reflects the status as of 2016 / "©Festo SECo. KG, all rights reserved): "The greenfield site"—a dream for every engineer, logistics specialist, and factory planner. For **Festo**, this was the case for the new building in Scharnhausen, where a modern technology plant was planned to meet not only the classic requirements of high quality and productivity, but also the company's ecological objectives. Festo succeeded in achieving outstanding ecological and economic results through energy-efficient factory planning, the integration of environmental and energy topics into the production system, and consistent implementation down to the shop floor level.

Alignment with Overall Ecological Objectives

The starting point was the company's overarching ecological goals: reducing energy-related CO_2 emissions by 20% by 2020 (baseline: 2008) and improving overall ecological performance along the process chain—measured using an *Environmental Performance Index*. The aim of this index is to make the ecological performance of companies or even countries quantitatively measurable. It calculates indicators such as ecosystem status, air, water, biodiversity, natural resources, and sustainable energy. The Environmental Performance Index considers the performance of the entire value chain, from raw material extraction and production to the use phase at the customer and product disposal. In this way, the concept of a circular economy is to be strengthened in the supply chain, encouraging suppliers and partners to act collectively.

To achieve these goals, it was clear from the factory planning phase that energy and resource efficiency would be a high priority in the new plant. By mapping energy value streams in all planned plant sections, interdisciplinary requirements could be taken into account during the planning stage. Both the technical building equipment and the requirements of the production facilities were visualized. The insights from these energy flow visualizations were evaluated for feasibility using a so-called "Total Cost of Ownership" (TCO) analysis. This helped, among other things, to demonstrate how a new building in Germany can increase resource efficiency and thus ensure long-term global competitiveness. A key success factor in the planning was the holistic consideration of building and production. This made it possible to introduce innovative approaches such as heat recovery from production using concrete core activation, combined heat and power plants, and optimized exhaust air management.

Integration of Energy and Environment into the Production System

After energy and environmental issues played a central role during the construction of the new plant, key ecological indicators were also permanently anchored in the production system, the "Festo Value Production" (FVP). In addition to the other operational pillars aimed at enabling optimal manufacturing, the energy and environment pillar was integrated.

Defining responsibilities and embedding new indicators in the production system strengthens the importance of environmental and energy topics. They have now become part of continuous improvement management. Through this integration, energy and environment are no longer isolated topics, but a collective responsibility that drives all areas of the company forward.

The indicators from the Environmental Performance Index play a crucial role here. By integrating them into the production system, many areas are now responsible for achieving better ecological performance in the future. Active efforts are to be made to identify and implement improvements in energy and resource use, emissions to soil, air, and water, and employee environmental awareness. The index then helps to regularly review the effectiveness of measures and ensure that targets are met. Above all, raising employee awareness is crucial for quickly and effectively identifying and implementing potential improvements.

Energy Management System

To support the various business units in achieving their energy efficiency targets, an energy management system was developed that includes energy experts from the key organizational units. The primary task of this expert team is to identify and reduce energy waste, establish energy standards, and design efficiency measures (Fig. 6.40).

The interdisciplinary expert team is intended to ensure that environmental objectives are achieved throughout the supply chain. For example, when planning and procuring

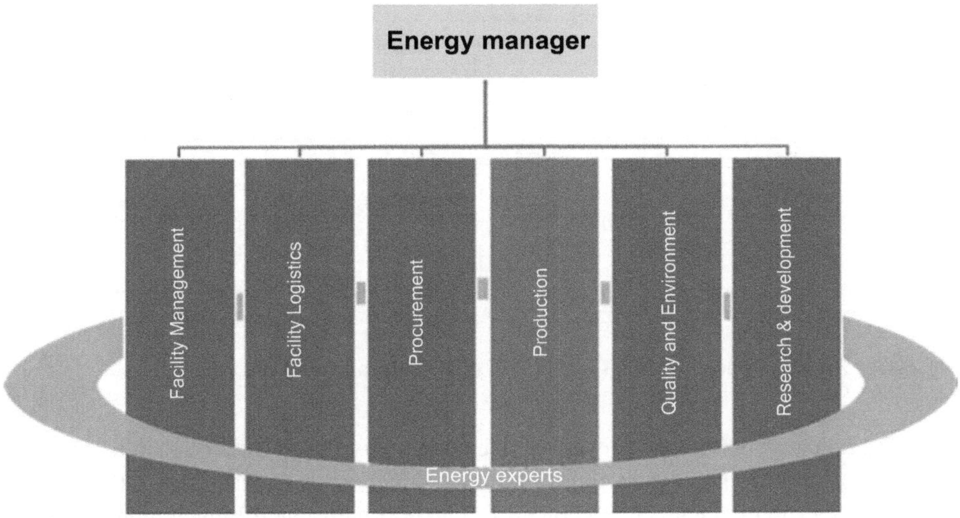

Fig. 6.40 Energy management within the organization. (© Festo SE & Co. KG, all rights reserved)

new machinery and equipment, energy efficiency is defined as one of the key criteria. Ongoing efficiency optimization measures are also implemented for older, existing machines, such as reducing pressure in the plant with the necessary adjustments to operating resources. On the building technology side, load management (staggered start-up of equipment) is used to avoid peak demand.

Operationalization to the Shopfloor Level

However, in order to hold all areas accountable for continuously improving energy efficiency, the topic was further operationalized. A key success factor here is the robust measurement infrastructure. From the outset, care was taken to ensure that energy consumption could be allocated to its source. This allocation makes it possible to define clear areas of responsibility, in which the respective production managers are required to implement improvements in energy efficiency. This source-based allocation also allows for the setting of annual targets and the integration of specific key performance indicators into target agreements.

In retrospect, creating transparency regarding consumption and waste proved to be the golden key to success. In the future, environmental performance indicators will be discussed during daily shopfloor management meetings, enabling Festo to significantly increase resource efficiency in many areas.

Through visualizations and effective communication, it can also be ensured that all employees in the company are constantly engaged with the topics of energy and environment. Visualization boards on the shopfloor allow information on energy and environmental issues to be accessed easily and in real time. Employees are encouraged to walk

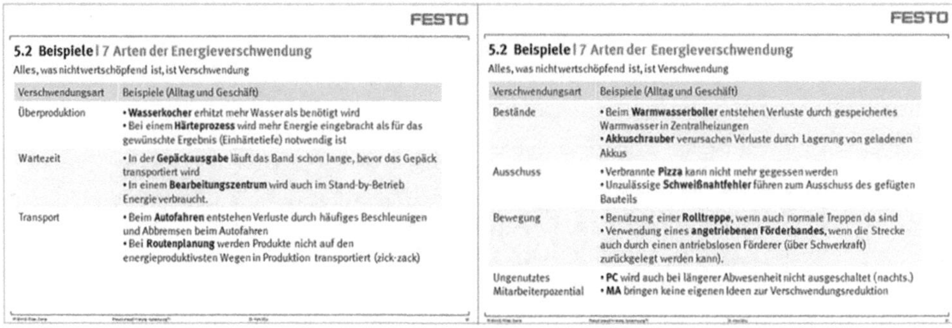

Fig. 6.41 7 types of energy waste. (© Festo SE & Co. KG, all rights reserved)

through production with "open" eyes, so that even minor optimizations, such as switching off machines during non-production times, are implemented. Such organizational measures already enable annual savings of up to €50,000 with just 20 machining centers. In 2016, the full rollout of the energy and environment pillar in shopfloor management took place to specifically raise employee awareness and achieve savings (Fig. 6.41).

Ultimately, the energy transparency system is a digital tool that was sustainably integrated into the FVP production system, ensuring that all components work together seamlessly.

The energy transparency system addresses and implements the aspects of visualization, organization, hardware/software, and data collection. Visualization is provided in real time and serves as the basis for monitoring key figures in the plant, from individual machines to entire buildings. These data help to optimize or compare consumption. Internal benchmarking can be carried out, for example, to determine why consumption varies under the same load. With further rollout, external comparisons with other plants and similar machines will also be possible (Fig. 6.42).

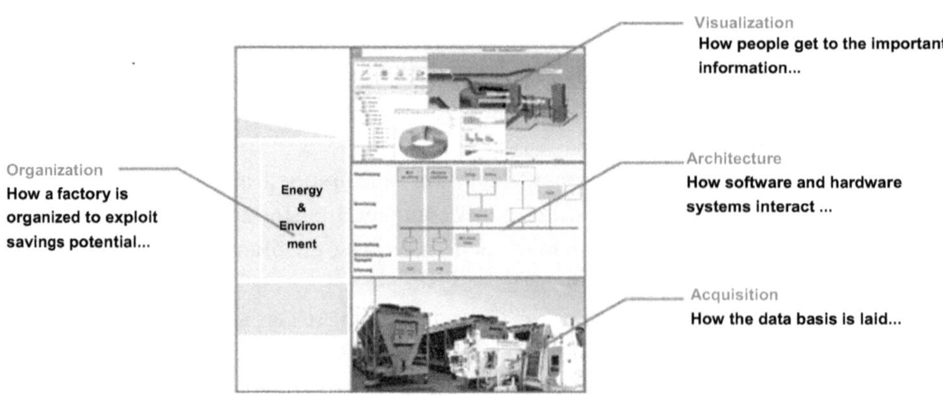

Fig. 6.42 Structure of the energy transparency system. (© Festo SE & Co. KG, all rights reserved)

Festo has succeeded in exemplary fashion in integrating holistic objectives—including those related to environment and energy—into its technology factory concept. The company has leveraged most of the opportunities offered by constructing a new plant and has firmly anchored the topic of resource efficiency in management systems and control loops. In this way, environmental objectives have been cascaded down to the shopfloor level, achieving an annual reduction in CO_2 emissions of up to 10% or 1,500 t CO_2. Ultimately, this project's success is attributable to the strong commitment of the entire workforce.

6.11 Siemens: Lean in the "Indirect" Area—Adapting Kata, Scrum, and Lean Methods

- Name: Siemens AG—Digital Industries, Motion Control, Electronics Factory Erlangen.
- Plant: Electronics Factory Erlangen (GWE), Frauenauracher Straße 80, 91056 Erlangen
- Employees at the plant: approx. 1000
- Industry: Drive and control technology
- Production processes: Assembly of printed circuit boards—SMT assembly (Surface-Mounting Technology), THT assembly (Through-Hole Technology), printed circuit board coating process, and final product assembly.

Through lean methods, numerous industrial companies have sustainably improved their production and logistics processes for years. It is now widely recognized that "lean" is not only successful in direct production environments. Leading companies have long since introduced lean practices in their administrative and indirect areas as well, thereby sustainably and effectively optimizing their entire value chain. Lean is also being used by service providers such as insurance companies, banks, or hospitals to optimize processes. Whether in a bank, an automotive manufacturer, or the purchasing department of a pharmaceutical company, the core questions remain the same: What adds value? What is the customer willing to pay for? Where does waste occur?

However, the central challenge in these indirect areas lies in making waste visible. Inventory or unnecessary travel times (as examples of two types of waste in production) are usually easier to identify than, for instance, long processing times in an accounting process or unnecessary decision loops (and thus longer lead times) in the marketing department.

At **Siemens AG—Digital Industries, Business Unit Motion Control, Electronics Factory Erlangen** – hereafter referred to as **Electronics Factory Erlangen (GWE)** –, the transfer of lean methods to indirect areas has been exemplary. After the "Holistic Production System" (GPS) had already been successfully implemented in production for over 10 years, the decision was made to introduce the GPS approach in indirect areas as well and to test this methodology in two pilot areas (Fig. 6.43).

Due to its thematic proximity to production, the initial focus was placed on logistics. The approaches tested there were then transferred to supporting areas and further evaluated. The idea behind this pilot approach was to roll out the new lean methods to other

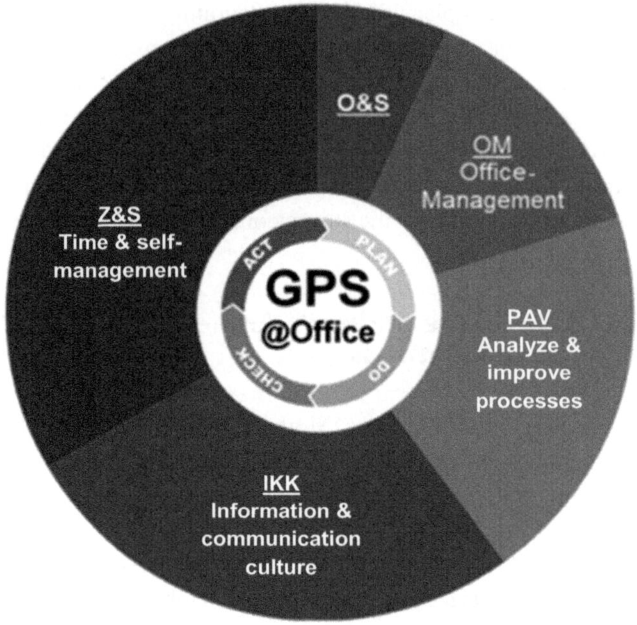

Fig. 6.43 Principles of GPS@Office. *Source:* Electronics Factory Erlangen (GWE)

functional areas, such as marketing, procurement, or accounting, only after successful implementation in production-related departments.

In implementing these changes, Electronics Factory Erlangen (GWE) adopted an innovative approach. In addition to classical lean methods, the latest concepts from Coaching Kata and Scrum were also utilized to optimize the indirect areas. A variant of the Coaching Kata was applied to ensure employee acceptance of the new lean and Scrum approaches.

In Coaching Kata, a coach guides employees purposefully toward a defined target state. The coach's main focus is to train employees to develop and contribute their own ideas as much as possible. The goal is to strengthen each employee's problem-solving skills so that, driven by self-motivation and determination, they are prepared to tackle increasingly challenging tasks.

The path to achieving the defined target state in Coaching Kata is not predetermined. Instead, it must be developed step by step through experimental work. Whenever there is uncertainty about how to proceed in a process or project, hypotheses are formulated using the Coaching Kata, which must then be confirmed or refuted in short cycles. The central guiding question is: "What is currently preventing us from reaching the defined target state?"

The Scrum methodology, on the other hand, originates from software development but is increasingly popular in agile project management and product development outside the software sector. The idea behind Scrum is to break down projects (and, if necessary, processes) into small work packages with manageable workloads (so-called "sprints"). Progress in each sprint is reviewed at short intervals in close coordination with the customer and adjusted as needed. In this context, the customer may be the actual end customer or an internal customer (e.g., the next department waiting for a specific input). By using small work packages that can be quickly reviewed and adapted, projects can be managed much more flexibly and agilely with the Scrum method.

It is precisely the combination of these two methods (Scrum and Coaching Kata) with the visualizations and control loops from lean management that has proven to be highly effective. By designing visualization boards in office areas that integrate all three methods, it is possible to make waste transparent even in indirect areas. Daily stand-up meetings also ensure that tasks are clearly defined and that cross-functional topics can be processed as smoothly as possible (Fig. 6.44).

In the initial design of visualizations and office boards in indirect areas, the team drew heavily on experience from production. However, it quickly became apparent that new forms of representation were needed in many areas. The key to successful implementation was to clearly define the specific objectives for each area in order to contribute to achieving the site strategy. Based on this, projects were defined, implemented step by step, and their progress visualized in the newly designed shopfloor management system (Fig. 6.45).

By establishing performance management systems in both production and indirect areas, it became possible to conduct short-cycle target-actual comparisons of departmental tasks, thereby making both causes of disruptions and waste transparent (Fig. 6.46).

Regular and effective communication is also one of the most important success factors in this project. Right at the start, the project objective was explained to employees: to create added value for the customer and to align the indirect areas accordingly, rather than, as feared, to reduce staff. The full rollout of GPS@Office took place one year after the successful pilot project.

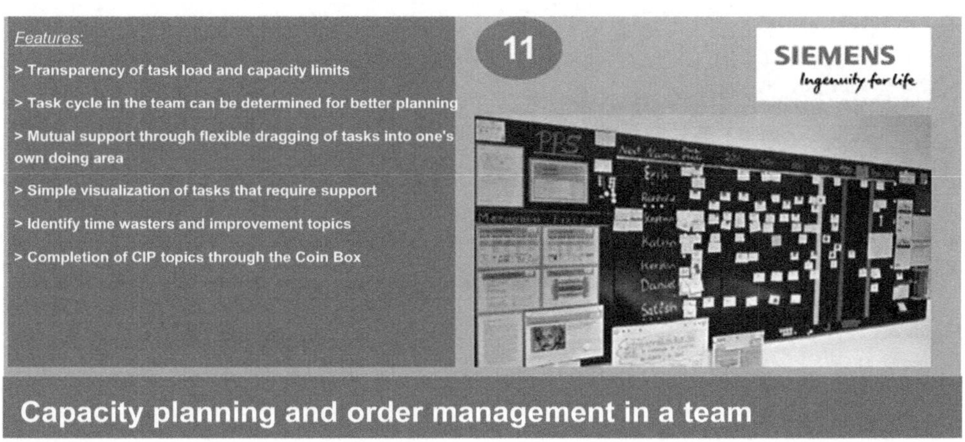

Fig. 6.44 Office board for GPS@Office. *Source:* Electronics Factory Erlangen (GWE)

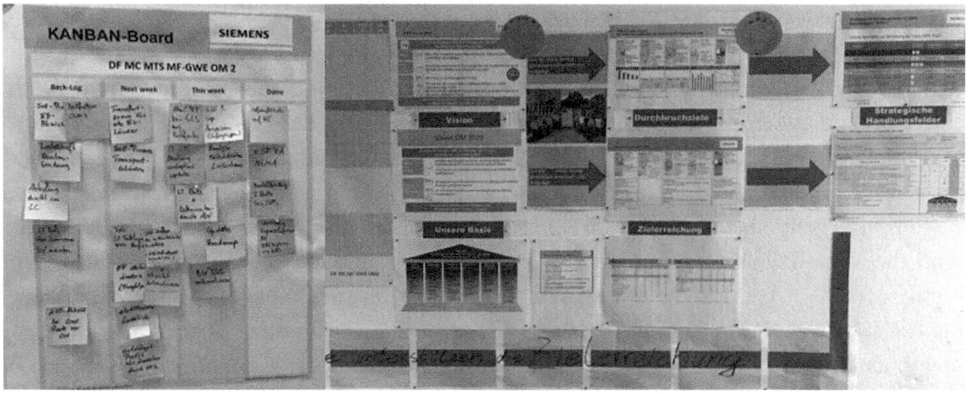

Fig. 6.45 Visualization and linking of projects with departmental objectives. *Source:* Electronics Factory Erlangen (GWE)

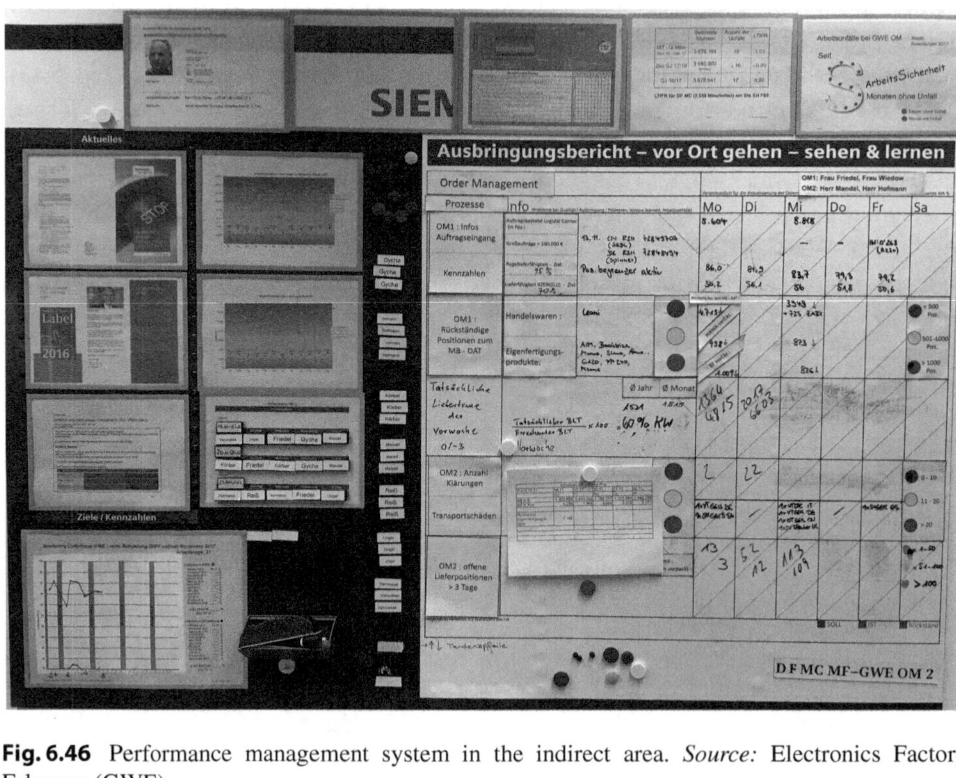

Fig. 6.46 Performance management system in the indirect area. *Source:* Electronics Factory Erlangen (GWE)

GPS@Office has now become an integral part of all indirect areas and enables customer- and value stream-oriented work in cross-functional teams. New communication methods, such as daily brief meetings for information exchange instead of lengthy, detailed minutes with wide distribution lists, are generally met with great approval. The overall performance of the company has also noticeably improved. By synchronizing all processes, delivery times to customers can be significantly reduced. Since strategically important suppliers have been involved earlier, material inventories have reached a record low since the introduction of GPS@Office. Overall, the new way of working at Electronics Factory Erlangen (GWE) has led to more efficient processes, reduced resource usage, and the realization of innovative solutions. All of these aspects also provide direct benefits in terms of sustainability.

6.12 TE Connectivity: How a Consistent Structure Can Make the Continuous Improvement Process Transparent and Measurable, Thus Securing the Achievement of Strategy andSustainability

- Name: TE Connectivity
- Location: Woert I Dinkelsbühl
- Employees at site: approx. 2000
- Industry: Automotive
- Production processes: Molding, coating, stamping, assembly

To structure the continuous improvement process, **TE Connectivity** follows the method of the Four Disciplines of Execution. This approach helps achieve strategic objectives and generate positive impacts on quality, service, and customer support. The four disciplines include:

- Focus on the essentials: Identifying the most important influencing factors and key metrics that can be proactively managed.
- Definition of lead metrics: Focusing on the relevant levers to ensure the achievement of desired outcomes and key metrics (lag metrics).
- Visualization of progress: Using visual tools (target vs. actual comparisons) to display progress and support decision-making.
- Establishment of accountability cycles: Regular review and adjustment of actions through reviews and control loops.

A central vehicle for implementing these principles is the company's own lean business system. This is supported by an overarching strategy aimed at a safe, sustainable, and connected future. Sustainability is firmly anchored in the company's vision.

TE Connectivity uses the Hoshin Kanri method to further operationalize strategic goals and focus improvement initiatives on the most essential topics. This is carried out in an annual rotating process.

Building on this, our TE Connectivity Lean System, "TE Connectivity Operating Advantage" (TEOA), enables the development of the site, concentrating on the optimization and transformation of value streams. This is achieved through the use of classic lean tools aimed at eliminating waste and optimizing processes (operational excellence), as well as through the use of modern technical tools such as automated guided vehicles and elements of the digital factory (technical excellence).

Derived from this methodology, TE Connectivity pursues a wide range of activities to drive the development of the site. Visualizing progress is a key component of continuous improvement.

This also applies to the site's sustainability goals. A good example is energy visualization, where energy consumption is monitored in detail. In various production areas such as electroplating, injection molding, and stamping, TE Connectivity is able to track and optimize energy usage. By connecting both old and new machines, energy consumption can be monitored and controlled at the part level, which also enables methodical and structured identification of optimization potential in these "green" topics.

Other examples where lean methods and indicator-based management using lead indicators help improve sustainability performance include monitoring compressed air consumption and regular preventive maintenance as part of TPM activities (Total Productive Maintenance), as well as fixed targets for reducing packaging and material usage. This also includes measures to minimize material consumption in stamping, increased use of recycled materials, and ongoing improvements in product design.

6.13 Welbilt Deutschland (Convotherm): Achieving "Green Production" Through Lean Management Projects

- Name: Welbilt Deutschland GmbH (brand: Convotherm)
- Location: Eglfing, near Weilheim/Upper Bavaria
- Employees at site: approx. 280
- Industry: Kitchen systems for the food service and catering sector
- Production processes: Sheet metal processing, assembly, and inspection

It all started with an idea: Professional chefs in large-scale kitchens needed new specialized technology for more efficient food preparation—the combi steamer! With this insight, Frank Dittmann and Werner Schwarzbäcker founded **Convotherm** on July 1, 1976. Since then, the company has developed into one of the world's leading brands in the field of combi steamers through continuous innovation and adherence to the highest quality standards. Chefs around the globe know and appreciate these universally applicable devices, which make it possible to prepare almost any dish quickly, gently, resource-efficiently, and in top quality (Fig. 6.47).

But Convotherm's focus is not only on the high quality and resource efficiency of the components processed. The effectiveness and efficiency of its own production processes are also continuously improved. In 2017, the company was recognized with the Lean

Fig. 6.47 The Convotherm plant in Eglfing. *Source:* Welbilt Deutschland GmbH

& Green Management Award in the category "General Manufacturing Industry: SMEs (Small and Medium-Sized Enterprises)." In 2021, Convotherm entered the competition again and once more took home the victory in the "General Manufacturing Industry: SMEs" category thanks to innovative and sustainable processes and further developments.

"We were very pleased to win the 'Lean & Green Management Award 2017,' but to be able to celebrate this success again four years later makes us incredibly proud and shows us that we are on the right path," says Stefan Dorsch, authorized signatory and Head of Production & Operations at Convotherm. For the company, sustainability and "green production" are of the utmost importance, as they are seen as part of corporate responsibility. This means that, for example, all administrative and external processes are also analyzed with regard to lean management and resource efficiency.

The numerous "Lean & Green" projects over the past 15 years have achieved the following results while doubling output:

- Production area remained unchanged.
- Avoidance of additional shifts and the associated costs (shift premiums, energy requirements, etc.). This was achieved through a lean project that increased the maximum number of units produced per shift from 28 to 38 devices.

- Productivity and efficiency increased by more than 30%, thanks to the established continuous improvement process in which all Convotherm employees are involved.
- Energy consumption reduced by approximately 12%. This was mainly achieved by switching to district heating, but ongoing incremental improvements have also been made through the continuous improvement process.
- OTIF (on-time in-full delivery) increased to a consistent level of over 98%.
- Material inventories reduced by more than 45%. Numerous lean logistics projects established alternative procurement methods such as consignment warehouses, supplier Kanban, and milk runs. This also significantly reduced the environmental impact by decreasing the number of delivery trucks, while still enabling daily deliveries. One truck now visits several suppliers daily to collect goods.
- Lead times reduced by 60% for mini devices and 25% for "Convotherm 4" devices, through targeted use of internal and external Kanban systems.
- Complete switch to reusable packaging (no repacking required in production, no unnecessary waste). Intensive discussions and workshops with suppliers, as well as the continuous improvement process, were key to achieving these goals.
- Significant improvements in ergonomics have led to fewer downtimes.
- Analysis of energy performance indicators to derive improvement measures.
- Continuous improvement process and suggestion system implemented throughout the company.

"Lean & Green" topics are an integral part of Convotherm's strategic direction and are broken down into annual targets accordingly. Progress towards these targets is monitored by the environmental and energy officers through quarterly audits. In addition, there is an interdisciplinary environmental and energy team at the site, which meets monthly to track project progress and decide on further measures.

Furthermore, environmental aspects and resource conservation play a crucial role, especially in new product developments. For example, a new AI-supported generation of devices was developed that uses a camera to detect which foods are placed in the cooking chamber and then automatically starts the appropriate program (Fig. 6.48).

As a result of optimized program sequences, it was possible to achieve, in addition to a reduction in energy consumption of approximately 28%, a shortening of preheating times by about 11%, baking times reduced by around 18%, and a remarkable reduction in finished goods waste by approximately 20%. This was made possible because employees can now hardly make any mistakes when operating or loading the devices. This is a typical example of how innovation and the use of modern technology can generate significant customer value while simultaneously conserving resources and reducing environmental impact (Fig. 6.49).

The savings achieved and the impact of the environmental and energy targets defined for 2021 and 2022 are explained in more detail below using several examples. For each topic, a person at the site is responsible for implementation:

Fig. 6.48 Convotherm-maxx pro-ConvoSense. *Source:* Welbilt Deutschland GmbH

1. New product lines with reduced energy consumption values ("Green Strategy")
   A completely new product line (Cumulus-"... maxx pro") is being developed with reduced energy consumption values (on average 2.5%). Specific target values are used to define optimal energy consumption for each device size and type. The anticipated reduction in energy consumption was achieved through the targeted and implemented improvements (triple glazing, LED lighting).
2. Online training included in the training program for service technicians
   Approximately 60% of the training sessions (~25 sessions with 10 participants each) from various training modules are planned to be held online. This will significantly reduce travel by car (an average of 400 km) and by plane from different countries; all manuals and information pages for the training are available digitally to online participants (no more paper printouts). In fact, 75% of the planned online training sessions were implemented as a contribution to this environmental goal.
3. Energy efficiency through low energy consumption
   New Intralogistics vehicles with standby mode are being introduced, which can only be started using the employee's personalized chip. After a defined period of inactivity, the vehicles switch to standby mode, saving an average of 25% battery power. This also reduces the frequency of recharging. The use of the appropriate charger also extends battery life. The described targets have been met.
4. Replacement of outdated production machinery
   The renewal of older machines in production is being advanced through the acquisition of a new laser machine and new spot welding machines. An estimated reduction in electricity and water consumption has also contributed significantly. Energy savings of approximately 10% are expected. Concrete data collection (measurement

Fig. 6.49 maxxpro-ConvoSense graphic. *Source:* Welbilt Deutschland GmbH

results) on energy savings is not yet possible. However, with the new, more energy-efficient machines, annual energy savings of up to approximately 15% are anticipated.

5. Company bicycles—"Good for fitness. Better for the environment."
   An offer for "bicycle leasing" is to be made available to employees. The goal is for approximately 30% of the workforce to take up the offer, thus making a significant contribution to environmental protection. Many colleagues had already expressed interest in company bicycles in advance. By the end of December 2022, 32 employees, or about 11.4%, had decided to participate and now use bicycles up to three times more frequently for commuting to work.

6.14 Witte Automotive Bulgaria: Leading "Lean & Green" from the Bottom Up in a Fast-Growing Environment

- Name: WITTE Automotive Bulgaria
- Plant: 7009 Ruse, Bulgaria
- Employees: Approx. 1200
- Industry: Automotive
- Manufacturing Processes: Injection molding, assembly

WITTE Automotive is a German company founded 120 years ago as a manufacturer of luggage locks. In the 1930s, the company began producing door handles and locks for the popular Volkswagen "Beetle," after which it fully shifted its focus to the automotive sector. Today, WITTE Automotive operates a total of six production plants—three in Germany, two in the Czech Republic, and one in Bulgaria. WITTE Automotive Bulgaria (WAB) is a subsidiary of the German parent company WITTE Automotive GmbH. Production began in 2010 and has continued to grow ever since. In 2023, sales reached €198 million and more than 85 million products were manufactured (Fig. 6.50).

Today, WITTE Automotive Bulgaria serves 165 different clients (19 OEMs and 146 Tier suppliers) across 350 locations, producing more than 8.5 million goods per month. The main product groups include: front and rear camera mechanisms and actuators, seat latches, automatic tolerance compensation systems (WITOL), front hood latches, tailgate latches, lock sets, and more. The plant has established a strong reputation for quality, efficiency, and customer satisfaction.

Starting in 2024, WITTE Automotive Bulgaria is expanding its core operations to include injection molding processes in its portfolio. With this expansion of its core business, WITTE Automotive Bulgaria is optimizing its production by implementing its own standards for manufacturing individual components and applying best-in-class processes for in-house production.

By the end of April 2024, WITTE Automotive Bulgaria will have 1156 employees. Of these, 223 are overhead staff and 933 are operators. The administrative staff is divided

Fig. 6.50 Witte Automotive. *Source:* WITTE Automotive Bulgaria

into central functions and departments supporting production, which facilitates easier allocation of tasks and responsibilities and helps organize the flow of information (Fig. 6.51).

Continuous improvement initiatives at WITTE Automotive Bulgaria began in 2015. Initially, these efforts were organized as an additional resource within the engineering department. In mid-2019, dedicated LEAN and Continuous Improvement (CIP) departments were established. Since 2021, the company has also set up a Product System Analysis (PSA) department and a Process System Analysis (PrSA) department, both focused on product and process improvement analysis.

Mindset and the right employees are the key success factors for the company's achievements. As a vital pillar of the group, the main focus for the next 15 years should be sustainable development. Sustainability is linked to retaining current talent, attracting new skilled employees for the next growth phase, and developing the next generation of leaders. WITTE Automotive Bulgaria follows the "Good to Great" principles, seeking the right roles and positions for employees after understanding their personalities and strengths. A LEAN leadership program was launched in 2018 for C-level and first-level management. From 2019 to 2023, the program was extended to second- and third-level management, senior specialists, and experts, and continues with operational production staff and high potentials. Starting in 2024, leadership training will continue with an expanded soft skills program for management staff. Since 2023, LEAN Six Sigma training for expert staff and leaders has also been introduced. WITTE Automotive Bulgaria is developing a program to train and educate employees based on LEAN leadership methods and has established local centers of expertise connected to LEAN, CIP, PSA, and PrSA.

As with all assembly plants worldwide, process performance is one of the most important KPIs for WITTE Automotive Bulgaria. The VSM and digitalization project

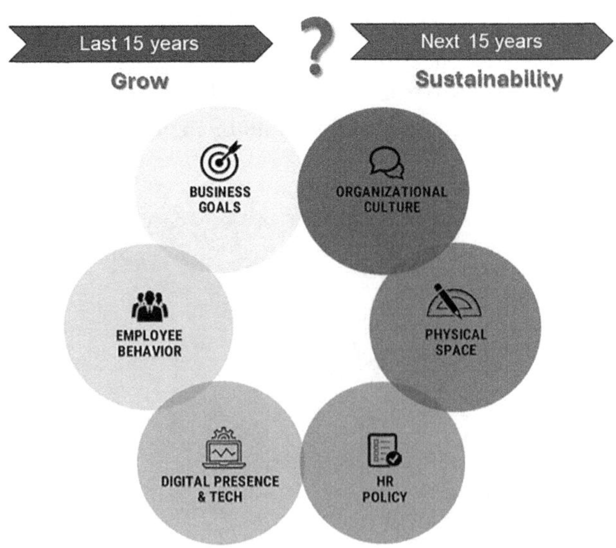

Fig. 6.51 From fast Growth to Sustainability. *Source:* WITTE Automotive Bulgaria

began as part of WITTE Automotive Bulgaria's commitment to Industry 4.0. To ensure the project's success, it was necessary to assemble a team of experts with diverse knowledge. This was made possible by the leadership programs already in place at WITTE Automotive Bulgaria. Before the internal digitalization project, all tracking and traceability of productivity (and other metrics) was done on paper. Many internal processes (apart from assembly) lacked traceability and tracking. The digitalization of internal processes at WITTE Automotive Bulgaria began in 2020 with the integration of the MES system and AMRs. The main goal of the project was to implement an intermediary software between people and the ERP system, integrating all production and logistics processes into a single system.

We aimed to involve more people in the projects—helping them adapt to the new situation, change their mindset, and accelerate the adoption of changes. The opinions of end users of any equipment are crucial for successful project implementation. Meetings were held to present conceptual ideas and implementation methods. After gathering feedback from direct users, changes were made to the project as needed. It is important to us that operators understand that improvements are designed to support them in the production process. At the end of this phase, end users were familiar with the project, had shared their opinions, and contributed to its successful implementation.

At WITTE Automotive, "Value Stream Mapping" (VSM) projects begin with statistics on criteria such as productivity, profit, customer orders, customer types, and more. These statistics are essential for selecting the right focus product. The decision on which product group to analyze in detail is based on these statistics. The main goal is to increase productivity and reduce waste for high-runner products. The first VSM projects began with GEMBA analyses of one of WITTE Automotive Bulgaria's high-runner products. We started from the loading of trucks with finished goods at the outbound warehouse, through the production processes, to the unloading of trucks with materials at the inbound warehouse. The following steps were carried out: "Process Diagram," "Process Map," and "Spaghetti Diagram." At the end of the VSM, 480 steps were identified, of which 24 were Value Added (VA) and 456 were Non-Value Added (NVA) (Fig. 6.52). Calculations of the distance traveled between all steps showed that the average distance per order is 129.5 km for an average quantity of 31,487 pieces per order. We analyzed all 456 NVA steps and divided them into two groups: "not value added but necessary" and "waste." Based on this, we identified the main types of waste for these products: transport, inventory, motion, waiting, and extra processing. For each type of waste, the percentage was determined based on the 456 VSM steps: transport (31%), inventory (2%), motion (15%), waiting (2%), and extra processing (8%). For transport, our target for each material is 3–4 moves from unloading the truck to the production line via the optimal route. The research showed that automating in-plant transport reduces unnecessary movements by operators. The team then focused on all possible technologies for transport automation and decided that the process required the implementation of Autonomous Mobile Robots/Automated Guided Vehicles (AMRs/AGVs) in the plant. Our goal was to adapt the improvement to our environment, not to adapt our environment to a new technology. The conclusion from

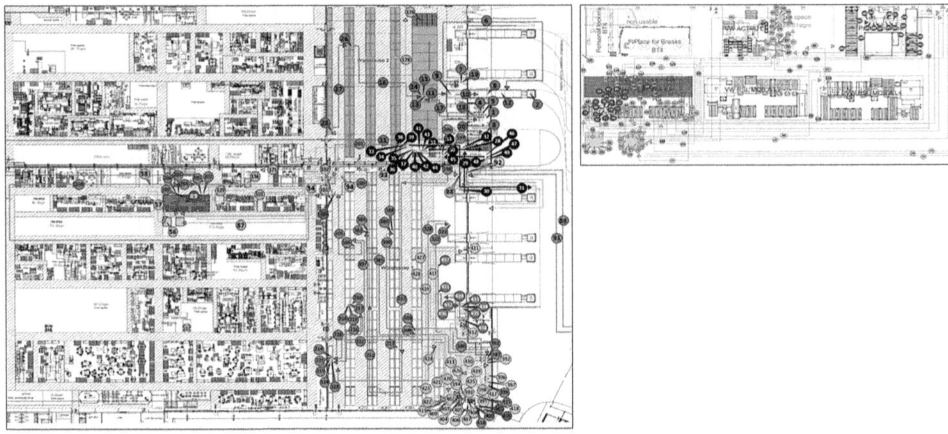

Fig. 6.52 Value Stream Mapping Overview (Processsteps). *Source:* WITTE Automotive Bulgaria

brainstorming sessions was that our transport processes would include three different fleets of vehicles: production AMRs, warehouse AMRs, and manually operated vehicles, all of which must be managed by a single system to avoid collisions. Before implementing new technology, it was important to understand the current state of material flows. We assessed the current situation and calculated the impact of implementing AMRs without changing the organization of internal flows. The calculations showed that such an approach would worsen productivity and increase idle runs by 40%. This was not a solution for us, so we began with footprint analyses of all flows.

We conducted research for an external solution (software) capable of managing three or more fleets with different navigation software. After numerous brainstorming sessions, we decided to develop our own in-house software for traffic management within the plant. The main objectives of our "WAB traffic management" are to calculate required times, predict routes, avoid collisions, reduce empty runs, and track all vehicles within the plant (regardless of whether they are automated or manually operated). The software provides AMRs with information on the shortest possible routes, prioritizes tasks based on production requirements, and selects the optimal storage bin for placing pallets in the warehouse, depending on the height and intended use of the material. The same software delivers identical information via tablet to operators of manually driven vehicles. At the production line, communication with the AMRs was handled by industrial computers. With this software, we have digitalized the KANBAN process to supply the production line with materials.

By working with VSM, waste in other supporting processes such as repacking of individual components, wrapping, and strapping became transparent. For example, the main repacking process at WAB was performed manually. Productivity was low and required significant man-hours. We decided that the process needed improvement—automating the necessary steps to reduce waste and increase productivity. We researched possible automation solutions with the goal of minimizing required labor. GEMBA preparation for this process previously involved 28 steps before starting. After project completion, GEMBA preparation required only 9 steps with minimal human intervention. Once the necessary steps were defined, we described them to several providers of automated repacking equipment. We automated the emptying of the master package with materials, filling materials into individual packages, printing and labeling, and weight control of both the master package and the repacked quantity. The machine is managed by an OMS system, which digitalizes the process and collects data for each package regarding timing, weight, number of deliveries, etc. This OMS system is connected to the ERP system via the WAB WMS system (Fig. 6.53).

Production digitalization (MES system) includes several functionalities and applications:

- Scan point—implementation of industrial terminals on production lines, which eliminated the use of paper for registering produced products and production line stoppages (previously two types of paper documents for each production line, per shift). Scan point is directly connected to the ERP system (SAP) and records data online.
- Production line dashboard—displays the most important KPIs of the production line. It is divided into two sections: KPIs relevant for operators and KPIs relevant for engineers. Operator KPIs foster internal competition between different shifts, resulting in increased productivity on the production line.
- Scan point reports—an application that helps administrators resolve issues quickly and efficiently, while also enabling operators to easily submit their ideas or report issues.

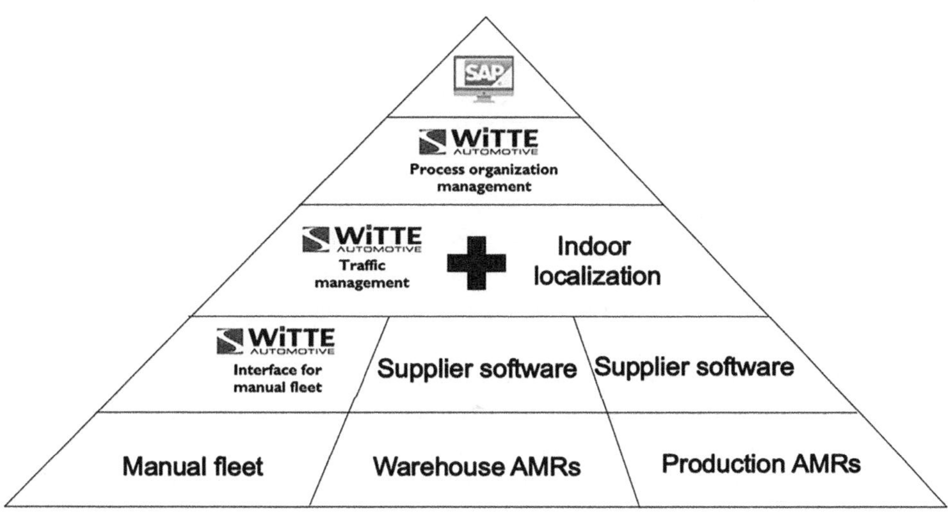

Fig. 6.53 WAB system integration. *Source:* WITTE Automotive Bulgaria

- Urgent needs—the purpose of this application is to provide direct information to the warehouse about materials required on the production lines to prevent production stoppages. It establishes a direct connection between production lines, inbound warehouse, and production shift managers through a desktop interface. The urgent needs application is directly connected to the Scan point devices on the production lines.
- "Production Intelligence" (PI)—this system provides real-time data analytics and manufacturing process control in a highly complex process environment. It facilitates traceability, prevents errors, and increases safety. With full implementation of Production Intelligence, we achieve "Digital Factory Status". PI functions include a digital dashboard for assembly lines, KPI visualization—OEE, performance, availability, productivity, quality, MTBF, QM error Pareto analysis, maintenance downtime Pareto and time consumption analysis, detailed fixture error analysis, production speed and micro-downtime monitoring, qualification matrix management, configuration data management, connectivity to SAP, PowerBI and data science tools such as KNIME, TensorFlow, as well as assembly line-specific reports and graphs in Grafana.
- Custom reports—this is an additional feature of Production Intelligence. It enables the creation of reports based on measured values from the production line, as well as easy tracking of specific parameters for finished products and rapid identification of process or part deviations.
- Monitoring of production stoppages—this dashboard is used by administrative functions within the production and maintenance teams—everyone can see the status of the production line, such as repairs, material needs, etc. This application helps maintenance teams respond and repair issues quickly.
- Production documentation—this application was developed to eliminate the use of paper for assembly and work instructions on the production lines. All documents required for work processes on the production line can be accessed digitally on monitors at the production line.
- AMR mission generation—AMR mission generation is fully integrated with the WMS. The AMR's API communicates to the WMS which material number is needed on the production line. The WMS automatically creates an order with pick-up and drop-off points.
- Time slot—time slot is an application that regulates inbound and outbound truck traffic at the plant. On average, 25 trucks pass through the plant daily. Before digitalization, all trucks arrived without scheduling, causing chaotic traffic in the yard. The application enables reservations for time slots at ramps for unloading and loading trucks.
- Internally developed WMS—WAB developed its own WMS system due to specific processes and the management of three different vehicle fleets. The WMS software interfaces with multiple systems such as refilling machines, the Kanban online board, urgent needs system, AMR system, and SAP. Components of the WMS include:
  - KANBAN card terminal—the development team created a user-friendly interface for scanning paper KANBAN cards. After scanning, the WMS automatically

creates an order for the material, and the mission is distributed based on vehicle workloads.
- For administrative functions, WAB aims to optimize routine task timing by implementing digital processes. In addition to the common use of "Confluence" and "Jira", we strive to digitalize paperwork and reduce manual tasks. As in production and warehouse, we aim to establish a strong connection between employees and the ERP system, without relying on additional applications such as Microsoft Office.

- Automatic exports and generation of information documents for appendices—the connection between SAP and Microsoft Office automatically generates documents in accordance with WITTE Automotive and Bulgarian legal standards, eliminating the need for manual writing or additional data export and import.
- Risk matrix—plant level—digitalization of the Excel table used to assess all plant risks. Tracks and notifies all deadlines. Notifications are sent via email to all employees responsible for the risk and related tasks. Before digitalization, the process required extensive data entry into Excel tables, which had to be checked and updated weekly.
- Digitalization help board—all software upgrades and applications are summarized on a single help board for easy access by all WAB employees.

At the end of the project, we will have three separate units—a fully integrated MES system managing all production processes, an internally developed WMS managing all logistics processes, and a separate administrative unit handling common daily administrative tasks. All three units will be connected to SAP. There is an established connection between the MES and WMS systems, which ensures timely information for all processes and reduces the execution time for each task on the shop floor.

One of the biggest enablers for the success of the project was the creation of multifunctional teams for each project. Every team member understood the importance of the project and accepted all assigned tasks. There was no need for constant supervision of the personnel involved; each team member monitored their own tasks and completed them on time. This was possible due to the habits and mindset fostered by WITTE Automotive Bulgaria through LEAN thinking. Effective management and the correct assessment of employees' personal and professional qualities are key to the success of any project. This enables the right selection of people, their placement in suitable positions, and high qualification, all of which guarantee project success. The motivation of participants, their persistence, and their understanding of the project's importance are also crucial factors. Spending more time on information gathering, analysis, and problem discussions is our approach to starting every project. An analytical approach to every task and accurate data assessment are prerequisites for success (Fig. 6.54).

Implementing a new project is significantly easier in an environment that is well standardized, with effective visual management and established working rules. We strive to standardize and facilitate operators' work to create convenience and foster a LEAN

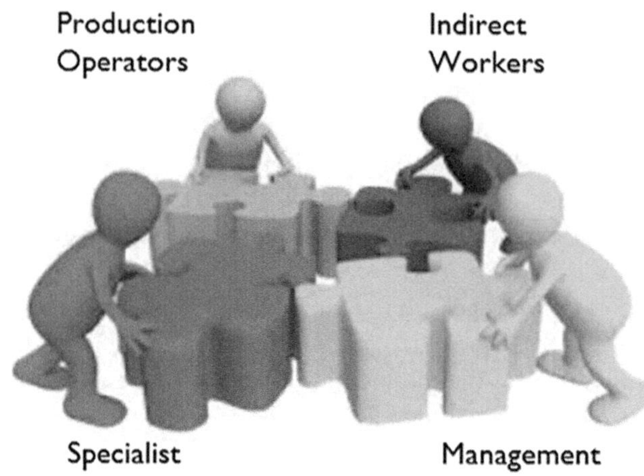

Fig. 6.54 Multi-functional team

mindset. Standardization and good visual management of the workplace, shop floor, and environment enable easy adaptation if employees need to move from one workplace or team to another. We have successfully instilled "5S" habits in all employees and taught them how easily everyone can apply LEAN tools.

Another success factor is that we do not automate waste; at WITTE Automotive Bulgaria, we eliminate waste and automate only value-adding or necessary processes. It is important for us to understand the need for automation, thoroughly prepare and analyze the situation, and make decisions based solely on collected data. Every project is built by multi-functional teams. The team includes employees from different departments of the plant, each bringing a different perspective to the project, which helps broaden the project scope and ensures rapid adaptation to changes and successful implementation.

Sustainability is not only centered on people and processes, but also on the environment. At the plant, we operate with 100% green energy, 15% of which is self-generated. In 2023, we completed the first phase of the photovoltaic system project. Electricity consumption was reduced by using LED lighting in production areas and motion sensors to control lighting usage. WAB has minimized its corporate carbon footprint (Fig. 6.55).

6.15 Volkswagen de México: How the Puebla plant is using "Lean & Green" best practices to improve resource efficiency in all areas

- Name: Volkswagen de México
- Plant: Vehicles Manufacturing Plant—Puebla
- Employees: approx. 14,470

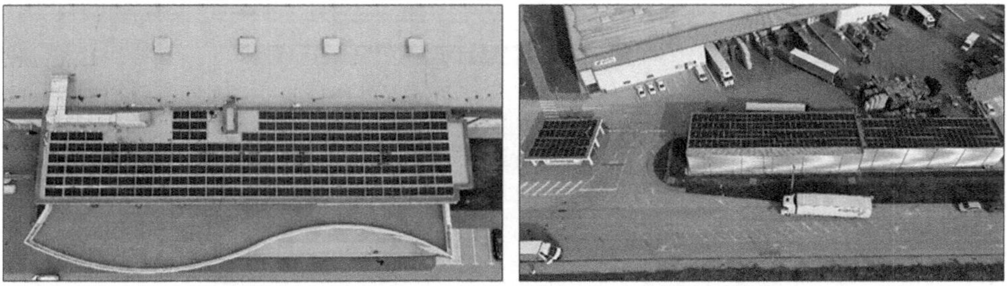

Fig. 6.55 Photovoltaic system at WAB. *Source:* WITTE Automotive Bulgaria

- Industry: Automotive
- Manufacturing Processes: Press shop, body shop, paint shop, assembly and finish lines in three different segments
- Products: Vehicles (VW Jetta A7, VW Tiguan SUV, and VW Taos SUV)

At **Volkswagen de México**, we are convinced that the responsible use of resources is fundamental to achieving sustainability—not only natural resources, but any resource used in our direct and indirect manufacturing processes. This includes the use of natural resources such as electricity, potable water, or natural gas, as well as intangible resources such as our workforce, investments in new projects, knowledge management, and leadership, among others.

The Volkswagen Production System

As the Volkswagen Group worldwide, we have a strategy to increase resource efficiency by jointly defining the "Volkswagen Production System." In this "Volkswagen Production System," we have consolidated standard tools and methodologies that enable us to optimize the rational use of our resources.

The "Volkswagen Production System" is implemented in waves, starting with our core business process—production—and then extending to adjacent areas such as indirect processes, new projects, the supply chain, and service at the brand's dealerships (Fig. 6.56).

Within the first wave, which includes manufacturing processes, Volkswagen de México has developed a strategy to eliminate waste and improve resource efficiency. This strategy is based on the use of tools such as workshops in all processes to identify and eliminate waste, continuous monitoring to improve response times through "shopfloor management," and problem-solving tools such as "lean Kata."

A key to improvement: Shopfloor Management

An important tool we use to improve manufacturing processes is "shopfloor management." This tool enables us to focus all efforts and resources on priority issues across

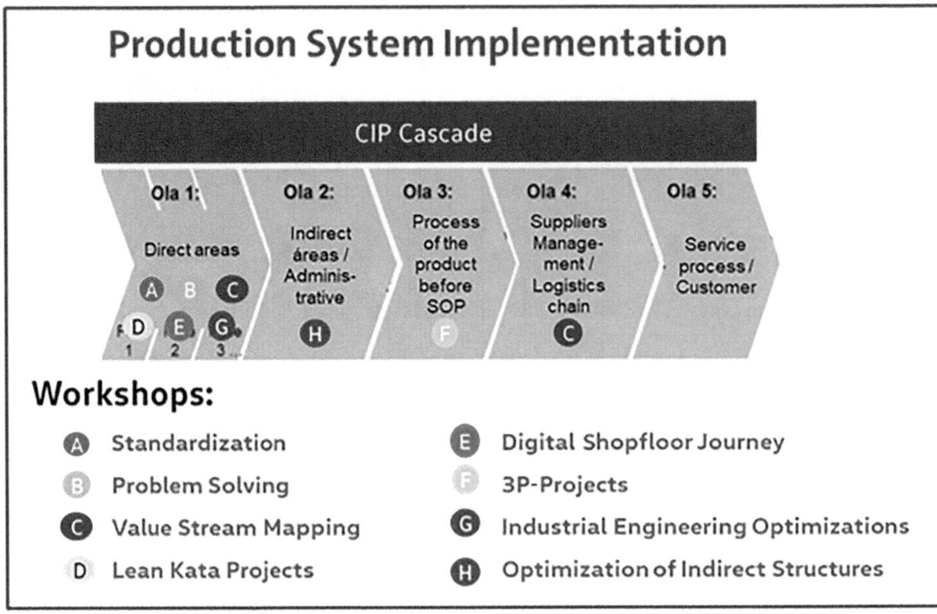

Fig. 6.56 Production System Implementation. *Source:* VW Production System

four dimensions: employee, process, quality, and finance within each manufacturing section.

Currently, we have implemented the shopfloor management tool in the manufacturing areas, which is designed to provide a forum where relevant issues in the control sections are discussed, corrective or preventive actions are defined, and specific topics related to its four dimensions are followed up.

To achieve this, the manufacturing processes are divided into control sections, each with a service structure consisting of personnel dedicated to automobile production and support areas such as maintenance, supply of production materials, supply of process materials, contracted services, quality control, planning, and finance.

Through shopfloor management, everyone involved in a control section is aligned with the objectives set for the various topics, with very short response times, as all actively participate in escalation meetings at different organizational levels, using the following key elements:

a) consistent goal deployment,
b) visualization and transparency of indicators,
c) use of a problem-solving tool, and
d) allocating the necessary time for meetings and activities.

One of the objectives of shopfloor management is to enhance communication and reaction speed to eliminate waste, and for this purpose it is managed at different levels within the organization. Each level has its own goals, responsibilities, and authorities, which are monitored using information boards.

Each level of shopfloor management meetings consists of two hierarchical levels that address issues related to their control sections, starting with the team leader and their coordinator and moving up to the plant manager. This sequence is carried out through meetings between each of these levels, where the main issues are resolved or, if necessary, escalated to the next hierarchical level for attention. The shopfloor management sequence takes place daily, starting at the beginning of the first production shift (Fig. 6.57).

Level 1 of shopfloor management addresses operational issues divided into two main categories: process and team. The process category primarily covers the management of volume and quality indicators, while the team category addresses personnel-related matters (Fig. 6.58).

At levels 2 and 3, the focus is broader, as issues in four categories are addressed: process, employee, quality, and finance. From the second level onward, cost issues also become an important indicator (Fig. 6.59).

The consistent application of this methodology has enabled the organization to ensure that each level can analyze and eliminate waste and issues within its own sphere of

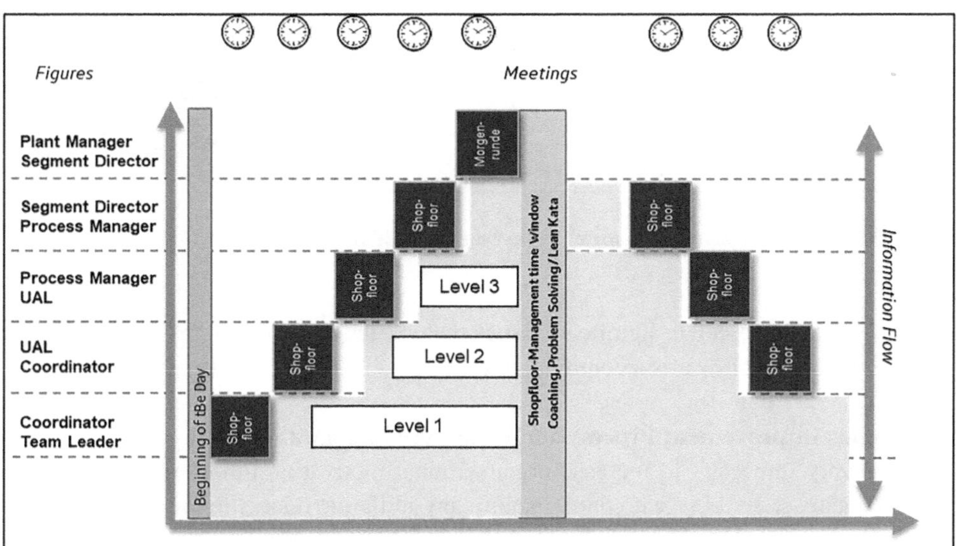

Fig. 6.57 Shopfloor management levels. *Source:* Volkswagen de México

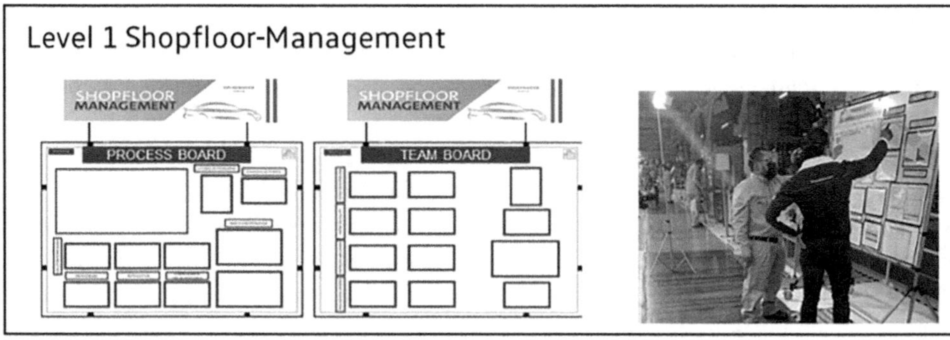

Fig. 6.58: Level 1. *Source:* Volkswagen de México

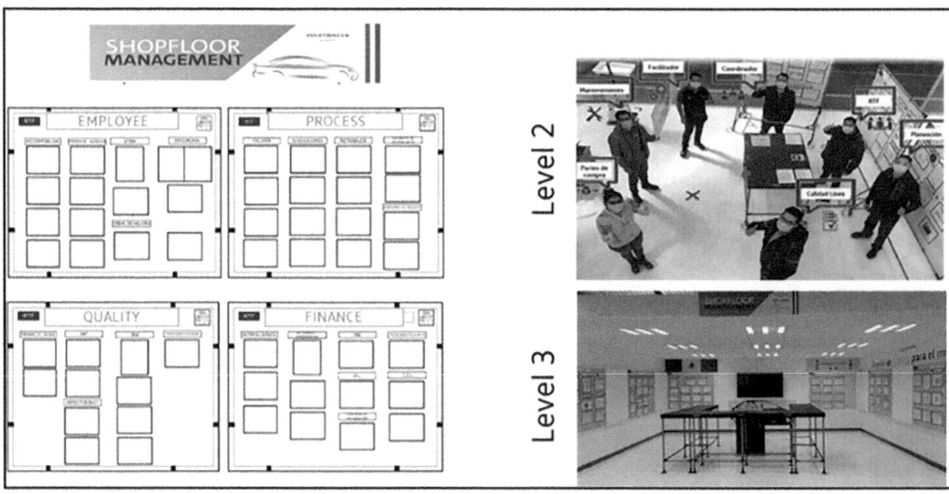

Fig. 6.59 Level 2 and Level 3. *Source:* Volkswagen de México

influence, and also escalate significant issues that exceed its responsibility, thereby aligning the organization towards a common goal.

Continuous Improvement Process and Employee Recognition

It is also very important to increase organizational motivation through recognition and ongoing feedback to those who participate in any initiative related to the company's sustainability.

To this end, Volkswagen de Mexico has implemented an annual event called the "Production Olympics," in which all areas of automobile manufacturing participate. The objective is to reward the best areas, taking into account ten categories that encompass the implementation of the production system (Fig. 6.60).

To determine the winner in each category, all areas are compared, seeking excellence in the implementation of all activities, establishing best practices, and sharing experiences. At the end of the competition, a large celebration is held with all the winners as part of the recognition of their efforts throughout the year. With this initiative, we are able to involve all our employees in the continuous improvement process.

The Zero Impact Factory

At Volkswagen, we are committed to the needs of present and future generations, which is why establishing an Environmental and Energy Policy that represents our vision has been essential.

The group's current strategy has the objective, in the coming years, of taking our products towards emission-free mobility for all. The Volkswagen Group stands firmly committed to the principles outlined in the Paris Climate Agreement and aligns its own activities with the 1.5-degree target. Our goal is to achieve net carbon neutrality by 2040 (reducing CO_2 emissions by 35% by 2030).

Fig. 6.60 The Production Olympics. *Source:* Volkswagen de México

The Strategy of Volkswagen de México, Zero Impact Factory, is based on the action fields of the Environmental Mission Statement of the VW Group (Fig. 6.61).

The vision of the "Zero Impact Factory" describes a factory that produces in a climate-, resource-, and environmentally friendly manner, thereby avoiding environmental impacts in vehicle and component production.

With a focus on climate protection and resource conservation, the Zero Impact Factory Strategy prioritizes monitoring key performance indicators (KPIs) related to environmental factors such as CO_2 emissions, volatile organic compounds (VOCs), energy usage, waste generation, and water consumption. These KPIs are integral components of the "Umweltentlastung Produktion" (UEP) indicator, which is monitored monthly to ensure the attainment of environmental goals (Fig. 6.62).

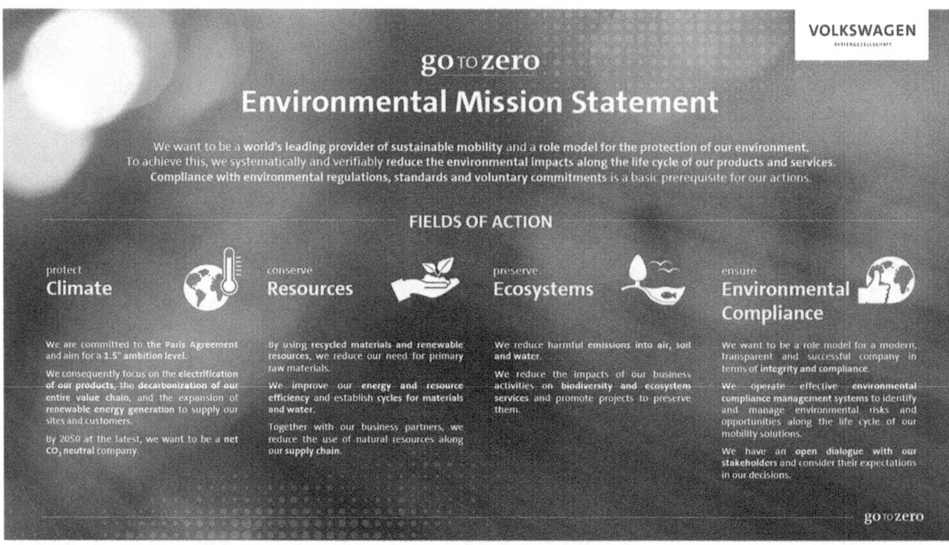

Fig. 6.61 Environmental Mission Statement of the VW Group. *Source:* Volkswagen

Fig. 6.62 Zero Impact Factory. *Source:* Volkswagen

Tracking spans across all levels of the organization, facilitated by our energy ambassadors from every department. Their role is pivotal in overseeing and monitoring resource consumption, emission generation, the implementation of energy efficiency projects, and ensuring the availability of information for informed decision-making (Fig. 6.63).

To mitigate CO_2 emissions, we prioritize the use of energy sources with minimal environmental impact, such as renewable energy. Since 2021, we have significantly increased our use of green electricity from the "La Bufa wind park," which now accounts for up to 70% of the energy consumed at our two plants, Puebla and Silao. This aligns with two key strategies: the Zero Impact Factory (target for 2025) and CO_2 neutrality (target for 2030). This initiative has contributed to a remarkable 68% reduction in CO_2 emissions per vehicle produced compared to the 2010 baseline.

To meet the group's goal, Volkswagen de México will undertake energy efficiency projects at the Silao Plant in the short term. These initiatives will enable the plant to rely entirely on renewable energy sources, transitioning from fossil fuels to solar power for electricity and replacing natural gas with biomethane. The projects will commence in 2024 and conclude in 2025.

Additionally, as part of our plan to minimize CO_2 emissions, Volkswagen de México has launched energy-saving projects. These efforts support our group-wide goal of achieving zero emissions by 2030. For example, we have introduced a new electric paint shop to stop using gas.

The Zero Plastic approach

At Volkswagen de México, we develop, produce, and distribute efficient motor vehicles and mobility services. In all these core processes we follow a life cycle approach to mitigate environmental risks, reduce our environmental impact, and optimize opportunities.

Energy Performance Indicators

Pos	Process	KPI FC 4+8 [kWh/Unit]	KPI Goal 2024 [kWh/Unit]	% of Compliance
1	Logistics	12.39	14.74	-15.9
2	Engines	23.89	27.81	-14.1
3	Axles and Components	10.22	11.15	-8.3
4	Assembly Segment II	46.51	49.84	-6.7
5	Assembly Segment III	62.25	66.64	-6.6
6	Presses	2.37	2.38	-0.4
7	Painting Segment I and II	204.21	204.2	0.0
8	Foundry	21.73	21.63	0.5
9	Painting Segment III	229.26	227.45	0.8
10	Guanajuato Plant	112	111	0.9
11	Segment II Bodies	62.54	61.95	1.0
12	Auxiliary Energies	158.36	156.42	1.2
13	Assembly Segment I	60.73	57.21	6.2
14	Finish Hall 7	5.17	4.83	7.0
15	Segment I Bodies	67.97	62.75	8.3
16	Catalytic Converters	1.99	1.83	8.7
17	Segment III Bodies	110.38	70.62	56.3
18	Pilot Plant	7.23	3.65	98.1

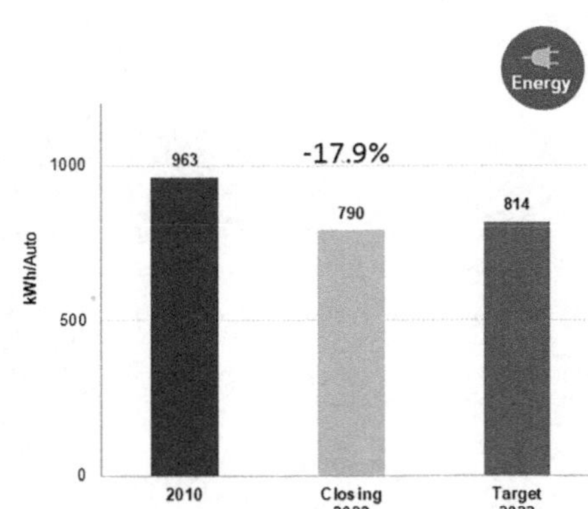

Fig. 6.63 Electricity Consumption per area. *Source:* Volkswagen de México

In our strategy, called "Way to Zero", logistics participates in 12 fields of action and one of them is focused on the efficient and sustainable management of our raw materials sent to us by our suppliers.

For 2 years we have focused on a project aligned with the reduction of waste generated by the use of plastics in our packaging of parts used for the construction of our automobiles and components.

We call this project "Zero Plastic" and the main objective is the complete elimination of this plastic in our packaging, with the priority being to maintain the quality of the piece from the shipment of our suppliers to delivery to the point of use in our production lines.

To meet the quality of our cars and components that our company offers to our customers worldwide, it is important that those materials detected with the use of plastic are evaluated, analyzed and verified by different internal areas such as logistics, quality, production, purchase; with the aim of not affecting its quality even when removing the protective plastic.

Therefore, a verification and approval flow was implemented for all areas involved. The process is shown in Fig. 6.64.

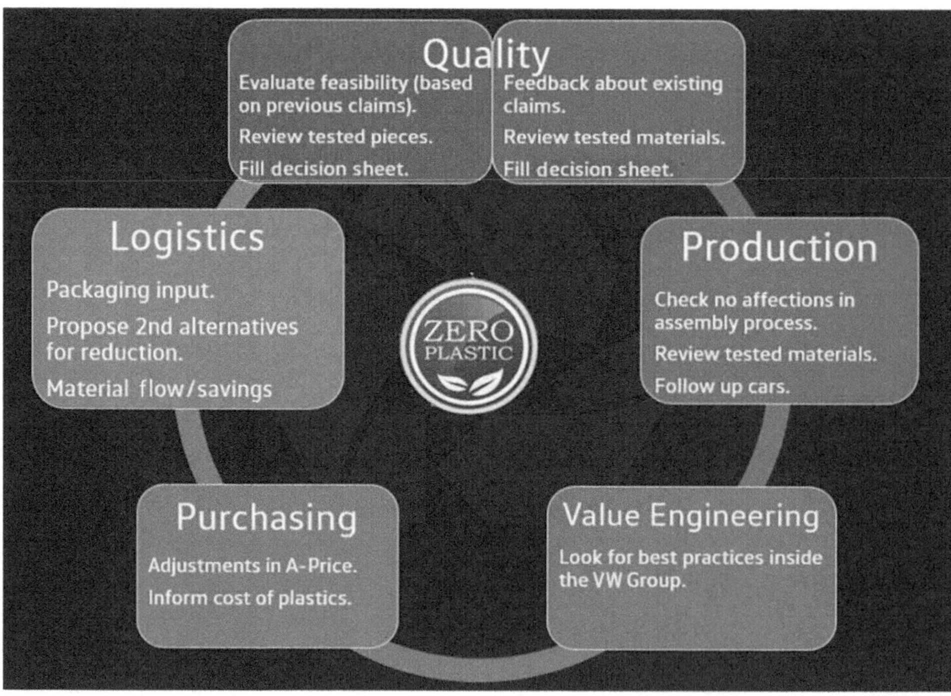

Fig. 6.64 Zero Plastic verification and approval process. *Source:* Volkswagen de México

Fig. 6.65 Zero Plastic Engine Protection. *Source:* Volkswagen de México

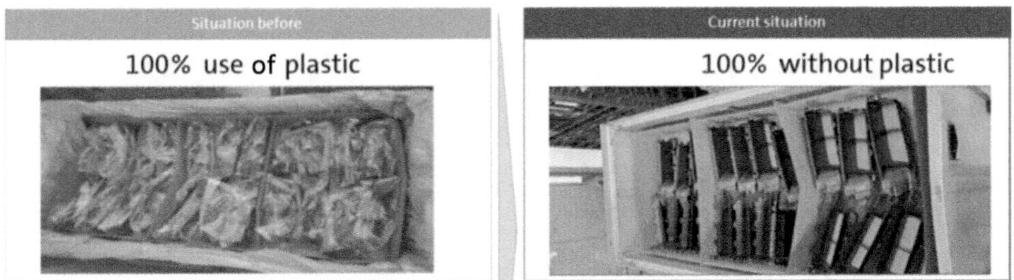

Fig. 6.66 Zero Plastic Radiator Deflector. (Source: Volkswagen de México)

In some cases, it is not possible to eliminate 100% of plastic, therefore protection alternatives such as foam, cardboard, reducing the use of plastic with a smaller gauge or sustainable alternatives such as bioplastic are analyzed. Below are some examples already implemented (Fig. 6.65 and 6.66).

Here the status of the tons of plastic reduced and the total objective for this year. This plastic reduction process has been replicated in our component plants in Guanajuato, Mexico and in the automobile plant in Chattanooga, USA (Fig. 6.67).

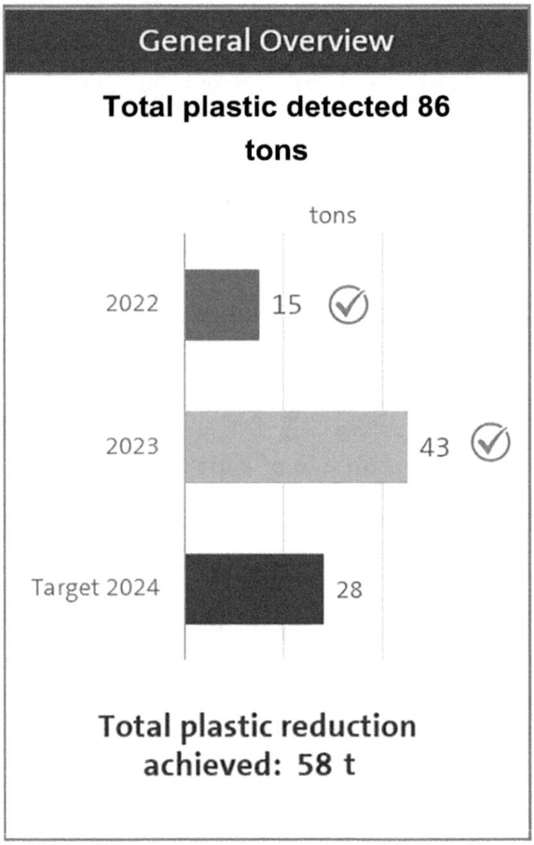

Fig. 6.67 Results of plastic reduction process. *Source:* Volkswagen de México

References

Wills, B. (2009). *Green intentions—Creating a green value stream to compete and win*. Productivity Press.

Conclusion

The integration of lean management and sustainability topics offers companies a wide range of opportunities to operationally embed ecological and social aspects, thereby contributing to the achievement of the 17 SDGs. The indications are clear that the pressure on companies to act in this regard will increase in the future (see Chap. 2). Growing environmental problems and limited resources are leading to stricter regulations for companies. In addition, there is a risk of losing credibility with consumers or investors and losing market share. On the other hand, successful integration of sustainability topics can create opportunities, enhance brand value, and reduce costs. Sustainability topics also often provide the basis for entirely new (future-proof) business models and are drivers of innovation in many areas. Nevertheless, many sustainability strategies remain at a "superficial" level, often driven and communicated primarily for marketing and sales purposes. The consistent operational integration into a company's own processes and supply chain remains a challenge for many organizations. Yet, this is precisely one of the key levers for making companies more future-proof. In doing so, companies can also make their contribution to achieving the broader sustainability goals (SDGs).

Lean management offers points of connection that can ensure sustainability is not viewed in isolation, but is instead advanced as part of the company-wide continuous improvement process (see Chap. 3). This is due in part to the focus on waste, which is closely linked to resource efficiency and can also be methodologically connected. Furthermore, a proper understanding of lean management goes beyond a toolbox of tools and methods and is closely associated with holistic excellence systems. This enables companies to build on existing methods, procedures, and control loops, which form the basis for a common language. Just as lean is not seen as the responsibility of individual departments in top-performing companies, integrating green topics can ensure that sustainability is not left to specific areas, but is understood as a responsibility shared by all.

Close, collaborative partnerships with suppliers also play a crucial role in holistic lean management. This, too, provides opportunities to anchor sustainability in the supply chain and actively initiate improvements—an aspect with which many companies still struggle today. A final positive link between "lean" and "green" is that green or

D. Reichert, *Lean & Green: Best Practice*, https://doi.org/10.1007/978-3-658-49880-1

sustainability topics offer the opportunity to generate a different or additional motivation for change and improvement processes. Optimizing processes and minimizing waste in "Lean & Green" are not only means to increase business success, but also improve the company's environmental and social impact, which in turn benefits society as a whole.

Once a company has decided to operate sustainably, it is important—starting from the definition of a sustainability strategy—to identify which specific approaches can help to drive the operational integration of social and ecological topics (see Chap. 4). The approaches presented have shown, with regard to machine effectiveness, material efficiency, and energy management, how a company's resource efficiency can be concretely improved by linking lean methods with green approaches. For machine effectiveness, it makes sense to expand classic TPM approaches. In energy management, the lean value stream method has proven to be practical, and for material efficiency, material flow analyses can serve as a starting point for achieving green improvements using various lean methods. Together with an overarching approach to embedding sustainability strategies, these are examples of how "lean" and "green" can be intelligently combined.

The fact that companies can be compared across industries in terms of both lean management implementation and sustainability topics is demonstrated by the annual "Lean & Green Management Award" (see Chap. 5). The assessment methods for the Lean & Green Management Award are based on a detailed and dynamic maturity model, which enables the evaluation of key business processes with respect to lean and green. In addition to the evaluation, the award's approach also facilitates practical knowledge transfer among participants.

However, how lean and green are actually implemented in companies depends heavily on corporate philosophy and the specific context. There is no "one-size-fits-all" approach, and companies will be required to develop their own solutions for both lean management systems and sustainability. The contributions presented illustrate the various strategic and operational areas in which lean & green can be realized (see Chap. 6). In all companies, however, it is evident that lean management and sustainability play a central role and positively reinforce each other—either because the implementation of lean management directly supports sustainability topics, or because lean and green are integrated in production systems or in the construction of new factories.

The economic and ecological successes achieved by these companies demonstrate that the intelligent integration of lean and green can significantly improve sustainability and resource efficiency in industry. This is a connection that is not yet sufficiently recognized and could be leveraged much more effectively through closer operational integration. To maximize synergies, both lean and green approaches should be embedded in holistic excellence systems and jointly advanced as part of the company's continuous improvement process. Sustainability is then consistently integrated into day-to-day operations, and the authenticity and effectiveness of strategies and reports are significantly enhanced.

This helps companies achieve more sustainable orientations more quickly and easily, thereby directly strengthening economic growth and decent working conditions (SDG 8), modernizing industries and infrastructures (SDG 9), and making production and consumption patterns more environmentally friendly (SDG 12). At the same time, reducing energy and material use supports climate protection measures (SDG 13). The "Lean & Green" integration thus holds potential that can contribute to greater future viability both at the level of individual companies and from an overall economic perspective.

GPSR Compliance

The European Union's (EU) General Product Safety Regulation (GPSR) is a set of rules that requires consumer products to be safe and our obligations to ensure this.

If you have any concerns about our products, you can contact us on ProductSafety@springernature.com

In case Publisher is established outside the EU, the EU authorized representative is:

Springer Nature Customer Service Center GmbH
Europaplatz 3
69115 Heidelberg, Germany

Batch number: 09371483

Printed by Printforce, the Netherlands